Intelligent Scheduling of Tasks for Cloud-Edge-Device Computing Systems

Editorial Board

Intelligent Scheduling of Tasks for Cloud-Edge-Device Computing Systems

Biao Hu

College of Engineering, China Agricultural University
Beijing, China

Mingguo Zhao

Department of Automation, Tsinghua University
Beijing, China

Zhengcai Cao

School of Mechatronics Engineering, Harbin Institute of Technology
Harbin, China

MengChu Zhou

The Helen and John C. Hartmann Department of Electrical and Computer Engineering, New Jersey Institute of Technology, Newark, NJ 07102, USA
The School of Information and Electronic Engineering, Zhejiang Gongshang University, Hangzhou 310018, China

IEEE Press
WILEY

Published by John Wiley & Sons, Inc., Hoboken, New Jersey.

For general information on our other products and services or for technical support, please contact our Customer Care Department within the United States at (800) 762-2974, outside the United States at (317) 572-3993 or fax (317) 572-4002.

Wiley also publishes its books in a variety of electronic formats. Some content that appears in print may not be available in electronic formats. For more information about Wiley products, visit our web site at www.wiley.com.

Library of Congress Cataloging-in-Publication Data has been applied for:

Print ISBN: 9781394361625
ePDF ISBN: 9781394361649
epub ISBN: 9781394361632
oBook ISBN: 9781394361656

Cover Design: Wiley
Cover Image: © BazziBa/stock.adobe.com

Contents

Foreword *ix*
About the Authors *xi*
Preface *xv*
Acknowledgments *xvii*
Acronyms *xix*
Glossary *xxi*

1 Introduction *1*
1.1 Cloud-edge-device Computing Systems *1*
1.2 Tasks *2*
1.3 Task Scheduling *3*
1.4 Outline of the Book *4*
1.5 Summary *5*

2 Scheduling Mixed Real-time Tasks in an Automotive System with Vehicular Network *7*
2.1 Introduction *8*
2.2 Related Work *10*
2.3 Models and Problem Formulation *12*
2.3.1 Software Model *12*
2.3.2 Hardware Model *12*
2.4 Hybrid Scheduler Design *13*
2.5 Schedulability Test *15*
2.5.1 Utilization-based Schedulability Test *15*
2.5.2 Demand-supply Analysis *15*
2.6 Offline Task Assignment *17*
2.6.1 Problem Formulation *17*
2.6.2 Hard Real-time Task Assignment *20*

2.6.3 Soft Real-time Task Assignment 22
2.6.4 Complexity Analysis 24
2.7 Online Job Assignment 24
2.7.1 Online Schedulability Test 24
2.7.2 Job Assignment Strategy 27
2.7.3 Complexity Analysis 28
2.8 Performance Evaluation 28
2.8.1 Compared Approaches 29
2.8.2 Schedulability Test Results 30
2.8.3 Online Job Assignment Tests 33
2.9 Summary 35

3 Workload-aware Scheduling of Real-time Independent Tasks in Cloud 37
3.1 Introduction 37
3.2 Related Work 41
3.3 Related Models 43
3.3.1 Virtual CPU Model 43
3.3.2 Real-time Job Model 43
3.3.3 Power Model of VM 44
3.4 Problem Formulation 44
3.4.1 Input 45
3.4.2 Output 45
3.4.3 Constraints 45
3.4.4 Objective 46
3.5 Scheduling Jobs in a Single Server 47
3.5.1 Power Analysis 47
3.5.2 Problem Transformation 47
3.5.3 Dynamic Programming 48
3.6 Scheduling Jobs in Multiple Servers 51
3.6.1 Server Energy Efficiency 51
3.6.2 Job Placement in Multiple Servers 52
3.7 Online Workload-aware Scheduling 53
3.7.1 Job Frequency Profile 54
3.7.2 Energy-efficient Job Accommodation Scheme 54
3.8 Performance Evaluation 58
3.8.1 Simulation Setup 58
3.8.2 Compared Approaches 58
3.8.3 Results 59
3.9 Summary 64

4 Energy-minimized Scheduling of Real-time Dependent Tasks in Cloud *65*
4.1 Introduction *65*
4.2 Related Work *68*
4.3 Problem Formulation *69*
4.3.1 Input *69*
4.3.2 Output *70*
4.3.3 Objective *71*
4.3.4 Constraints *71*
4.4 Energy-efficient Scheduling Without Real-time Constraint *74*
4.4.1 Energy Consumption-minimized Task Placement Plan *74*
4.4.2 Partition Scheduling *75*
4.5 Scheduling with Real-time Constraint *78*
4.5.1 Task Placement Adjustment Strategy *79*
4.5.2 Start Time Adjustment *82*
4.5.3 Schedule Adjustment in a Backward Way *84*
4.6 Performance Evaluation *85*
4.6.1 Simulation Setup *86*
4.6.2 Compared Approaches *87*
4.6.3 Results *88*
4.7 Summary *93*

5 Workload-aware Scheduling of Real-time Dependent Tasks in Vehicular Edge Computing *95*
5.1 Introduction *95*
5.2 Related Work *97*
5.3 Models and Problem Formulation *99*
5.3.1 Vehicular Computing Model *99*
5.3.2 Application Model *100*
5.3.3 Power Model *101*
5.3.4 Response Time Model *102*
5.3.5 Problem Formulation *102*
5.4 Decentralized Auction-bid Scheduling Scheme *103*
5.4.1 Auction-bid Strategy *103*
5.4.2 Task Prioritization *104*
5.4.3 Task Assignment and Execution *104*
5.4.4 Power Management *106*
5.5 GS Scheme *107*
5.5.1 Task Execution of Multiple Applications *107*
5.5.2 Application Group and Allocation *108*
5.6 Evaluation *110*

5.6.1 Simulation Setup *110*
5.6.2 Performance Results *111*
5.7 Summary *117*

6 Scheduling Multiple-criticality Dependent Tasks in Vehicular Edge Computing System *119*
6.1 Introduction *119*
6.2 Related Work *122*
6.3 Problem Formulation *123*
6.3.1 Input *123*
6.3.2 Output *125*
6.3.3 Constraints *125*
6.4 Response Time Analysis *126*
6.4.1 Task's Response Time in a VM *127*
6.4.2 Application's Response Time *127*
6.5 Scheduling at Level-1 Mode *128*
6.5.1 Application Decomposition *128*
6.5.2 State-transition Equation *129*
6.5.3 Dynamic Programming *131*
6.6 Mixed-criticality Scheduling *132*
6.6.1 Mixed-criticality Schedulability Test *132*
6.6.2 Online Management by Frequency Prediction *133*
6.7 Performance Evaluation *134*
6.7.1 Compared Approaches *134*
6.7.2 Results *135*
6.8 Summary *139*

7 Real-world Applications of Scheduling Technologies *141*
7.1 Introduction *141*
7.2 Traffic Management *141*
7.3 Smart Agriculture with Internet of Things *143*
7.4 Healthcare Monitoring Systems *144*
7.5 Summary *145*

8 Summary and Future Research *147*
8.1 Summary *147*
8.2 Future Research *147*

References *149*
Index *165*

Foreword

Edge computing, in concert with cloud computing and on-premises systems, is redefining the future of intelligent distributed computing. In fact, the increasing demand for real-time processing, privacy preservation, low-latency responses, bandwidth saving, and energy-efficient computation has driven the development of cloud-edge-device computing systems, as a new computing paradigm that seamlessly integrates the capabilities of cloud data centers, edge nodes, and end-user devices. This architectural evolution offers tremendous potential across domains such as smart cities, autonomous vehicles, healthcare 4.0, industrial Internet of Things (IIoT), and cyber-physical systems.

In recent years, the research and industrial communities have recognized the urgent need for intelligent scheduling strategies that can dynamically allocate computational tasks across this heterogeneous infrastructure. While cloud platforms provide abundant computational power, they often fall short in latency-critical applications. Edge nodes, closer to the data source, offer rapid response but are resource-constrained. Device-level processing adds immediacy and contextual awareness but poses severe energy and computing limitations to devices. Balancing these trade-offs calls for advanced scheduling mechanisms that are not only context-aware but also adaptable, scalable, and robust.

This book, *Intelligent Tasks Scheduling for Cloud-Edge-Device Computing Systems*, addresses these challenges with remarkable depth and clarity. It begins by laying a strong foundation of the cloud-edge-device paradigm and its role in enabling responsive and intelligent services. Building upon this groundwork, the book systematically presents a variety of scheduling techniques tailored to different task types, including real-time, independent, and mixed-criticality, each thoughtfully designed to address constraints related to energy consumption, timing, and resource availability.

This book represents the collaborative work of a team of experienced and forward-looking researchers who are recognized contributors to the fields of IoT, real-time systems, and edge-cloud computing. Their insights, drawn from both academic and applied contexts, provide a timely and valuable contribution to this growing area of study. I commend the authors for producing a comprehensive, well-organized, and technically rigorous book that will be of significant interest to graduate students, researchers, system designers, and practitioners working in intelligent distributed systems and IoT.

Giancarlo Fortino, Ph.D. & Professor
Fellow of IEEE
University of Calabria, Italy
June 2025

About the Authors

Biao Hu is an Associate Professor in the Department of Mechanical Engineering at the College of Engineering, China Agricultural University (CAU), Beijing, China. He received his B.S. in Automation from the Harbin Institute of Technology (2010), M.S. in Automation from Tsinghua University (2013), and Ph.D. in Informatics from the Technical University of Munich (TUM) (2017).

Dr. Hu's research interests span Internet of Things (IoT) systems, real-time scheduling, edge intelligence, and robotics. His work focuses on intelligent task scheduling across cloud-edge-device platforms, energy-efficient scheduling for real-time and embedded systems, and intelligent control systems in cyber-physical environments.

Before joining CAU in 2021, Dr. Hu served as an Associate Professor at the Beijing University of Chemical Technology and worked as a researcher at Fortiss GmbH, an affiliated research institute of TUM focused on software-intensive systems and robotics.

He is a prolific researcher with a strong record of publications in leading journals such as *IEEE Transactions on Industrial Informatics, IEEE Transactions on Cloud Computing, IEEE Transactions on Services Computing*, and *IEEE Transactions on Parallel and Distributed Systems*. His contributions include foundational work on workload-aware scheduling, hybrid task frameworks for automotive systems, and real-time parallel processing for heterogeneous platforms.

In addition to his research, Dr. Hu is actively engaged in academic service. He is a Senior Member of IEEE and serves as a Handling Editor for the *Journal of Circuits, Systems, and Computers*. He has been a reviewer for numerous prestigious journals and international conferences in the fields of computing, artificial intelligence, and embedded systems.

Mingguo Zhao is a Professor at the Department of Automation, Tsinghua University, and the Director of both the Robot Control Laboratory at the Navigation and Control Institute and the Cross-Disciplinary Center for Brain-Inspired Robotics at the Center for Unmanned Systems. He has made significant contributions to the fields of intelligent robotics, brain-inspired control, and autonomous systems over the past two decades.

Dr. Zhao received his B.Eng. degree in Mechatronic Engineering in 1995, M.Eng. degree in Spacecraft Design in 1997, and Ph.D. in Mechatronic Engineering in 2001 from Harbin Institute of Technology. After completing his postdoctoral research at Tsinghua University, he joined the Department of Automation, where he has since progressed from Assistant Researcher to Full Professor.

His research is centered around the development of brain-inspired computing theory and platforms for general artificial intelligence and their applications to robotic control. He is especially known for his work on dynamic bipedal walking, neuromorphic robotic architectures, autonomous bicycles, and human-robot interaction.

His work has been recognized with several prestigious awards, including the Geneva International Invention Exhibition Silver Medal (2017), the National Teaching Achievement Award (2014), and the Ministry of Education's Natural Science Award (2015). Dr. Zhao continues to explore the convergence of brain-inspired computing and robotics, driving forward innovations that aim to bridge the gap between biological intelligence and artificial systems.

Zhengcai Cao is a Professor at the School of Mechatronics Engineering, Harbin Institute of Technology, and a distinguished expert recognized by national talent programs in China. His research focuses on intelligent robotics, embodied AI, and humanoid robots. Over the past decades, he has led over 10 national and provincial research projects, including a Key Project of the National Natural Science Foundation and National Key R&D Program. He has authored or co-authored more than 30 articles in IEEE Transactions and holds over 20 patents and 10 software copyrights. His research has earned him multiple awards, including the Second Prize of the National Science and Technology Achievement Award in Natural Science (2022), the First Prize of the Chinese Association of Automation Natural Science Award (2020), and the Second Prize of the China Machinery Industry Science and Technology Invention Award (2022).

As a dedicated educator, Professor Cao has spearheaded five major education reform projects, and his courses—*Principles of Automatic Control* and *Robotic Control Technology*—have been recognized as top-quality courses by the Ministry of Education and Beijing Municipal Commission of Education. He is the chief editor of the widely used textbook *Principles of Automatic Control*. His teaching achievements have been recognized with multiple national and provincial awards, including the Special Prize for Teaching Achievement in Petrochemical Higher Education (2020) and the Second Prize for Teaching Achievement from the Chinese Association of Automation (2022).

Professor Cao is an IEEE Senior Member and serves as Associate Editor for several top-tier journals, including *IEEE Transactions on Cybernetics, IEEE Transactions on Neural Networks and Learning Systems, IEEE Transactions on Intelligent Transportation Systems*, and *IEEE/CAA Journal of Automatica Sinica*. He holds key roles in several national academic organizations, including board membership in the Chinese Association for Artificial Intelligence and standing committee membership in the Chinese Association of Automation's Symbiotic Robotics Committee. He is also a core member of the National Major Research Program on Symbiotic Robotics by the National Natural Science Foundation of China.

MengChu Zhou received his B.S. degree in Control Engineering from Nanjing University of Science and Technology, Nanjing, China in 1983, M.S. degree in Automatic Control from Beijing Institute of Technology, Beijing, China in 1986, and Ph.D. degree in Computer and Systems Engineering from Rensselaer Polytechnic Institute, Troy, NY in 1990. He joined New Jersey Institute of Technology (NJIT), Newark, NJ in 1990, and has been a Distinguished Professor of Electrical and Computer Engineering since 2013. His research interests are in intelligent automation, machine learning, Petri nets, robotics, Internet of Things, big data, cloud/edge computing, transportation, and energy systems. He has over 1400 publications, including 17 books, over 900 journal papers (over 700 in IEEE transactions), and 32 book chapters. He holds 31 patents and has several pending ones. His recently co-authored books include *Learning Automata and their Applications to Intelligent Systems*, IEEE Press/Wiley, Hoboken, NJ, 2024 (with J. Zhang), and *Device-Edge-Cloud Continuum Paradigms, Architectures and Applications*, Springer Nature, 2023 (with C. Savaglio, G. Fortino, and J. Ma).

He served as Editor-in-Chief of *IEEE/CAA Journal of Automatica Sinica*. He is presently Senior Editor of *IEEE Transactions on Intelligent Transportation Systems*, and Associate Editor of Research, *IEEE Transactions on Industrial Informatics, IEEE Internet of Things Journal*, and *Frontiers of Information Technology & Electronic Engineering*. He is founding Chair/Co-chair of the Technical Committee on AI-based Smart Manufacturing Systems and Technical Committee on Humanized Crowd Computing of IEEE Systems, Man, and Cybernetics Society (SMC), Technical Committee on Semiconductor Manufacturing Automation of IEEE Robotics and Automation Society (RAS).

He is a recipient of the Excellence in Research Prize and Medal from NJIT, Humboldt Research Award for US Senior Scientists from Alexander von Humboldt Foundation, and Franklin V. Taylor Memorial Award and the Norbert Wiener Award from IEEE SMC Society, Computer-Integrated Manufacturing UNIVERSITY-LEAD Award from Society of Manufacturing Engineers, Distinguished Service Award from IEEE Robotics and Automation Society, and Edison Patent Award from the Research & Development Council of New Jersey. He is a life member of the Chinese Association for Science and Technology, USA and served as its President in 1999. He is a Fellow of IEEE, International Federation of Automatic Control (IFAC), American Association for the Advancement of Science (AAAS), Chinese Association of Automation (CAA), and the National Academy of Inventors (NAI).

Preface

The convergence of cloud, edge, and device-level computing has redefined how data is generated, processed, and utilized across a wide range of intelligent systems. From autonomous vehicles navigating complex environments to wearable devices enabling real-time healthcare diagnostics, the underlying computing architecture has grown more heterogeneous and distributed than ever before. Within this layered ecosystem, one of the most pressing and foundational challenges is intelligent task scheduling, determining where, when, and how computational tasks should be executed to meet application requirements under varying constraints.

This book is the culmination of years of research and development at the intersection of real-time systems, distributed computing, and optimization. It is motivated by the growing need for scalable, efficient, and intelligent scheduling mechanisms that are adaptable to the dynamic environments of modern computing infrastructures. Our goal is to provide a rigorous, systematic, and application-driven treatment of the scheduling problem in cloud-edge-device architectures, with a special focus on real-time and mixed-criticality scenarios.

The book is designed with both academic rigor and practical relevance in mind. It integrates theoretical foundations with algorithmic innovations and performance evaluations. It spans diverse scheduling contexts, including mixed-criticality systems in vehicular networks, energy-aware workload placement in cloud servers, and decentralized coordination in edge-based cyber-physical systems.

Each chapter offers a self-contained investigation into a unique scheduling challenge, progressing from fundamental models and complexity analysis to concrete strategies and real-world case studies. Wherever possible, we bridge the gap between abstract theory and tangible implementation to support both researchers and system designers.

We hope this book serves as a valuable reference and catalyst for future innovation in this rapidly evolving domain. Whether you are a graduate student entering the field, a researcher seeking deeper insights, or a practitioner designing next-generation intelligent systems, we invite you to explore the chapters ahead and contribute to the advancement of intelligent scheduling in cloud-edge-device computing systems.

This work would not have been possible without the insights and collaboration of our colleagues, students, and industry partners, whose perspectives and contributions have shaped the trajectory of this research. We also extend our gratitude to the growing global community of scholars working in the fields of edge computing, real-time systems, and distributed intelligence, whose pioneering work continues to inspire and guide our own.

This work was supported in part by the STI2030-Major Projects 2021ZD0201401 and 2021ZD0201402, Tongxiang Institute of Artificial General Intelligence under Grant TAGI2-A-2024-0006, and FDCT (Fundo para o Desenvolvimento das Ciencias e da Tecnologia) under Grant No. 0147/2024/AFJ.

Biao Hu
China Agricultural University, Beijing, China

Mingguo Zhao
Tsinghua University, Beijing, China

Zhengcai Cao
Harbin Institute of Technology, Harbin, China

MengChu Zhou
New Jersey Institute of Technology, Newark, NJ, USA

Acknowledgments

This work would not have been possible without the insights and collaboration of our colleagues, students, and industry partners, whose perspectives and contributions have shaped the trajectory of this research. In particular, we would thank our collaborators, Prof. Jing Bi of Beijing University of Technology, Prof. Haitao Yuan of Beihang University, and Prof. Gang Chen of Sun Yat-Sen University. We also extend our gratitude to the growing global community of scholars working in the fields of edge computing, real-time systems, and distributed intelligence, whose pioneering work continues to inspire and guide our own.

This work was supported in part by the STI2030-Major Projects 2021ZD0201401 and 2021ZD0201402, and in part by Tongxiang Institute of Artificial General Intelligence under Grant TAGI2-A-2024-0006.

Acronyms

AutoSAR	AUTomotive Open System Architecture
DAG	Directed Acyclic Graph
DPM	Dynamic Power Management
DVFS	Dynamic Voltage Frequency Scaling
ECU	Electronic Control Unit
EDF	Earliest Deadline First
FP	Fixed Priority
GA	Genetic Algorithm
HEFT	Heterogeneous Earliest Finish Time
IoT	Internet-of-Things
MCS	Mixed-Criticality System
MINLP	Mixed-Integer Nonlinear Programming
NSGA	Non-dominated Sorting Genetic Algorithms
PSO	Particle Swarm Optimization
QoS	Quality-of-Service
RSU	Roadside Unit
vCPU	virtual Central Processing Unit
VEC	Vehicular Edge Computing
VM	Virtual Machine

Glossary

$c_{j,k}$	the count of virtual CPUs allocated to *k*th virtual machine in *j*th server
d_i	the deadline of *i*th task or *i*th job
e_i	the execution time of *i*th task
f_i	the arrival frequency of *i*th task or job
f_k^i	the frequency of processing *i*th application corresponding to *k*th level
$\hat{f}_i^q$	the arrival frequency of *i*th job at *q*th period
$\Delta\hat{f}_i^q$	*i*th job frequency increment at *q*th period
l_j^i	computation load of *j*-task from *i*th application
s_i	the start execution time of *i*th task
t_r	task release time
$w_{i,j}$	the execution time of *i*th task by *j*th processing unit
$x_{i,j}$	the placement indicator of *i*th task on *j*th processing unit
$A_{j,k}$	the coefficient of *k*th resource on *j*th server
$B_{j,k}$	the amount of *k*th resource on *j*th server
C_j	number of available vCPUs in *j*th server
C_{S_p}	available computation resource of *p*th server
C_i	criticality level of *i*th application
E_i	the energy consumption of *i*th virtual machine
J_i^{Δ}	*i*th job with frequency $\Delta\hat{f}_i^q$
$P_{j,k}$	power of *k*th virtual machine in *j*th server

S_j	jth server
$\mathcal{S}^{\Delta_i}$	server set for accommodating J_i^{Δ}
$\mathcal{T}_l$	the set of lth level tasks
$\mathcal{T}_l^j$	the set of lth level tasks placed on jth server
T_j^i	jth task of ith application
$\mathcal{U}_j$	utilization of jth processing unit
$V_{j,k}$	kth virtual machine in jth server
$V_{p,q}$	qth virtual machine of pth server
$\alpha_{i,j}$	power constant of processing ith task on jth processing unit
α_j	static power coefficient of jth processing unit
β_j	dynamic power coefficient of jth processing unit
$\lambda_{i,j}$	computation efficiency of processing ith task by jth processing unit
$\lambda_{i,j}^{\flat}$	execution efficiency of jth processing unit on processing ith task
τ_i	ith task period
ϱ_i	the amount of computing resources to ith task
Λ_j	the jth processing unit
Ξ_i	the set of task nodes of ith application

1

Introduction

Cloud-edge-device computing systems are at the forefront of modern technology, serving as a critical enabler for diverse applications ranging from real-time data processing to autonomous vehicles. This chapter provides an overview of these systems, outlines the key tasks they perform, discusses scheduling challenges, and sets the stage for the subsequent chapters of this book.

1.1 Cloud-edge-device Computing Systems

The evolution of computing paradigms has led to the integration of cloud computing, edge computing, and device-level processing into a cohesive ecosystem. Each layer in this triad has distinct capabilities and plays a complementary role in modern applications:

- **Cloud Computing:** It offers virtually unlimited computational resources and storage, making it ideal for data-intensive analytics, centralized control, and long-term archiving. For example:
  - In smart grid management, cloud platforms analyze historical electricity usage data to forecast demand and optimize distribution.
  - In precision medicine, cloud-based systems store and analyze genomic data from thousands of patients to identify patterns and recommend personalized treatments.
- **Edge Computing:** It operates closer to data sources, reducing the latency associated with transmitting data to the cloud and responding in real time. It is well-suited for latency-sensitive applications, such as:
  - In manufacturing, edge devices process data from industrial sensors to detect anomalies like overheating or mechanical wear in real time.
  - In video surveillance, edge nodes perform real-time face or license plate recognition to trigger immediate alerts without involving cloud servers.

Intelligent Scheduling of Tasks for Cloud-Edge-Device Computing Systems, First Edition.
Biao Hu et al.
Published 2025 by John Wiley & Sons, Inc.

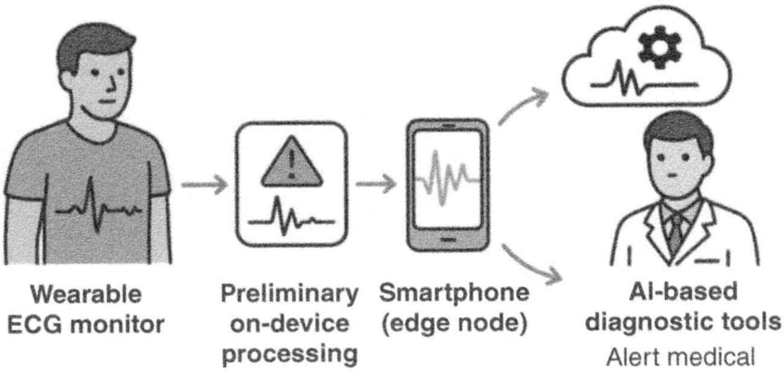

Figure 1.1 Wearable electrocardiogram (ECG) assisted with edge computing.

- **Device-level Processing:** It involves computation directly on endpoint devices, such as embedded systems, smartphones, or Internet of Things (IoT) sensors. These devices are crucial for collecting and preprocessing data:
  - In home automation, a smart thermostat uses on-device sensors to detect occupancy and adjust temperature settings autonomously.
  - In environmental monitoring, a water quality sensor embedded in a river can analyze basic chemical parameters locally and only send alerts when thresholds are breached.

This hierarchical architecture enhances system responsiveness and reduces unnecessary data transmission. For example, in a smart transportation system, vehicles continuously collect data on location, speed, and traffic conditions. Edge units installed on road infrastructure aggregate this information to manage traffic lights and avoid congestion. Meanwhile, the cloud aggregates and analyzes long-term traffic patterns to inform urban planning and infrastructure development.

Another emerging application is in remote healthcare. As shown in Figure 1.1, a wearable electrocardiogram (ECG) monitor detects irregular heart rhythms and processes preliminary results on-device. If anomalies are detected, the data is passed to a nearby smartphone (acting as an edge node) for detailed processing. If a critical pattern is confirmed, the data is transmitted to the cloud for analysis by artificial intelligence (AI)-based diagnostic tools and alerting medical personnel.

1.2 Tasks

Tasks in cloud-edge-device systems are the atomic units of computation. They can be simple or complex, and their characteristics often determine their ideal placement in the architecture. Based on execution dependencies and timing requirements, tasks fall into the following categories:

- **Real-time Dependent Tasks:** These require strict timing and often involve data dependencies between tasks. Examples include:
  - In an autonomous drone delivery system, real-time video analysis for obstacle detection must be followed by trajectory adjustment within milliseconds.
  - In augmented reality (AR) applications, rendering and positioning of virtual objects must occur in sequence and with minimal delay to maintain a smooth user experience.
- **Independent Tasks:** These have no interdependencies and can be executed in parallel or out of order. They are ideal for distributed scheduling. Examples include:
  - In financial services, fraud detection models may process user transaction logs independently to detect suspicious patterns.
  - In scientific simulations, multiple Monte Carlo simulations with different seed values can run in parallel across cloud servers.
- **Mixed-criticality Tasks:** These combine tasks of varying urgency and importance, requiring differentiated handling:
  - In aerospace systems, navigation control (high-criticality) must be prioritized over cabin temperature regulation (low-criticality).
  - In e-health applications, a fall detection alert from a wearable must take precedence over routine vitals logging.

Effectively categorizing and managing these tasks enables systems to make informed decisions about task offloading, redundancy, and scheduling. For instance, in a connected vehicle network, engine diagnostics (low-criticality, batch tasks) can be deferred to the cloud, while lane-change detection (high-criticality, real time) is executed at the edge or device level.

1.3 Task Scheduling

Scheduling governs how tasks are allocated across the cloud-edge-device hierarchy. Efficient scheduling is essential for optimizing energy, meeting deadlines, and ensuring a seamless user experience. Several key challenges must be addressed:

- **Energy Efficiency:** Energy conservation is vital, especially for battery-powered devices and sensors. Scheduling strategies may:
  - Batch low-priority data uploads to the cloud during low-energy-cost periods.
  - Utilize low-power modes on edge devices when not actively processing.

  For example, a wildlife tracking system on GPS collars may only activate data transmission when the animal moves beyond a geofence, thereby extending battery life.

- **Resource Utilization:** Balancing load prevents both overload and underuse. Effective strategies include:
  - Offloading heavy analytics tasks to the cloud during peak edge load.
  - Prefetching and caching frequently accessed data at edge nodes.

  In smart retail, when a surge of users interacts with a digital kiosk, computation for recommendations can be load-balanced to nearby edge nodes while preserving UI responsiveness.
- **Real-time Constraints:** Meeting deadlines is essential in safety-critical applications. For instance:
  - In telemedicine, patient monitoring systems must deliver abnormal health event notifications within seconds.
  - In cooperative adaptive cruise control, vehicle-to-vehicle communication delays must be minimal to avoid collisions.
- **Workload Variability:** Real-world systems must dynamically adapt to changing workloads. Scheduling algorithms can:
  - Use machine learning to predict upcoming workloads and pre-allocate resources accordingly.
  - Apply load-shedding strategies when resources are temporarily unavailable.

  In cloud gaming, servers may preload player profiles and game state during anticipated high-traffic periods (e.g., evenings or weekends) to maintain consistent performance.

Advanced scheduling frameworks are increasingly leveraging AI-driven optimization and feedback loops. For example, reinforcement learning-based schedulers can continuously learn optimal task placement strategies under varying network, compute, and energy constraints.

1.4 Outline of the Book

This book explores the design, implementation, and optimization of scheduling techniques in cloud-edge-device computing systems. It systematically addresses the challenges of real-time task execution across heterogeneous computing layers through theoretical models, algorithmic innovations, and practical applications. The content is organized as follows:

- Chapter 2 focuses on scheduling mixed real-time tasks in automotive systems with vehicular networks. It introduces a hybrid scheduler and provides offline and online task assignment strategies, along with complexity analysis and schedulability testing.

- Chapter 3 explores workload-aware scheduling of real-time independent tasks in cloud environments. It discusses virtual CPU and power models, formulates the scheduling problem, and presents solutions for both single and multiple server settings with energy-efficient strategies.
- Chapter 4 examines energy-minimized scheduling for real-time-dependent tasks in the cloud. It provides task placement strategies that balance real-time constraints with power consumption goals, utilizing both forward and backward scheduling techniques.
- Chapter 5 transitions to vehicular edge computing and discusses scheduling strategies for real-time-dependent tasks. It introduces decentralized auction-based methods and group scheduling to support multiple applications with power-aware task execution.
- Chapter 6 delves into the complexity of scheduling mixed-criticality dependent tasks in vehicular edge systems. This chapter presents task decomposition, frequency prediction, and dynamic programming techniques to ensure real-time guarantees in multimode operational environments.
- Chapter 7 bridges theory and practice by illustrating real-world applications of scheduling technologies in domains such as smart cities, industrial automation, healthcare monitoring, and autonomous systems.
- Chapter 8 summarizes the key contributions and insights from the preceding chapters and outlines potential directions for future research, including adaptive scheduling, AI-assisted task management, and cross-layer orchestration.

Each chapter concludes with a summary to reinforce key concepts and facilitate understanding, while extensive performance evaluations and case studies ground the discussion in practical relevance.

1.5 Summary

The cloud-edge-device computing paradigm has transformed the digital landscape by enabling distributed intelligence and responsive services. As modern applications grow in complexity and require low latency, high availability, and energy efficiency, the importance of effective task scheduling becomes paramount.

This introductory chapter has laid the foundation for understanding the structure and objectives of cloud-edge-device systems, categorized task types, and highlighted critical scheduling challenges such as energy efficiency, resource utilization, real-time constraints, and workload variability. These insights establish the context for the detailed exploration that follows.

The subsequent chapters of this book will delve deeper into task scheduling strategies tailored to different scenarios and system architectures. Through rigorous analysis, algorithm design, and practical application, this book aims to equip readers – researchers, practitioners, and advanced students alike – with the tools and knowledge to design more efficient and intelligent cloud-edge-device computing systems.

2

Scheduling Mixed Real-time Tasks in an Automotive System with Vehicular Network

As vehicles incorporate increasingly advanced autonomous driving capabilities, the role of vehicular networks in ensuring both safety and real-time performance of on-board computing tasks becomes critical. While existing research on vehicular networks primarily focuses on enhancing network communication and resource allocation, it often overlooks the crucial role of on-board computing in vehicle safety. Addressing this gap, this chapter introduces a hybrid scheduling framework designed to guarantee the completion of all hard real-time tasks while minimizing deadline misses for soft real-time tasks. The proposed scheduling system consists of local and global schedulers. The local schedulers ensure the timely execution of hard real-time tasks, while the global scheduler dynamically allocates soft real-time jobs based on real-time network conditions. Depending on the available processing capacity of the vehicular network, incoming jobs are either scheduled for execution or discarded. To optimize task allocation, we propose a novel approach that integrates a utilization-based schedulability test with demand-supply analysis, enabling efficient offline task assignment. To maximize the number of soft real-time tasks that meet their deadlines, our framework dynamically computes demand and supply bounds at runtime, leveraging real-time execution data to mitigate scheduling inefficiencies inherent in worst-case offline assumptions. Experimental results demonstrate that, compared to a genetic algorithm, our approach significantly reduces computational overhead while achieving superior offline task assignment. Additionally, the online scheduling mechanism successfully recovers many soft real-time jobs that would otherwise be dropped by the offline algorithm.

Intelligent Scheduling of Tasks for Cloud-Edge-Device Computing Systems, First Edition.

Published 2025 by John Wiley & Sons, Inc.

2.1 Introduction

In recent years, the increasing adoption of computing-intensive applications, such as autonomous driving, coupled with a global vehicle user base exceeding one billion, has placed significant strain on the communication and computing resource management of vehicular networks. To address these challenges, cloud and edge computing technologies have been integrated into vehicular networks. Cloud servers offer vast computing power to handle resource-intensive applications, while edge servers provide low-latency, high-bandwidth solutions for flexible and real-time services [1–3]. Consequently, a key challenge in such systems is optimizing the utilization of computing resources to effectively support diverse applications while ensuring the highest possible quality of service (QoS).

Vehicular networks leverage vehicle-to-roadside and roadside-to-cloud communication to support autonomous driving while ensuring traffic safety and efficiency. Numerous roadside units equipped with edge servers are deployed along roadways to handle vehicles' computational requests. When an edge server lacks sufficient capacity, these requests can be offloaded to remote cloud servers for processing. Vehicular network applications encompass a wide range of functions, including vehicle navigation, traffic flow control, congestion management, and accident warnings. Broadly, these applications can be categorized into automotive applications, which originate from vehicle operations, and traffic applications, which stem from traffic monitoring and regulation. Each application type has distinct QoS requirements and must be prioritized accordingly. For many automotive applications, real-time performance is crucial to ensuring driving safety, particularly as autonomous driving capabilities continue to advance. In this chapter, we focus on optimizing the scheduling of automotive applications to enhance their efficiency and responsiveness.

A vehicular network comprises three layers of computing resources with varying capabilities to support automotive applications: vehicular on-board computing, edge computing, and remote cloud computing. Vehicular on-board resources, located within the vehicle itself, provide direct computing power for automotive applications. Roadside units, connected to vehicles via wireless communication, serve as intermediaries that facilitate offloading computational tasks. Meanwhile, cloud servers aggregate data from multiple roadside units and vehicles, enabling more comprehensive traffic regulation and optimization. Existing research [4–8] predominantly focuses on computation resource allocation and task assignment optimization, often assuming that all applications, regardless of origin, can freely utilize all three computing layers. However, this assumption is overly optimistic and impractical. In reality, vehicles are typically self-interested and reluctant to share their computing resources due to concerns about security, privacy, and economic factors. A more realistic scenario is that each vehicle processes only its own automotive applications. If its on-board computing resources are insufficient, certain tasks can be offloaded to an edge or cloud server for processing. This chapter aims to develop an efficient scheduling framework tailored to this practical scenario, ensuring optimal resource utilization while maintaining security and performance constraints.

Modern vehicles are increasingly equipped with a diverse range of automotive applications designed to enhance passenger comfort and entertainment. These applications can generally be classified into hard real-time and soft real-time categories based on the severity of consequences resulting from timing failures. Hard real-time applications have strict timing requirements, as any failure to meet deadlines can pose serious risks to human safety. In this context, "sufficiently guaranteed" means that all hard real-time tasks must consistently meet their timing constraints. Examples include steering control, airbag deployment, and anti-lock braking systems. In contrast, soft real-time applications do not have life-threatening consequences if their timing constraints are not met. However, delays can affect the overall user experience, reducing comfort and entertainment quality. Examples include in-car gaming, radio streaming, and multimedia playback.

In this chapter, we address the challenge of efficiently scheduling mixed real-time automotive applications by maximizing the utilization of computing resources within a vehicular network. We model these applications as tasks that generate jobs either periodically or aperiodically, each requiring a specific execution time. The hardware architecture of modern vehicles consists of numerous heterogeneous electronic control units (ECUs) [9]. According to the Automotive Open System Architecture (AUTOSAR) standard [10], ECUs are evolving into general-purpose processors capable of handling a variety of tasks with different levels of efficiency. While our proposed scheduler operates on the vehicle side, it can offload certain jobs to roadside units or cloud servers when necessary. However, since the characteristics of these external servers do not directly impact the scheduling mechanism, they are not considered in our analysis. The core problem we investigate is how to efficiently allocate a mix of real-time tasks across a vehicle's ECUs or determine when to offload them to external computing resources. Our objective is to strictly ensure the timing requirements of all hard real-time tasks while minimizing deadline misses for soft real-time tasks, thereby optimizing overall system performance.

The task assignment problem in a homogeneous multiprocessor system is analogous to the bin packing problem and is known to be nondeterministic polynomial time (NP)-hard [11]. In automotive systems, tasks consist of both hard and soft real-time types, each requiring distinct handling strategies. A simple approach is to prioritize hard real-time tasks over soft ones. While this ensures the strict timing requirements of hard real-time tasks, it can be suboptimal for soft real-time tasks, particularly those with urgent deadlines that may need to be processed before certain hard real-time tasks with higher timing tolerances. Another challenge arises from aperiodic task releases. To guarantee their timing constraints, system schedulability is typically evaluated under the worst-case assumption that these tasks arrive as frequently as possible. While this ensures strict deadline adherence, it also leads to significant resource underutilization, as real-world workloads rarely exhibit such extreme conditions. To address this, a scheduler must be adaptive, dynamically adjusting task execution based on real-time system behavior rather than static worst-case assumptions. Furthermore, heterogeneous ECUs in modern vehicles add another layer of complexity compared to homogeneous multiprocessor systems. Different ECUs have varying processing capabilities, making efficient task allocation even more challenging. While some existing studies [5, 12, 13] have proposed partial solutions to these issues, none provide a comprehensive approach suitable for our specific problem.

To ensure that all hard real-time tasks meet their requirements while minimizing the timing failures of soft real-time tasks, this work proposes a hybrid scheduling framework that integrates offline schedulability testing with online job assignments. This framework makes two key contributions to the field of automotive task scheduling:

1. **Formulation of the Mixed Real-time Task Scheduling Problem:** For the first time, the scheduling of mixed real-time automotive tasks within the context of a vehicular network is formally addressed. A hybrid scheduling framework has been introduced, consisting of global and local schedulers, which ensures that all hard real-time tasks meet their deadlines while minimizing the number of soft real-time tasks that miss their deadlines.
2. **Two-stage Task Assignment Scheme:** The proposed scheme consists of two stages: offline stage: a combination of the utilization-based schedulability testing and demand-supply analysis is employed to quickly find assignments for all hard real-time tasks and some soft real-time tasks. Online stage: using real-time information about task releases and executions, demand-bound analysis is applied to efficiently utilize remaining computing resources and adaptively schedule unassigned jobs.

2.2 Related Work

The core concept of a vehicular network is to enable vehicles on the road to form a communication network using wireless self-organizing technologies, facilitating the exchange and dissemination of various types of information [14, 15]. With the advancement of autonomous driving, vehicles now need to collect and process an increasing amount of information in real time. As a result, vehicular networking and computing technologies have significantly expanded the available computing resources for executing these tasks [2, 16, 17]. Consequently, efficiently utilizing these diverse resources to enhance the QoS for these tasks has become a critical challenge. Given its importance, numerous techniques have been proposed in the literature to optimize system performance from various perspectives. Since this chapter focuses on the design of an automotive task scheduling framework, we review relevant work on task scheduling and resource allocation within vehicular networks.

To overcome the limitations of vehicular on-board hardware, vehicles are assumed to be capable of offloading computing-intensive tasks to peripheral servers. In various scenarios, depending on the optimization goals, several solutions have been proposed for the simultaneous allocation of resources in edge computing. For example, in Jiang et al. [4], an optimal policy is introduced for minimizing deadline violations in vehicular clouds by using a task replication technique. However, this approach requires frequent information exchanges, which can result in high communication overhead. Addressing the lack of efficient incentives and task assignment mechanisms, Zhou et al. [6] propose a contract-matching approach to motivate vehicles to share their resources and minimize network delays. In Ning et al. [18], a partial computation offloading and task scheduling algorithm is presented, aiming to maximize overall system-wide profit while considering the incentive compatibility and individual rationality of vehicular users. Additionally, a priority scheme for task scheduling with dependencies is introduced in Liu et al. [7], ensuring that application completion time constraints and processing tasks with dependency requirements are met.

While these studies predominantly focus on task offloading strategies within vehicular networks, they often fail to address the inherent unreliability of wireless communication for task offloading, which makes it unsuitable for safety-critical automotive tasks.

To address the task scheduling problem with varying requirements, the concept of a mixed-criticality system has been introduced, enabling both safety-critical and non-safety-critical tasks to share the same hardware infrastructure [19]. In such systems, task interference can be mitigated by defining different levels of task execution and employing a mode-switching scheme [12, 20, 21]. However, from a practical standpoint, many of the approaches proposed by the mixed-criticality research community deviate significantly from industrial standards and practices [22]. Furthermore, these approaches do not explore the potential benefits of utilizing peripheral servers to enhance task QoS.

With the increasing demand for computing power in the automotive sector, automakers and tier-one suppliers are incorporating multicore ECUs into automotive hardware architectures. These systems feature heterogeneous processing capabilities, enabling the execution of diverse tasks with varying levels of efficiency. In Monot et al. [23], low-complexity heuristics are proposed for partitioning tasks and organizing sequencer tasks to execute the runnable set on each core. To balance load and ensure task deadlines under contingency conditions, a mixed harmonic runnable scheduling algorithm, which includes partitioned scheduling, is discussed in Lee et al. [24]. Other studies, such as Bello et al. [25], Xie et al. [26, 27], and Quan et al. [28], focus on shortening completion times, minimizing energy consumption, and improving the reliability of automotive applications with task dependencies. However, these approaches do not address task scheduling based on real-time task execution information.

We conclude that there is not a scheduling framework that makes use of computing resources in a vehicular network to meet the timing requirements of hard and soft real-time automotive tasks. In particular, how to reclaim system computing resources online to serve the released jobs adaptively remains open. This work intends to solve them.

2.3 Models and Problem Formulation

2.3.1 Software Model

2.3.1.1 Task Model

Tasks in an automotive system can be either hard real time or soft real time, and their release pattern can be either periodic or aperiodic. Hence, there are generally four types of tasks, which are periodically released hard real-time tasks, aperiodically released hard ones, periodically released soft real-time tasks, and aperiodically released soft ones.

We use (τ_i, w_i, d_i) to denote task T_i's characteristics, where τ_i denotes its period, w_i denotes its worst-case execution time, and d_i denotes its deadline. Note that, for aperiodic tasks that have no strict period, τ_i denotes the minimum time interval between its two successive releases. We further assume that a task's deadline is equal to its period, i.e., $d_i = \tau_i$, implying that it must be completed before the next same task arrives.

2.3.1.2 Job Model

Every time a task is released, a corresponding job is generated. For example, if task $T_i(\tau_i, w_i, d_i)$ is released at time t, we use $J(t_r, T_i)$ to denote the job characteristics, where t_r is its release time, i.e., $t_r = t$, and its absolute deadline is $t_r + d_i$; T_i is its parent task. A job meets the real-time requirement if it finishes before its absolute deadline, i.e., $f(J) \leq t_r + d_i$, where $f(J)$ represents its finish time.

2.3.2 Hardware Model

2.3.2.1 Vehicular Network Model

On the hardware side, a vehicular network includes three layers of computation units that can be used to execute tasks, i.e., the vehicle itself, roadside units, and a cloud server. Because vehicles are always moving, they are connected with roadside units via wireless communication only, while roadside units are connected to a cloud server in various ways. Automotive tasks coming from a vehicle can stay in it or be offloaded to a roadside unit or a cloud server. For offloaded ones, vehicles get the response back after they have been processed. However, a hidden danger for them is that this response can be delayed for a long time or cut off due to the fact that the wireless communication is not always reliable, particularly due to moving vehicles.

2.3.2.2 Vehicular Computation Model

In the vehicle layer, the automotive system is composed of a set of different types of ECUs, where an ECU is a processor that can process an automotive job. In general, different ECUs have different computation power to execute a job, and we use Λ_j to denote an ECU and use $\lambda_{i,j}$ to represent its computation efficiency of processing T_i. If job $J(t_r, T_i)$ runs on this ECU, its worst-case execution time is $w_i/\lambda_{i,j}$.

2.3.2.3 Roadside and Cloud Computation Model

We suppose that when a vehicle is going to offload its task to a roadside unit or cloud server, its finish time is immediately estimated and returned to the vehicle. Such a finish time estimation technique can be achieved by learning-based approaches, as shown in Cheng et al. [29, 30] and Liu et al. [31]. For example, when the request for processing $J(t_r, T_i)$ is submitted to a roadside unit, the unit estimates its finish time as $g(J)$, and if it is submitted to the cloud server, the cloud server estimates its finish time as $h(J)$. Here, we intentionally ignore the finish time estimation scheme in a roadside unit and cloud server, and focus on the scheduler design in the automotive system only. In this way, we have

$$f(J) = \begin{cases} g(J), & J \text{ is run in roadside unit} \\ h(J), & J \text{ is run in cloud server} \end{cases}. \tag{2.1}$$

2.4 Hybrid Scheduler Design

Our goal is to design an automotive scheduler that can minimize the number of soft real-time tasks missing their deadlines, while sufficiently guaranteeing that all hard real-time tasks meet their deadlines. Toward this goal, considering that wireless communication is not reliable, hard real-time tasks should be processed only by a vehicle itself. Soft ones can be offloaded for better service.

AUTOSAR suggests preemptive static priority and partitioned scheduling for safety-critical tasks on multicore implemented ECUs.[1] The automotive computing

1 www.autosar.org

system can then be generalized as a heterogeneous multiprocessor system, where a task can be assigned to a processor for its execution. The system is scheduled by a global scheduler and many local ones. The former assigns a task to a processor, while a local scheduler at each individual processor schedules the assigned tasks [32]. Here, we consider that a processor has its own local scheduler and memory space, where job migration among processors is not permitted. In this chapter, we take the fixed priority (FP) as a local scheduler, and focus on designing a global scheduler, i.e., deciding how to assign tasks to the processors and which job should be offloaded.

A hybrid scheduling framework is proposed as shown in Figure 2.1. Tasks are first assigned via schedulability test offline. The assigned tasks are sent to the specific processor deployed with FP local scheduler, while unassigned tasks need to be handled by the global scheduler dynamically online. Here, processors' free slack is calculated by using demand-supply analysis online. This slack is reclaimed to serve the released jobs from unassigned tasks, and it has no impact on the schedulability of assigned tasks. If such a processor is not found, the released job is either offloaded or discarded, depending on the estimated finish time of a roadside unit and cloud server.

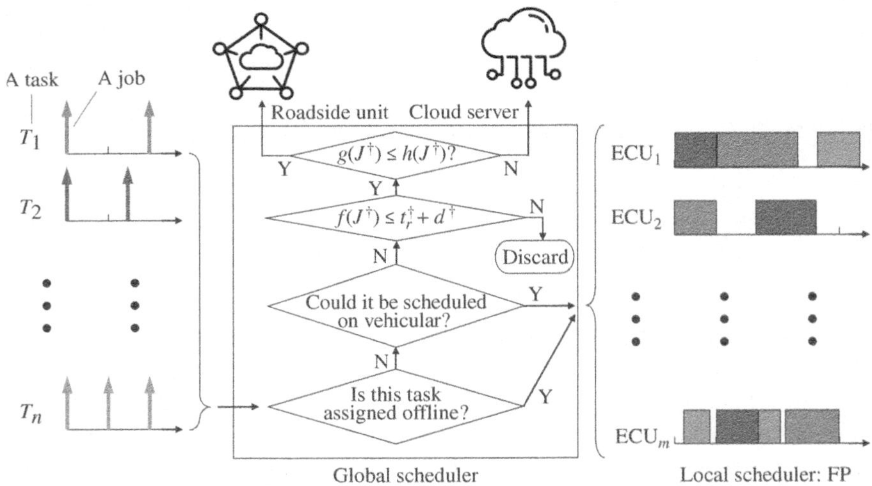

Figure 2.1 The hybrid scheduling framework, where $J^\dagger$ denotes the jobs from an unassigned task, $t_r^\dagger$ denotes its release time, and $d^\dagger$ denotes its deadline.

2.5 Schedulability Test

For periodic tasks scheduled by FP, an optimal priority assignment is to follow a rate-monotonic scheme, i.e., tasks with higher release frequencies (smaller periods) have higher priorities than tasks with lower release frequencies (larger periods). In this chapter, we adopt this scheme to assign priorities. Tasks in a processor are called schedulable if they can all meet their deadlines at any time. There are generally two approaches to test the schedulability of periodic tasks: one is based on utilization and the other is based on demand-supply analysis.

2.5.1 Utilization-based Schedulability Test

Liu and Layland [33] have proved that for a set of n periodic tasks with unique periods, a feasible schedule that always meets deadlines exists if the CPU utilization is below a specific bound (depending on the number of tasks).

Theorem 2.1 *Liu and Layland [33] Consider a set of n tasks where w_i and τ_i are the worst-case execution time and period of task T_i on a processor Λ, $i = 1, 2, \ldots, n$, respectively. The schedulability test condition for rate-monotonic scheduling is*

$$\sum_{i=1}^{n} \frac{w_i}{\tau_i} \leq n(2^{1/n} - 1). \tag{2.2}$$

Note that this test also fits for tasks that are released aperiodically but with a minimum release distance [34]. In addition, (2.2) is a sufficient but not necessary condition for schedulability, which means, there would be some task sets that are schedulable without satisfying (2.2). To tightly test the schedulability, we can use demand-supply analysis.

2.5.2 Demand-supply Analysis

For a task T_i with period or minimum release distance τ_i, its release times within Δ is bounded by

$$\alpha(T_i, \Delta) = \left\lfloor \frac{\Delta + \tau_i}{\tau_i} \right\rfloor, \; \forall \Delta > 0, \tag{2.3}$$

where $\alpha(T_i, 0) = 0$ and $\lfloor x \rfloor$ is round down of x [13]. For instance, when $\Delta = 0$, a task can be activated only once, and when $\Delta \in [3,\ 4) \cdot \tau_i$, a task can be activated at most four times.

Definition 2.1 The *workload-bound function* [13] models the number of execution time units requested by a task over any interval of length Δ.

Because each released task needs w_i units of execution time, the *workload-bound function* of task T_i within Δ is then bounded by

$$\varsigma(T_i, \Delta) = \left\lfloor \frac{\Delta + \tau_i}{\tau_i} \right\rfloor \cdot w_i, \ \forall \Delta > 0, \tag{2.4}$$

where $\varsigma(T_i, 0) = 0$ [13].

Definition 2.2 The *demand-bound function* [13] models the minimum execution time units over any interval of a length Δ that must be provided to a set of tasks to ensure their schedulability.

Because each released task has a deadline d_i, this demand is bounded by

$$\varrho(T_i, \Delta) = \left\lfloor \frac{\Delta + \tau_i - d_i}{\tau_i} \right\rfloor \cdot w_i, \ \forall \Delta \geq 0, \tag{2.5}$$

with $d_i = \tau_i$, we have

$$\varrho(T_i, \Delta) = \left\lfloor \frac{\Delta}{\tau_i} \right\rfloor \cdot w_i, \ \forall \Delta \geq 0.$$

Definition 2.3 The *supply-bound function* [13] models the minimal number of execution time units available over any interval of a length Δ for a processor.

For example, for a task T_1 that has the highest priority in a processor, the available resource to this task is the whole computation service from this processor, i.e.,

$$\beta(T_1, \Delta) = \Delta,$$

where $\beta(T_1, \Delta)$ denotes the supply-bound function of task T_1 over an interval of Δ. For tasks whose priorities are not the highest, their supply-bound functions are the computing resources left over after processing all higher-priority tasks.

Theorem 2.2 *Chakraborty et al. [35] If the supply-bound function of a task is equal to or larger than its demand-bound function, i.e.,*

$$\beta(T_i, \Delta) \geq \varrho(T_i, \Delta), \tag{2.6}$$

this task is schedulable where $\beta(T_i, \Delta)$ denotes the supply-bound function of task T_i over an interval of Δ.

Without loss of generality, we suppose that $T_1, T_2, \ldots, T_n$, are ordered from the highest priority to the lowest one. As shown in Figure 2.2, computing resources

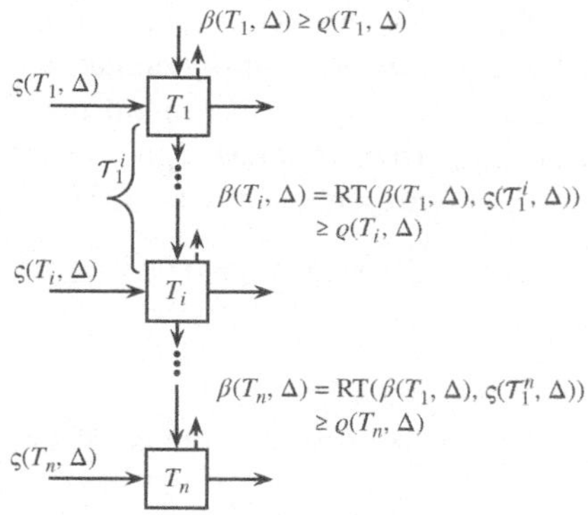

Figure 2.2 Demand-supply schedulability test for fixed-priority scheduling.

are used from T_1 to T_n successively. We can use the real-time calculus to get the supply-bound function for a specific task T_i [35]:

$$\begin{aligned}\beta(T_{i+1}, \Delta) &= \mathrm{RT}(\beta(T_1, \Delta), \varsigma(\mathcal{T}_1^i, \Delta)) \\ &= \sup_{0\leq\lambda\leq\Delta} \{\beta(T_1, \lambda) - \varsigma(\mathcal{T}_1^i, \lambda)\}, \ \forall i \in \{2..n\}\text{'}\end{aligned} \tag{2.7}$$

where

$$\beta(T_1, \Delta) = \Delta, \ \varsigma(\mathcal{T}_1^i, \Delta) = \sum_{j=1}^{i-1} \varsigma(T_j, \Delta),$$

where $\mathcal{T}_1^i$ represents the task set, including tasks from T_1 to T_{i-1}. The calculation of RT in (2.7) gets the supply-bound function that is left after processing all its higher-priority tasks. To guarantee the schedulability of every task, its supply-bound function must be equal to or greater than its demand-bound function, i.e.,

$$\beta(T_i, \Delta) \geq \varrho(T_i, \Delta), \ \forall \Delta, \ \forall i \in \{1..n\}. \tag{2.8}$$

2.6 Offline Task Assignment

Once tasks are assigned to processors offline, they stay on their processors permanently. Thus, the computation overhead for the global scheduler can be greatly reduced if more tasks can be assigned offline. For this aim, we will discuss how to assign as many tasks as possible offline next.

2.6.1 Problem Formulation

In the system, we suppose that there are n hard real-time tasks denoted as $T_1, T_2, \ldots, T_n$, and n' soft real-time tasks denoted as $T'_1, T'_2, \ldots, T'_{n'}$. Without loss of generality, $T_1, T_2, \ldots, T_n$ and $T'_1, T'_2, \ldots, T'_{n'}$ are both ordered in ascending order of their periods. Besides, there are m processors denoted as $\Lambda_1, \Lambda_2, \ldots, \Lambda_m$. We use $x_{i,j}$ and $y_{i',j}$ to represent the assignment of hard real-time tasks and soft real-time tasks, respectively. In particular, if task T_i has been assigned to processor Λ_j, $x_{i,j} = 1$. Otherwise, $x_{i,j} = 0$. This scheme also fits for $y_{i',j}$. Because a task can be assigned to one processor only, we have $\sum_{j=1}^{m} x_{i,j} = 1\,(1 \le i \le n)$ and $\sum_{j=1}^{m} y_{i',j} = 1\,(1 \le i' \le n')$.

In our heterogeneous multiprocessor system, the execution time of task T_i on processor Λ_j is

$$c_{i,j} = x_{i,j} \cdot \frac{w_i}{\lambda_{i,j}},$$

where we have $c_{i,j} = 0$ if T_i is not assigned to Λ_j. Then, the utilization of processor Λ_j can be computed as

$$\mathcal{U}_j = \sum_{i=1}^{n} x_{i,j} \cdot \frac{w_i}{\lambda_{i,j} \cdot \tau_i} + \sum_{i'=1}^{n'} y_{i',j} \cdot \frac{c'_{i'}}{\lambda'_{i',j} \cdot \tau'_{i'}}, \tag{2.9}$$

where $c'_{i'}$, $\tau'_{i'}$ and $\lambda'_{i',j}$ denote the worst-case execution time, period, and computation efficiency of the task $T'_{i'}$, respectively. The first part of (2.9) is the utilization taken by hard real-time tasks, and the second part is the utilization taken by soft ones. The task count at this processor is

$$n_j = \sum_{i=1}^{n} x_{i,j} + \sum_{i'=1}^{n'} y_{i',j}. \tag{2.10}$$

According to Theorem 2.1, tasks at Λ_j are schedulable if

$$\mathcal{U}_j \le n_j(2^{1/n_j} - 1).$$

Hence, in order to make all tasks schedulable, we have to find $x_{i,j}$ and $y_{i',j}$ that meet the below conditions:

$$\begin{cases} \mathcal{U}_j \le n_j(2^{1/n_j} - 1), & j = 1, \ldots, m \\ \sum_{j=1}^{m} x_{i,j} = 1, & i = 1, \ldots, n \\ \sum_{j=1}^{m} y_{i',j} = 1, & i' = 1, \ldots, n' \end{cases}, \tag{2.11}$$

where $\mathcal{U}_j$ and n_j are presented in (2.9) and (2.10).

Unfortunately, there may not exist a feasible solution to meet the above conditions, especially in the overloaded situation where there are too many tasks but few processors in a system. To sufficiently guarantee that there is a solution in any case, we deliberately introduce a virtual processor into the system, where the virtual processor is able to accommodate any task without utilization limitations. In this way, the total count of processors becomes $m + 1$, and the above constraints then become

$$\begin{cases} \mathcal{U}_j \leq n_j(2^{1/n_j} - 1), & j = 1, \ldots, m \\ \sum_{j=1}^{m+1} x_{i,j} = 1, & i = 1, \ldots, n \\ \sum_{j=1}^{m+1} y_{i',j} = 1, & i' = 1, \ldots, n' \end{cases}. \tag{2.12}$$

Theorem 2.3 *There must exist a solution that meets the constraints of (2.12).*

Proof: Here, we present a solution that meets the above constraints in any case. Let

$$x_{i,j} = 0,\ x_{i,m+1} = 1,\ y_{i',j} = 0,\ y_{i',m+1} = 1,$$

where $i = 1, \ldots, n$, $i' = 1, \ldots, n'$, and $j = 1, \ldots, m$. We find that this solution assigns all tasks to the virtual processor. Hence, $\mathcal{U}_j = 0$ and $n_j = 0$, $\forall j = 1, \ldots, m$. The three conditions of (2.12) are thus met.

Although a virtual processor can guarantee the existence of a solution, there are still two problems yet to be solved, which are how to maximize the number of tasks that are schedulable in real processors and how to guarantee that all hard real-time tasks are schedulable. This requires us to set an optimization target that can maximize the number of tasks assigned to real processor, and strengthen the constraint that hard real-time tasks can be assigned to real processors only. We thus reformulate our problem to an optimization problem with constraints, i.e.,

$$\begin{aligned} \max \quad & \sum_{i=1}^{n}\sum_{j=1}^{m} x_{i,j} + \sum_{i'=1}^{n'}\sum_{j=1}^{m} y_{i',j} \\ \text{subject to}: \quad & \begin{cases} \mathcal{U}_j \leq n_j(2^{1/n_j} - 1), & j = 1, \ldots, m \\ \sum_{j=1}^{m} x_{i,j} = 1, & i = 1, \ldots, n \\ \sum_{j=1}^{m+1} y_{i',j} = 1, & i' = 1, \ldots, n' \end{cases}. \end{aligned} \tag{2.13}$$

This is a nonlinear integer program, where the optimization goal denotes the total count of tasks assigned to real processor $\Lambda_1, \Lambda_2, \ldots, \Lambda_m$; the first constraint guarantees the schedulability of tasks in real processors; the second constraint guarantees that hard real-time tasks can be assigned to real processor only; and the last constraint guarantees that a soft real-time task must be assigned to one of processors, including the virtual one.

This optimization problem is not easy to solve, because on the one hand, there is not an efficient solver to solve a nonlinear integer program, and on the other hand, the extra virtual processor increases the variables that make the problem more complicated. Besides, the utilization constraint is a sufficient condition, instead of a necessary condition, for testing tasks' schedulability. There can be cases that real processors can actually accommodate more tasks, while being excluded by this constraint. Here, we adopt a divide-and-conquer strategy to solve these problems. We try to assign hard real-time tasks first, and then soft real-time tasks, by adopting both utilization-based schedulability tests and demand-supply analysis.

2.6.2 Hard Real-time Task Assignment

In the worst case, all soft real-time tasks miss their deadlines, but all hard real-time tasks meet their deadlines. For this reason, we can first focus on the assignment of hard real-time tasks, and study how to assign soft real-time tasks afterward.

Since all hard real-time tasks need to be assigned, it makes no sense to set the optimization goal as the task count. In order to leave more utilization space for soft real-time tasks, the utilization taken by hard real-time tasks should be minimized. In addition, a nonlinear constraint is not good for optimization. We find that $n(2^{1/n} - 1)$ is a monotonically decreasing function with n and converges to 0.693 when $n \to +\infty$, i.e.,

$$\mathcal{U}_j > 0.693, \quad \lim_{n \to +\infty} \mathcal{U}_j = 0.693. \tag{2.14}$$

The first constraint of (2.15) can then be transferred to a linear constraint by replacing $n_j^h(2^{1/n_j^h} - 1)$ with 0.693, i.e., $\mathcal{U}_j^h \leq 0.693$. In this way, the nonlinear integer program is successfully changed to linear integer program, i.e.,

$$\begin{aligned} \min \quad & \sum_{j=1}^{m} \mathcal{U}_j^h \\ \text{subject to :} \quad & \begin{cases} \mathcal{U}_j^h \leq 0.693, & j = 1, \ldots, m, \\ \sum_{j=1}^{m} x_{i,j} = 1, & i = 1, \ldots, n \end{cases} \end{aligned} \tag{2.15}$$

where $\mathcal{U}_j^h = \sum_{i=1}^{n} x_{i,j} \cdot \frac{w_i}{\lambda_{i,j} \cdot \tau_i}$ and $n_j^h = \sum_{i=1}^{n} x_{i,j}$.

Because the first constraint of (2.15) is a sufficient but not necessary condition for schedulability, we need to further use the demand-supply analysis to accommodate more tasks to pass the schedulability test. It includes two steps.

1. Through the binary search, a feasible q is found out to make T_1 to T_q meet (2.15). Assign these tasks according to $x_{i,j}$.
2. For tasks from T_{q+1} to T_n, assign them to processors via the demand-supply schedulability test.

In the first step, as a linear integer program can be efficiently solved by some excellent solvers, we try to assign tasks as many as possible by solving (2.15). As shown in Algorithm 2.1, if not all tasks can pass the schedulability test by (2.15), tasks with the smaller periods have the preference for further investigation, while tasks with larger periods are intentionally filtered out. This can be achieved via binary search because T_1 to T_n have been ordered by their periods. Note that, once tasks have been assigned to a processor, their scheduling priorities are also automatically decided with the rate-monotonic scheme.

Algorithm 2.1: Step 1 of Task Assignment for Real-time Tasks

Require: $T_1, \ldots, T_n, \Lambda_1, \ldots,$ and Λ_m
Ensure: Task Assignment

1: Use binary search to find out q such that T_1 to T_q pass the schedulability test of (2.15), and assign T_1 to T_q to processors according to $x_{i,j}$ from the solution of (2.15);
2: **if** $q = n$ **then**
3: Success and return;
4: **else**
5: Assign tasks T_{q+1} to T_n by Algorithm 2.2;
6: **end if**

In the second step, for these tasks that do not meet (2.15), we assign them via (2.6). Tasks are successively tested from T_{q+1} to T_n. Because the processor with the lowest utilization has the highest chance to accommodate a new task, the processor choice is thus prioritized by their utilization. The real-time calculus [35] is used to derive its supply-bound function and demand-bound function by the rate-monotonic scheduling scheme. Once a processor is found to be feasible for a new task, this new task is assigned to it, and the algorithm turns to assigning the next task. This procedure continues until all tasks have been assigned. If there is a task that cannot be accommodated by any processor, the algorithm fails, as shown in Algorithm 2.2.

In general, the utilization-based schedulability test is fast but conservative to judge system schedulability, which means that some tasks are misjudged to be not schedulable. Hence, our designed two-step scheme first makes use of utilization-based schedulability test of (2.15) to assign tasks as many as possible, and leave unassigned tasks to be processed by the accurate but slow demand-supply analysis. This can shorten the time overhead of assigning tasks.

Algorithm 2.2: Step 2 of Task Assignment for Real-time Tasks

Require: $T_1, \ldots, T_n, \Lambda_1, \ldots,$ and Λ_m
Ensure: Task Assignment
for $k = (q+1)..n$ **do**
  Sort processors to $\Lambda_1^\flat$, $\Lambda_2^\flat$, .., and $\Lambda_m^\flat$ in the ascending order of utilization;
  for $j = 1..m$ **do**
    Test the schedulability of T_k on the processor $\Lambda_j^\flat$ via (2.6);
    if T_k can be scheduled in $\Lambda_j^\flat$ **then**
      Assign T_k to $\Lambda_j^\flat$;
      if $k = n$ **then**
        Succeed and return;
      else
        Break;
      end if
    else if $j = m$ **then**
      Fail to assign this task;
    end if
  end for
end for

2.6.3 Soft Real-time Task Assignment

Except for testing the schedulability of hard real-time tasks, soft real-time tasks can also be taken into the schedulability test. Analogously, we can reformulate the optimization problem as

$$
\begin{aligned}
\min \quad & \sum_{j=1}^{m} \mathcal{U}_j \\
\text{subject to :} \quad & \begin{cases} \mathcal{U}_j \leq 0.693, & j = 1, \ldots, m \\ \sum_{j=1}^{m} x_{i,j} = 1, & i = 1, \ldots, n \\ \sum_{j=1}^{m} y_{i',j} = 1, & i' = 1, \ldots, n' \end{cases},
\end{aligned}
\tag{2.16}
$$

where $\mathcal{U}_j$ is computed by (2.9). Note that constraint (2.16) is likely to hold only when all hard real-time tasks have been assigned by solving constraint (2.15) solely, i.e., $q = n$ in Algorithm 2.1. Otherwise, there is not a feasible solution to meet constraint (2.16) because $\sum_{i=1}^{n} x_{i,j} \cdot \frac{w_i}{\lambda_{i,j} \cdot \tau_i} \leq 0.693$ does not hold. We now discuss the two cases, respectively.

Case 1: $q = n$. In this case, we try to assign soft real-time tasks as many as possible by solving constraints (2.16). Analogous to Step 1 of Algorithm 2.1, we can use the binary search to find out q' such that there is a feasible assignment for soft real-time tasks from T'_1 to $T'_{q'}$ via solving (2.16). For these soft real-time tasks that are left unassigned, i.e., $T'_{q'+1}$ to $T'_{n'}$, we assign them to processors individually in a procedure similar to Stage 2 of Algorithm 2.2. For these soft real-time tasks that remain unschedulable in the end, they should be handled by the global scheduler online.

Case 2: $q < n$. In this case, there is not a solution for meeting (2.16). However, we can set $q' = 0$, and on the basis of hard real-time task assignment, soft real-time tasks are assigned to processors in the same way as assigning $T'_{q'+1}$ to $T'_{n'}$ of Case 1.

The aforementioned procedures of assigning soft real-time tasks are presented in Algorithm 2.3. It should be noted that in Case 1, there are two options about deciding $x_{i,j}$ ($\forall i \leq n,\ j \leq m$). One is to use the value from the solution of (2.15), and the other is to consider them as variables and decide their value by solving constraints (2.16). The former reduces the computation burden of deciding $y_{i,j}$, while the latter can often find a better option to accommodate more soft real-time tasks than the former.

Algorithm 2.3: Task Assignment for Soft Real-time Tasks

Require: $T'_1, \ldots, T'_{n'}, \Lambda_1, \ldots, \Lambda_m$
Ensure: Task Assignment

if $q = n$ **then**
    Use binary search to find out q' such that T'_1 to $T_{q'}$ pass the schedulability test of (2.16), and assign T'_1 to $T_{q'}$ to processors according to $y_{i,j}$ from the solution of (2.16);
    if $q' = n'$ **then**
        Return;
    end if
else
    $q' = 0$;
end if
Assign tasks $T'_{q'+1}$ to $T'_{n'}$ by Algorithm 2.2;

2.6.4 Complexity Analysis

Our proposed Algorithms 2.1–2.3 involve the integer linear program that is classified as an NP-complete problem [36]. Although there are some excellent solvers such as simplex, they all have exponential worst-case complexity. For assigning hard real-time tasks using Algorithms 2.1 and 2.2, the worst case is checking every possible solution candidate. Due to the fact that a task can possibly be assigned to any one of the processors, there are m options for each task. Together, there are m^n options in total. Thus, the worst-case complexity is $O(m^n)$.

As regards assigning hard and soft real-time tasks using Algorithm 2.3, there are m processors and $n + n'$ tasks. The worst-case complexity is thus $O(m^{n+n'})$. Considering that this algorithm works offline, such complexity has no effect on the system performance at runtime. Besides, from the experimental results of Section 2.8.2, we find that the average computation time to find an assignment solution is less than 1 second when the platform has less than 80 tasks and over 30 processors. This demonstrates that our proposed approach can work very efficiently.

2.7 Online Job Assignment

The task assignment offline can sufficiently guarantee the schedulability of assigned tasks. The schedulability test is based on the assumption that tasks are released as frequently as possible and every released job takes up the worst-case execution time. In reality, this assumption is too pessimistic because released jobs likely need less execution time, and aperiodic tasks are released less frequently, thus leaving a lot free slack for the global scheduler to insert the unassigned tasks. As shown in Figure 2.3, all tasks are first assigned to a partitioned ECU, and the job assignment online tries to save these unassigned tasks to run with extra capacity from ECU, edge server and cloud server. In this section, we discuss how to use the free slack to serve the unassigned tasks online, such that their deadlines can be met in the greatest margin.

2.7.1 Online Schedulability Test

We have derived the bound function of workload, demand, and supply for task T_i offline under the worst-case assumption in Section 2.5.2. However, with the online information of task execution, these bound functions can be refined. For the sake of brevity, $[\![a]\!]_b$ represents max(a, b), and $[\![a]\!]^c$ denotes min(a, c).

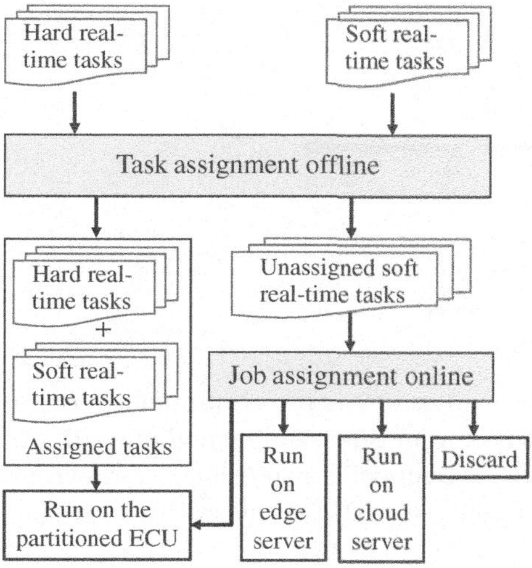

Figure 2.3 Scheduling flowchart.

Theorem 2.4 *At any time t, for a task T_i whose currently released job has been finished, its workload-bound function from time t and onward is*

$$\varsigma(T_i, \Delta, t) = \left[\!\!\left[\left\lfloor \frac{\Delta + t - r_i(t)}{\tau_i} \right\rfloor \right]\!\!\right]_0 w_i,$$

and its demand-bound function from time t and onward is

$$\varrho(T_i, \Delta, t) = \left[\!\!\left[\left\lfloor \frac{\Delta + t - r_i(t) - d_i}{\tau_i} \right\rfloor \right]\!\!\right]_0 w_i.$$

If the currently released job has not been finished, its workload-bound function from time t and onward is

$$\varsigma(T_i, \Delta, t) = (w_i - e_i(t)) + \left[\!\!\left[\left\lfloor \frac{\Delta + t - r_i(t)}{\tau_i} \right\rfloor \right]\!\!\right]_0 w_i, \tag{2.17}$$

and its demand-bound function from time t and onward is then

$$\begin{aligned} \varrho(T_i, \Delta, t) = & \left[\!\!\left[\left\lfloor \frac{\Delta}{r_i(t) + d_i - t} \right\rfloor \right]\!\!\right]^1 \cdot (w_i - e_i(t)) \\ & + \left[\!\!\left[\left\lfloor \frac{\Delta + t - r_i(t) - d_i}{\tau_i} \right\rfloor \right]\!\!\right]_0 w_i \end{aligned}, \tag{2.18}$$

where $r_i(t)$ and $e_i(t)$ are the release time and already finished execution of the latest released job of T_i at t, respectively.

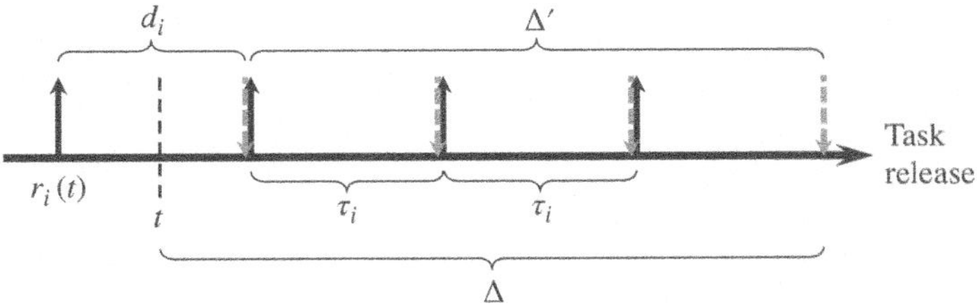

Figure 2.4 Task worst-case release pattern at time t.

Proof: Because the demand-bound function must bound the maximum execution demand of jobs from T_i within any interval from time t online and onward, we suppose that the future jobs are released as frequently as possible, as shown in Figure 2.4. The release time of last released job is $r_i(t)$, and this released job may have finished or not. We have two cases.

Case 1: The released job has finished, and it does not need further execution. The maximum number of released jobs within Δ is $\lfloor(\Delta' + \tau_i)/\tau_i\rfloor$, where $\Delta' = \Delta + t - r_i(t) - \tau_i$. Then, the workload of future jobs is bounded by

$$\varsigma(T_i, \Delta, t) = \max\left(0, \lfloor\frac{\Delta + t - r_i(t)}{\tau_i}\rfloor\right) \cdot w_i = \left[\!\left[\lfloor\frac{\Delta + t - r_i(t)}{\tau_i}\rfloor\right]\!\right]_0 \cdot w_i,$$

and the demand of future jobs is bounded by

$$\varrho(T_i, \Delta, t) = \max\left(0, \lfloor\frac{\Delta + t - r_i(t) - d_i}{\tau_i}\rfloor\right) \cdot w_i = \left[\!\left[\lfloor\frac{\Delta + t - r_i(t) - d_i}{\tau_i}\rfloor\right]\!\right]_0 \cdot w_i.$$

Case 2: The released job has not finished. The demand-bound function should also include the demand of this unfinished job. We denote this unfinished job as J_i. The upper bound of the remaining execution time of J_i is $(w_i - e_i(t))$, and it has to be finished before $r_i(t) + d_i$. Thus, this demand can be concluded as

$$\varrho(J_i, \Delta, t) = \min\left(1, \lfloor\frac{\Delta}{r_i(t) + d_i - t}\rfloor\right) \cdot (w_i - e_i(t)) = \left[\!\left[\lfloor\frac{\Delta}{r_i(t) + d_i - t}\rfloor\right]\!\right]^1 \cdot (w_i - e_i(t)).$$

In a nutshell, the workload-bound function and demand-bound function of T_i with the unfinished job are concluded as (2.17) and (2.18).

With the workload-bound and demand-bound functions of every task, we can use the real-time calculus to get the supply-bound function of each task. To guarantee the schedulability of every task, its supply-bound function must be equal to or greater than its demand-bound function, i.e.,

$$\beta(T_i, \Delta, t) \geq \varrho(T_i, \Delta, t), \ \forall \Delta, \ \forall i \in \{1..n\}. \tag{2.19}$$

2.7.2 Job Assignment Strategy

For tasks that are not assigned offline, their released jobs need to be assigned by the global scheduler online. Here, we suppose that different jobs from the same task can be assigned to different processors, but an assigned job cannot migrate to another processor. The principle of assigning a job is that its deadline should be met, without failing other tasks. Here, we find out a feasible processor via the schedulability test online.

Suppose that an unassigned task $T^\dagger$ releases a job $J^\dagger$ at time t, the demand-bound function of this job can be found as

$$\varrho(J^\dagger, \Delta, t) = \left[\left[\left\lfloor \frac{\Delta}{d^\dagger} \right\rfloor \right]\right]^1 \cdot c^\dagger,$$

where $d^\dagger$ and $c^\dagger$ are the job's deadline and worst-case execution time. We test whether this job can be assigned to a processor from Λ_1 to Λ_m individually. For example, if Λ_j is chosen to accommodate this job, we first set this job with the lowest priority, and gradually increase its priority until all tasks in Λ_j and the job itself are schedulable via the following test:

$$\begin{cases} \beta(T_i^j, \Delta, t) \geq \varrho(T_i^j, \Delta, t), & \forall i \in \{1..n^j\} \\ \beta(J^\dagger, \Delta, t) \geq \varrho(J^\dagger, \Delta, t) \end{cases}, \tag{2.20}$$

where T_i^j denotes the job at Λ_j, n^j denotes the job count, and $\beta(T_i^j, \Delta, t)$ and $\beta(J^\dagger, \Delta, t)$ are obtained by the real-time calculus.

If there are multiple processors that are feasible, the newly released job can be assigned to the processor that first passes the test. If no processor can pass the schedulability test, the global scheduler can request offloading it a roadside unit or a cloud server. If the estimated finish time is smaller than its deadline, this job is offloaded to the one with smaller finish time. Otherwise, this job is discarded, as shown in Algorithm 2.4.

Algorithm 2.4: Online Job Assignment

Require: Newly job $J^{\dagger}$, Task assignment made already (offline)
Ensure: Job assignment

for $j = 1..m$ **do**
  if constraint (2.20) holds **then**
    Assign job $J^{\dagger}$ to processor Λ_j;
    Return
  end if
end for
if $f(J^{\dagger}) \leq t + d^{\dagger}$ **then** ▷ $f(J^{\dagger})$ represents its estimated finish time, as shown in Eq. 2.1
  if $g(J^{\dagger}) \leq h(J^{\dagger})$ **then** ▷ $g(J^{\dagger})$ and $h(J^{\dagger})$ represent its estimated finish time from roadside unit and cloud server, respectively.
    Offload job $J^{\dagger}$ to the roadside unit;
  else
    Offload job $J^{\dagger}$ to cloud server;
  end if
else
  Discard job $J^{\dagger}$;
end if

2.7.3 Complexity Analysis

The worst case of assigning a job is to check every possible priority option in each processor. There are n^j options in a processor Λ_j assigned with n_j tasks. For every priority option, the real-time calculus of (2.7) is applied to do the supply-demand analysis for n_j times. Thus, the worst-case complexity is $O(mn_j^2)$. Because there are $n + n'$ tasks that are distributed on m processors, the average value of n_j is estimated to $\frac{n+n'}{m}$, and then the worst-case complexity is $O\left(\frac{(n+n')^2}{m}\right)$. This complexity is acceptable when the system size is not too large. The experimental results of Section 2.8.3 demonstrate that in a system with 200 tasks and 30 processors, most of jobs are assigned within 1 second, and the average computation time is less than 0.1 second. Therefore, it should be practicable to use the proposed approach in real automotive systems.

2.8 Performance Evaluation

The performance of our proposed hybrid scheduling framework is evaluated from two sides, where one is the schedulability test and the other is the job assignment online. Task sets that are common in automotive systems [37] are used for this evaluation, where we mainly compare our approaches with some state-of-the-art ones and perform sensitivity analysis and make various trade-offs.

Task period (unit: ms) is chosen at random from two base period sets that are {20, 40, 80, 200, 400, 800} ms and {25, 50, 100, 250, 500, 1000}. The ratio of hard real-time tasks and soft real-time tasks is 1:1. These parameters are typically found in automotive systems [38]. Task deadlines are set to be equal to their periods. The worst-case execution time of each task follows an unbiased distribution with the use of the Uunifast algorithm [39]. The actual execution time is a random value from $(\alpha, 1)$ of its worst-case execution time, where $0.2 \leq \alpha \leq 1$. The computation efficiency of a processor is a random number within [0.5, 1.5].

2.8.1 Compared Approaches

We have formulated the schedulability test as a nonlinear integer program as shown in (2.13), and two heuristic approaches combining utilization-based and supply-demand analysis are proposed to solve it. Besides, a genetic algorithm (GA) and an exact computing method can also be applied to solve this problem. In detail, the compared approaches of testing schedulability are as follows:

- **UT-SD:** By using the utilization-based test of (2.15) and then supply-demand analysis, this approach first assigns hard real-time tasks and then tries to assign soft real-time tasks as many as possible, as presented in Algorithms 2.1–2.3.
- **UT-SD⁺:** Analogous to UTSD, this approach also applies Algorithms 2.1–2.3 to assign tasks. However, unlike UT-SD, which applies the assignment of hard real-time tasks from (2.15) to solve the assignment problem of soft real-time tasks from (2.16), UT-SD⁺ finds their assignment using (2.16) without assignment information from (2.15).
- **EXACT:** This approach first transfers (2.13) to a linear integer program by setting the utilization limit as 0.693, and then tries to assign tasks from the virtual processor to the real one, only if the re-assignment does not violate the schedulability of assigned tasks.
- **GA:** It sets the optimization goal of (2.13) as the fitness function, and encodes task assignment as a float value within (0, 1). The population size is set to 100, iteration count is 50000, and mutation probability is 0.1.

Several metrics can be used to evaluate their performance. They include the rate of assigned tasks among all tasks offline, the computation time of finding task assignment, the rate of jobs saved for the online execution, and the computation time of deciding job assignment online. The rate of assigned tasks is calculated as $\frac{n_a + n'_a}{n + n'}$, where $n + n'$ denotes the total number of tasks and $n_a + n'_a$ denotes the number of tasks that find their assignment by the offline test. The rate of saved jobs is calculated as $\frac{n_a^{\Delta}}{n^{\Delta}}$, where n^{Δ} denotes the number of all jobs during an interval of Δ and n_a^{Δ} denotes the number of jobs that are processed (instead of being discarded).

2.8.2 Schedulability Test Results

We investigate the effect of task set size, processor count, and total task utilization on the schedulability test performance of compared approaches, where task utilization refers to its execution time divided by its period, i.e., $\frac{w_i}{\tau_i}$, and total task utilization $\mathcal{U}$ is the utilization sum of all tasks, i.e.,

$$\mathcal{U} = \sum_{i=1}^{n+n'} \frac{w_i}{\tau_i},$$

where w_i is the execution time and τ_i is the activation period of a task T_i.

For every parameter configuration, we perform 20 experiments on a randomly generated task set and use the average rate of assigned tasks among all tasks and average computation time of finding the solution as the experimental results.

2.8.2.1 Effect of Task Set Size

In this simulation, we vary the task set size from 50 to 200 by setting the processor count to 20 and the total task utilization to 16. The experimental results are presented in Figures 2.5a and 2.6a, where we find that the assignment rate of UT-SD and UT-SD$^+$ is almost the same and as high as 100%. This indicates that both are very effective to assign tasks. It appears counter-intuitive that their assignment rate has a slight increase with respect to task count increment. This is, however, reasonable because the total task utilization has been fixed to 16, and the larger the task count is, the smaller task utilization is. A smaller granularity of task utilization makes it easier to assign tasks to processors. From their computation time of Figure 2.6a, we find that UT-SD needs the least computation to find a solution. Especially when the task count is smaller than 80, it is very fast to assign tasks. This is because UT-SD first solves a small-size problem of (2.15), and its solution is very helpful to reduce the complexity of solving (2.16). The success rate of EXACT approach is not high because it does not use the demand-supply analysis to assign tasks. This also verifies that demand-supply analysis is effective to improve the system schedulability. EXACT approach needs more computation than UT-SD and UT-SD$^+$ to find a solution that is not as good as theirs. The assignment rate of GA is better than EXACT approach when the task count is less than 90. However, its computation is the largest.

2.8.2.2 Effect of Processor Count

In this simulation, we vary the processor count from 10 to 50 by setting the task set size to 200 and the total task utilization to 16. The results are presented in

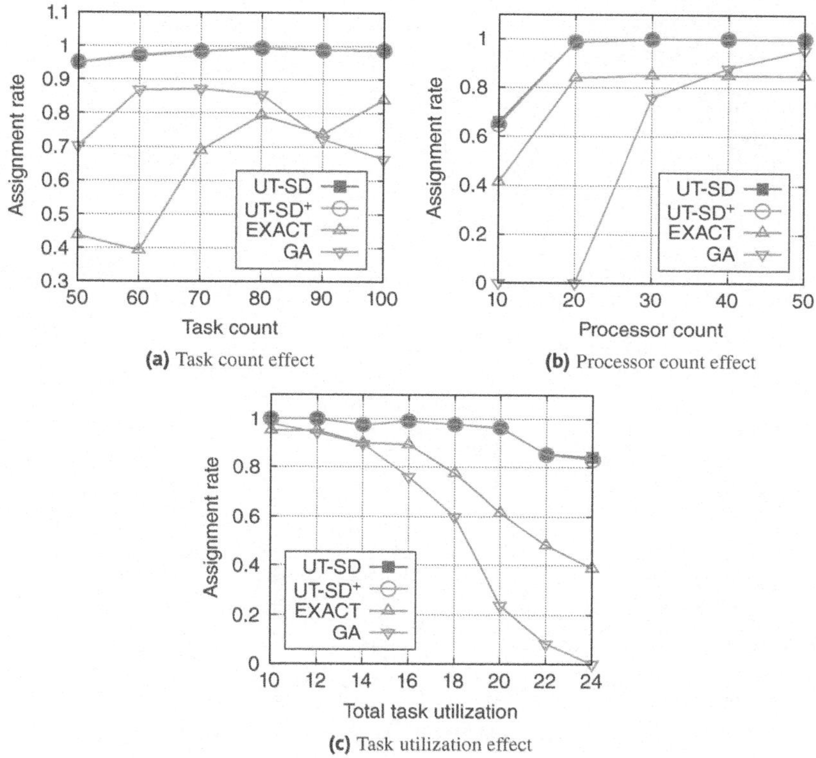

Figure 2.5 Average rate of assigned tasks among all tasks by UT-SD, UT-SD+, and EXACT approaches on synthetic automotive benchmark with varying parameters.

Figures 2.5b and 2.6b in a log-scale of vertical axis, where we find that the assignment rate of UT-SD and UT-SD$^+$ is almost the same and as high as 100% when the processor count is more than 20. The assignment rate of UT-SD and UT-SD$^+$ is 0.62 when the processor count is 10. This is because the total utilization is 16, and a system with 10 processors can only accommodate around 60% of all tasks. Figure 2.6b shows that the computation time of UT-SD, UT-SD$^+$, and EXACT declines exponentially with the processor count increment, which shows that increasing the processor count not only makes it easier to accommodate tasks but also greatly reduces the difficulty to find a solution. This is because the total task utilization is fixed to 16, and more processors mean more chances to accommodate them. Thus, the computation time declines with the increasing processor count. GA achieves a similar trend in assigning tasks, but its computation is high and does not decline, due to the fact that it has to iteratively search for 50000 times with a population size of 100.

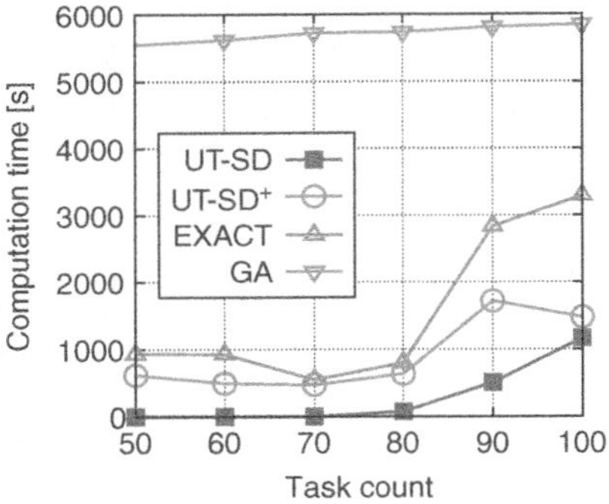

(a) Task count effect

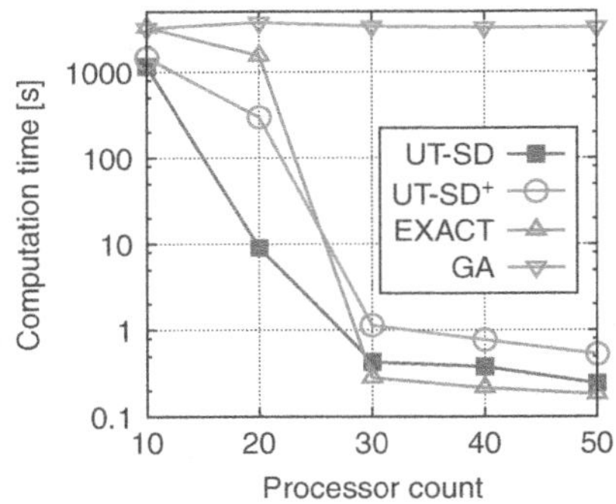

(b) Processor count effect

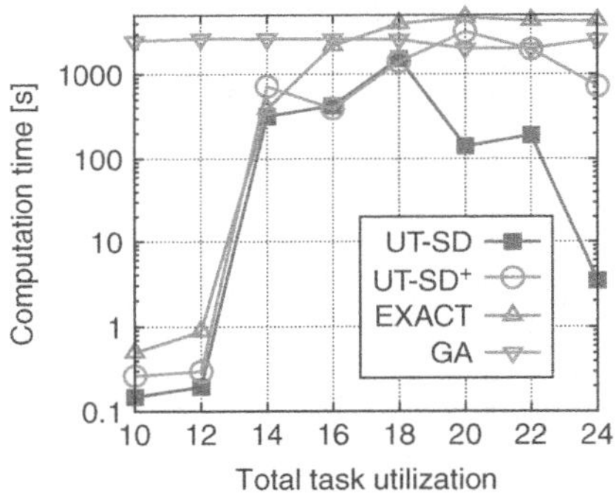

(c) Task utilization effect

Figure 2.6 Assignment rate and average computation time of compared approaches with varying parameter configurations.

2.8.2.3 Effect of Total Task Utilization

In this simulation, we vary the total task utilization from 10 to 24 by setting the task set size to 100 and the processor count to 20. The results are presented in Figures 2.5c and 2.6c, where it shows that UT-SD and UT-SD^{+} still perform very closely in assigning tasks. They can use the computing resources to the fullest by making the assignment rate close to 1 when the total task utilization is 20. Even when it is over 20, the utilization of assigned tasks in the system is also 20 because there are only 20 processors. The EXACT approach performs very badly by achieving only around 60% utilization of assigned tasks. The computation time is presented in Figure 2.6c, where its vertical axis is also log-scaled. It shows that the three approaches need computation time less than 1 second when total task utilization is below 12. However, it rises very sharply when it increases to 14. It also shows that there is a big fluctuation in computation time. In general, when it is close to the system's maximum capability, the computation time is the largest for the three approaches. But when it is over such a maximum level, there is a large chance to fail, thus reducing the search time. The assignment rate of GA drops more quickly than its peers, and its computation is almost the largest among them.

From the above results, we find that UT-SD$^+$ takes more computation time than UT-SD to achieve a performance that is similar to UT-SD with respect to assigning tasks. It illustrates that assigning hard real-time tasks first is useful for the computation reduction, and the supply-demand analysis can compensate for the loss of utilization-based schedulability test. EXACT approach does not apply supply-demand analysis, thus failing to assign many tasks that could be schedulable.

2.8.3 Online Job Assignment Tests

The schedulability test guarantees that all assigned tasks can meet their deadlines, even under the worst-case scenario. To perform some or all unassigned tasks, we assign their jobs online, based on the actual task execution. We know that tasks' actual execution time is more likely to be less than the worst-case assumption, and their released periods are also more likely to be longer than the assumed minimum period. Thus, we investigate the effect of actual execution time and actual release periods on the performance of our proposed job assignment scheme online. The data is collected within a simulation length of 10000 seconds, which means that the system starts at time 0 and stops at the 10000th second.

2.8.3.1 Effect of Actual Execution Time

In this simulation, we test the effect of actual execution time by varying α from 0.2 to 1. In particular, the actual execution time is drawn from $[\alpha \cdot w_i,\ w_i]$ randomly, where w_i is its worst-case execution time. It is tested in a platform with 18 processors, 100 tasks whose total utilization is 20 and they are released with the minimum period. Because the system is overloaded, there must be some soft real-time tasks that are not assigned offline. For these unassigned tasks, their released jobs are assigned online to the vehicle, roadside unit, or cloud computing server. The rate of soft real-time jobs that are successfully assigned to them is presented in Figure 2.7, where we find that the rate of saved jobs by the vehicle declines with increasing α. The rate of totally saved jobs also declines with increasing alpha. This is because the actual execution time becomes large with increasing α, resulting in less free slack for an automotive system to save soft real-time jobs. On the contrary, these unsaved jobs have to be offloaded to an edge and cloud computing system to execute with increasing α, and the rates of saved jobs by them also increase.

2.8.3.2 Effect of Actual Release Period

In this simulation, we test the effect of actual release time by varying β from 1 to 2. In particular, its actual release interval is drawn from $[\tau_i,\ \beta \cdot \tau_i]$ randomly, where

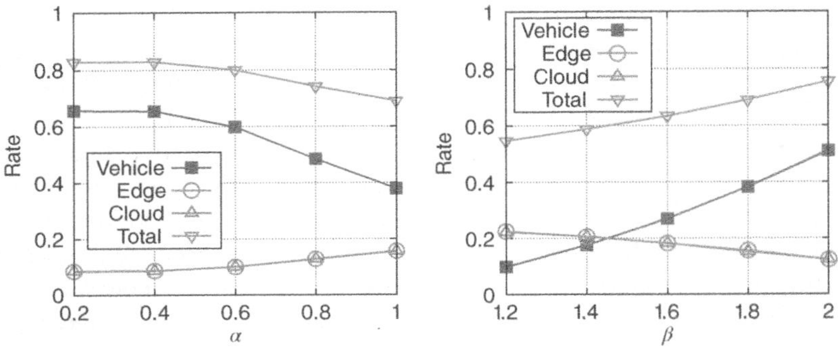

(a) Task execution time **(b)** Task release period

Figure 2.7 The rate of soft real-time jobs that are successfully assigned to vehicle, edge, or cloud computing system.

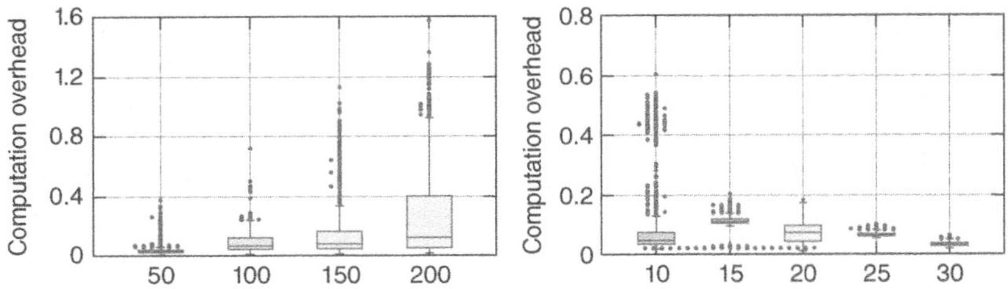

(a) Total task count **(b)** Total processor count

Figure 2.8 The computation time overhead of assigning a soft real-time job.

τ_i is its minimum period. It is also tested in a platform with 18 processors, 100 tasks whose total utilization is 20 and their execution time is set to be the worst-case scenario. The rate of successfully saved soft real-time jobs is presented in Figure 2.7b, where we observe that the rate of saved jobs on vehicle increases greatly with increasing β. This is because a larger release period reduces the system scheduling burden, and makes it easier to accept more jobs. However, as more jobs are saved by vehicles, there are less jobs that are left to the edge or cloud computing systems to process. Thus, their rates of saved jobs decrease.

2.8.3.3 Effect of Task Count on Computation Time

In this simulation, we test the effect of system's total task count on the computation time of assigning a soft real-time job online. It is tested in a platform with 18 processors, by varying task count from 50 to 200 whose total utilization is 20. The boxplot of experimental results is presented in Figure 2.8a, where we observe that the average computation overhead of assigning a soft real-time job online increases with the total task count, due to the reason that there are more tasks in a processor and it involves more demand-supply analysis online. Besides, we observe that there can be quite a large variability of computation overhead, even on a system with the same number of tasks. This is because processors are checked one by one, where the best case is checking only one processor, and the worst case is checking all processors.

2.8.3.4 Effect of Processor Count on Computation Time

In this simulation, we test the effect of a system's processor count on the computation time of assigning a soft real-time job online. It is tested in a platform with 100 tasks by varying processor count from 10 to 30. The total task utilization is always 10% larger than the processor count such that the system is always overloaded and there are some soft real-time jobs to be assigned online. The boxplot of experimental results is presented in Figure 2.8b, where we observe that the computation overhead declines with the total processor count. This does not comply with our expectation. However, it is reasonable because the task count is fixed to 100, and more processors result in fewer tasks on a processor. Thus, it needs less computation to do the demand-supply analysis on a processor. Besides, when fewer tasks are assigned to a processor, there is a larger opportunity to accommodate a new job on a processor.

2.9 Summary

An automotive system is a safety-critical environment that involves a mix of hard and soft real-time tasks. With the rapid expansion of vehicular networks, some soft real-time tasks can be offloaded to edge or cloud servers, allowing more computational resources to be dedicated to handling hard real-time tasks. In this context, this chapter proposes a hybrid scheduling framework that integrates local schedulers within each processor and a global scheduler responsible for assigning soft real-time jobs. The hybrid framework utilizes a two-stage task assignment approach. During the offline stage, a combination of utilization-based schedulability tests and demand-supply analysis is used to efficiently assign hard real-time tasks and some soft real-time tasks. At the online stage, the global scheduler dynamically adapts to real-time task execution information by deriving a demand-bound function to handle unassigned soft real-time tasks. If these tasks cannot be processed by on-board processors, they are offloaded to edge or cloud servers. Extensive experimental results demonstrate the significant advantages of this hybrid scheduling framework.

3

Workload-aware Scheduling of Real-time Independent Tasks in Cloud

Cloud computing is a transformative paradigm that delivers high-quality computational services to users. However, its energy consumption significantly impacts service costs, making energy efficiency a critical consideration. This chapter explores strategies to minimize energy consumption while ensuring adequate response times for real-time independent tasks in the cloud. The problem is formulated as a nonlinear integer program and, through the derivation of a state-transition equation, is transformed into an unconventional 0-1 knapsack problem. A dynamic programming approach is then employed to solve it efficiently. Beyond this optimization framework, we propose an energy-efficient job accommodation scheme designed to handle dynamic workloads with varying frequencies throughout the day. Unlike existing approaches that abruptly shut down old virtual machines and provision new ones for incoming tasks, our scheme prioritizes job allocation on existing virtual machines, creating new instances only when necessary. Conversely, during periods of reduced workload, tasks running on energy-inefficient servers are migrated to other machines, allowing some servers to be powered down to conserve energy. This adaptive and smooth adjustment of computing resources maintains service quality while optimizing energy usage. Experimental results demonstrate that the proposed approach outperforms a particle swarm optimizer and two heuristic-based methods in job accommodation efficiency and energy savings, highlighting its effectiveness in workload-aware scheduling for real-time cloud computing environments.

3.1 Introduction

Cloud computing is a fundamental technology for deploying a wide range of applications and a key service paradigm that delivers computing, storage, and network resources on demand. By leveraging cloud services, enterprises can outsource their computing needs, eliminating the high upfront costs associated with purchasing

Intelligent Scheduling of Tasks for Cloud-Edge-Device Computing Systems, First Edition.

Published 2025 by John Wiley & Sons, Inc.

information technology (IT) infrastructure while also reducing the burden of software and hardware maintenance and upgrades.

While cloud computing offers a promising solution to various computational challenges, its high service costs remain a significant barrier to widespread adoption. These costs generally include both deployment and operational expenses, with electricity consumption accounting for approximately 42% of total operational costs [40]. Due to their substantial energy demands, cloud data centers contribute to approximately 2% of global carbon dioxide (CO_2) emissions [41]. Reducing energy consumption is therefore essential not only for lowering cloud service costs but also for mitigating environmental impact. However, minimizing energy consumption often requires shutting down cloud servers, which can compromise the quality of service (QoS). This inherent trade-off between energy efficiency and service quality presents a critical challenge [42, 43]. In this chapter, we explore strategies to optimize energy usage in cloud computing systems while maintaining high QoS standards.

The dynamic, complex, and unpredictable nature of cloud environments presents significant challenges for effective power management [44]. In a cloud computing system, users submit computation-intensive jobs or request services from a cloud data center, with demand fluctuating based on the frequency of job submissions. For instance, in an intelligent traffic system, vehicles frequently request services from a cloud data center [45]. The request frequency is closely tied to traffic flow, with the number of vehicles per hour during peak times being significantly higher than at midnight [46]. To optimize energy efficiency, job scheduling must be highly adaptable. For example, some cloud servers can be powered down during off-peak hours, while all available servers should be utilized during periods of high demand. This dynamic approach ensures energy savings without compromising service availability.

A virtual machine (VM) is a basic unit in cloud computing, providing a defined amount of CPU power, memory, and bandwidth to execute computational tasks. Many previous studies [47–50] have adopted a model where a separate VM is created for each computation job and then destroyed upon completion. However, this approach is often impractical and leads to significant resource wastage [51]. First, provisioning a new VM takes approximately 10 seconds, while incoming computation jobs can arrive at much higher frequencies, making frequent VM creation and termination inefficient. Second, assigning a dedicated VM to each job is not resource-efficient, as a single VM can execute multiple jobs concurrently. For instance, consider a system where hardware resources are divided into identical units, with each virtual CPU (vCPU) representing one such unit. Suppose there are two jobs: the first has a period of 5 ms, an execution time of 2 ms on a VM with one vCPU, and a response time requirement of 3 ms. The second job has a period of 10 ms, an execution time of 3 ms on a VM with one vCPU, and a response time requirement of 10 ms. If each job is assigned its own VM, two vCPUs are required to meet their deadlines, as shown in Figure 3.1a. However, by prioritizing the first job, both tasks can be consolidated onto a single VM while still meeting their response time requirements, effectively saving one vCPU, as presented in Figure 3.1b. This demonstrates that efficient workload consolidation can significantly reduce resource consumption while maintaining performance guarantees.

Unlike separation scheduling, where each VM runs only a single job, job grouping allows multiple jobs to be assigned to a single VM. This approach, known as job group scheduling, is a promising solution for reducing computational resource requirements and, consequently, lowering energy consumption. However, effectively grouping jobs and provisioning VMs with sufficient computational resources to meet deadlines is a challenging problem. Real-time task assignment in multiprocessor systems is already known to be NP-hard [11, 52], and the problem considered in this study is even more complex, as it simultaneously involves computation scheduling, resource allocation, and energy consumption minimization. Furthermore, since computation job frequencies fluctuate significantly throughout the day, the scheduling approach must be capable of making quick, adaptive adjustments to accommodate these variations. These adjustments should be both robust and smooth to ensure the continuity and reliability of service. Effective VM management is critical, as frequent VM creation and destruction can introduce significant computational and time overhead. Thus, optimizing VM utilization while maintaining system performance and energy efficiency remains a key challenge in cloud computing.

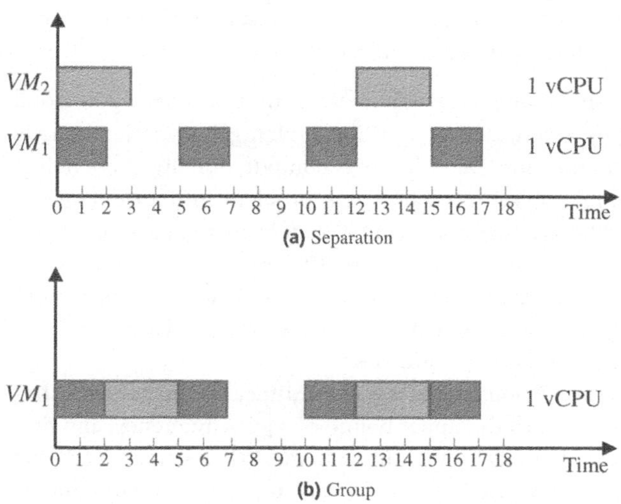

Figure 3.1 Diagram showing (a) separation scheduling and (b) group scheduling.

Numerous job scheduling approaches have been developed to optimize energy consumption in cloud computing systems [1, 47, 53–60]. In Shi et al. [47], task placement and resource allocation are leveraged to minimize the completion time of parallel jobs under energy consumption constraints. An online scheduler periodically assigns dynamic jobs and allocates the residual computing capacity of each server, though it does not account for the overhead introduced by resource allocation. To manage burst workloads, Hu et al. [55] propose a peak load scheduling control method utilizing a two-tier request queue. For the energy-efficient partial computation offloading problem, Bi et al. [1, 59] introduce a particle swarm optimizer (PSO) based on genetic learning to jointly optimize task offloading between cloud data centers and edge devices, as well as resource allocation within the data center. Similarly, Yuan et al. [60] present a simulated annealing-based bee algorithm, built on a G/G/1 queuing model, to reduce energy costs through fine-grained resource provisioning and task scheduling. In mobile-edge computing networks, Yang et al. [56] transform the problem of completion time and energy minimization into an equivalent form solvable via an iterative algorithm. While other methods, such as those proposed in Fang et al. [58], Chen et al. [57], and Wang et al. [53, 54], effectively balance completion time and energy efficiency, they are challenging to implement in environments with highly dynamic workloads and stringent real-time performance requirements.

Unlike existing approaches that either focus solely on scheduling static tasks or employ online schedulers without accounting for resource allocation overhead, this chapter introduces a workload-aware scheduling approach that adaptively manages server power modes to minimize energy consumption while maintaining QoS. The key contributions of this study are as follows:

- We formulate the problem of energy-efficient real-time scheduling in cloud computing as a nonlinear integer program. Since solving this problem exactly or with intelligent optimization algorithms is computationally challenging, we transform the single-server job scheduling problem into an unconventional 0-1 knapsack problem. By deriving a state-transition equation, we enable the use of dynamic programming to efficiently obtain high-quality solutions. Additionally, we extend this solution to a multiserver environment through a voluntary admission scheme that ranks servers based on their energy efficiency for processing specific jobs.
- To manage fluctuations in job frequency at runtime, we introduce a frequency profile, which defines the upper bound of a job's frequency, and propose an energy-efficient job accommodation scheme. When system workload increases, this scheme prioritizes the use of existing VMs to accommodate new jobs. Conversely, when workload decreases, it transfers jobs from energy-inefficient servers to more efficient ones, allowing some servers to be powered down. This ensures that every job can always access at least one available VM, preventing service interruptions and maintaining QoS.

- We evaluate the proposed approach against a PSO and two heuristic methods. Experimental results show that our approach achieves the highest success rate in executing and completing jobs with minimal energy consumption. Moreover, its computation time is two orders of magnitude lower than that of the PSO. Additionally, we analyze the impact of the profile period on scheduling performance, demonstrating that shorter profile periods can further reduce overall system energy consumption.

3.2 Related Work

Cloud computing offers diverse service modes and deployment models, making it adaptable to various user needs across different scenarios. Its key advantages, including cost-effectiveness, on-demand scalability, and ease of management, have led to a growing adoption of cloud-based services. However, several challenges remain unresolved. In the following section, we review existing studies that address the energy minimization problem through power management, VM creation, and task assignment, which are three critical aspects that this study aims to optimize.

Energy savings in cloud computing can generally be achieved through two primary techniques: deactivating idle servers or reducing their operating frequency. The former, known as dynamic power management (DPM) [61, 62], involves powering down servers when they are not in use, while the latter, dynamic voltage and frequency scaling (DVFS) [63, 64], adjusts processor frequency and voltage to lower power consumption. Server power consumption is often correlated with the number of active computing resources and workload intensity. Based on this relationship, several studies have developed power models to optimize energy efficiency [47, 65, 66]. The accuracy of such models has been validated [67], and we adopt one in this study. A straightforward approach proposed in Daraghmeh et al. [68] dynamically switches servers on and off based on task arrival rates. However, this method lacks guarantees on task completion time. In Mao et al. [69], an online joint radio and computational resource management algorithm is introduced to minimize the long-term average weighted energy consumption of mobile devices and mobile-edge computing servers. This method determines optimal CPU-cycle frequencies in each time slot but focuses solely on transmission power and bandwidth allocation, without considering hardware resource allocation for VMs.

A VM is a basic unit that executes tasks in cloud and edge computing systems, and managing each VM effectively is crucial for load balancing and energy minimization. In Xiao et al. [70], a novel coalitional game-theoretic approach based on merge-and-split techniques is proposed to save energy through dynamic VM consolidation. This approach partitions physical machines into groups based on their workload levels and employs a coalitional game-based algorithm to optimize VM consolidation, thereby ensuring high energy efficiency for physical machines. Similarly, Mohiuddin and Almogren [71] use VM consolidation to migrate workloads and place idle physical servers into a hibernation mode, further reducing energy consumption. While both approaches effectively achieve load balancing across servers, they do not consider the real-time requirements of tasks. In Al-Wesabi et al. [72], the problem of resource allocation for dynamic dataflows is framed as an optimization problem with energy and resource constraints, and several heuristics are proposed to solve it. However, these heuristics do not address the creation of VMs or the associated resource allocation. On the other hand, Al-Wesabi et al. [72] propose a unified meta-heuristic optimization algorithm for efficient resource allocation in cloud computing systems. However, this algorithm overlooks the real-time performance needs of tasks.

Task assignment is crucial for energy minimization in cloud and edge computing systems. Its complexity arises from the combinatorial nature of the problem and the tight coupling with resource allocation. In Guo et al. [73], an energy-efficient resource allocation scheme is proposed for a multiuser mobile-edge computing system, where the energy consumption at the base station for executing and transmitting tasks is weighted. The energy consumption minimization problem for all tasks is transformed into a three-stage flow-shop problem, which is solved using Johnsons algorithm and convex optimization techniques. In Xu et al. [74], the problem is decoupled into two subproblems: task offloading and resource allocation, with an iterative search approach used to find a joint solution. However, both of these approaches struggle to schedule tasks with highly variable arrival rates throughout the day. To optimize energy consumption on edge-cloud integrated computing platforms while maintaining service-level agreements, Materwala et al. [75] propose an evolutionary genetic algorithm. This method focuses on computation offloading rather than optimizing resource allocation on cloud servers. A deep reinforcement learning approach is introduced in Yan et al. [76] to minimize energy consumption in task assignment. However, this method does not always ensure adequate real-time performance. In Materwala and Ismail [77], task execution time and system energy are treated as a bi-objective optimization problem, and an evolutionary algorithm-based approach is used to solve it. Additionally, Hussain et al. [78] and Zhou et al. [79] propose a two-stage energy-efficient task scheduling algorithm and a game-theoretic approach, respectively, to allocate cloud resources for task execution. However, all these methods are not well-suited for managing dynamically arriving tasks.

Energy-aware VM placement and task scheduling methods are classified and evaluated in Saurav and Benedict [80], Ismail and Materwala [81]. Based on the findings from these studies and the previous review, we can conclude that scheduling jobs in groups is still an emerging area of research. Moreover, the challenge of adaptively allocating computational resources and managing server power modes to minimize energy consumption in cloud computing systems while ensuring QoS remains an important issue to address.

3.3 Related Models

In this section, we present the cloud computing vCPU model, real-time job model, and energy consumption model, which are primarily based on Shi et al. [47]. The power model used is consistent with those in Shen et al. [66], Kim et al. [65], and Krishnan et al. [67]. There are two key modifications in the job execution model: (1) The computation jobs considered in this study are real-time jobs, which are released periodically and have deadline constraints, as opposed to jobs without such time-sensitive requirements; and (2) Multiple jobs can be grouped together and assigned to a single VM, rather than each job running on an individual VM.

3.3.1 Virtual CPU Model

A data center consists of numerous heterogeneous computing servers, denoted by the set $\mathcal{S} = \{S_1, S_2, ..., S_m\}$, where S_j represents the jth server. These servers offer various types of computing resources, such as CPUs, memory, and disks. In this study, we define a vCPU as a basic resource unit that includes a certain allocation of CPU, memory, and disk resources. Each server has its own set of computing resources, and C_j represents the number of available vCPUs on server S_j. A VM can accommodate a varying number of vCPUs, with a higher number of vCPUs corresponding to greater computational power.

3.3.2 Real-time Job Model

We use $\mathcal{J} = \{J_1, J_2, ..., J_n\}$ to denote the set of requested computation jobs. Jobs here are limited to computation-intensive jobs, and for each job J_i, we use (f_i, l_i, d_i) to represent its release frequency, computation load, and relative deadline, respectively. In particular, f_i indicates that this job is released according to the frequency f_i, and l_i indicates the number of million instructions required for each released job. This job's relative deadline is d_i, which requires that its response time should not be greater than d_i. The execution time of processing a job depends on the server and the number of computation resources devoted to it. This type of real-time job model can be representative of various Internet-of-Things applications, such as video processing, speech recognition, and navigation. These applications release the workload periodically, and their processing rates should not be lower than their release frequencies. For example, a video releases images at a rate of approximately 30 frames per second, and the rate of image processing should reach that rate. In addition, an image often needs a certain amount of computation to finish, which is often inversely proportional to the number of resources allocated to it. Different servers have different execution efficiencies for the same job; for example, if

$c_{j,k}$ vCPUs from S_j are devoted to processing J_i, the execution time is $\tau_i = \frac{l_i}{\lambda_{i,j} c_{j,k}}$, where $\lambda_{i,j}$ is server S_j's execution efficiency when executing J_i. Each released job must be finished before its deadline. Such a job model has been adopted in plenty of previous literatures, such as Chen et al. [82], Shi et al. [47], Hu and Li [83], Hussain et al. [78], Zheng et al. [84], Zhang et al. [85, 86], Chen et al. [87], Wang et al. [88], Cui et al. [89], Elashri and Azim [90], and its effectiveness has been verified by performing experiments on real platforms [88–90].

3.3.3 Power Model of VM

The power consumption of a VM is composed of static power $\bar{P}$ and dynamic power $\tilde{P}$, where $\bar{P}$ is consumed once a VM has been created, and $\tilde{P}$ is consumed only when the VM is processing a job. $\bar{P}$ and $\tilde{P}$ are both dependent on the server and a dedicated computing resource. For example, a VM $V_{j,k}$ is created from the server S_j to executing jobs J_1, J_2, ..., $J_{n'}$, where n' $(n' \leq n)$ denotes the total number of jobs in this VM. If the computing resource dedicated to $V_{j,k}$ is $c_{j,k}$, the static power of $V_{j,k}$ is $\bar{P}_{j,k} = \alpha_j \cdot c_{j,k}$ and its dynamic power is $\tilde{P}_{j,k} = \beta_j \cdot c_{j,k}$, where α_j and β_j are the static and dynamic power coefficients of server S_j. Assume this VM has worked for Δ, and its energy consumption is

$$\begin{aligned} E_{j,k}(\Delta) &= \bar{P}_{j,k} \cdot \Delta + \tilde{P}_{j,k} \cdot \Delta \cdot U_{j,k} \\ &= \alpha_j \cdot c_{j,k} \cdot \Delta + \beta_j \cdot c_{j,k} \cdot \Delta \cdot U_{j,k}, \end{aligned} \tag{3.1}$$

where $\Delta \cdot U_{j,k}$ is the portion of Δ used to execute jobs ranging from J_1 to $J_{n'}$. $U_{j,k}$ is the utilization of $V_{j,k}$:

$$U_{j,k} = \sum_{i=1}^{n'} \frac{f_i l_i}{\lambda_{i,j} c_{j,k}}. \tag{3.2}$$

Then, we know that the average power of $V_{j,k}$ within Δ is

$$P_{j,k} = \frac{E_{j,k}(\Delta)}{\Delta} = \alpha_j \cdot c_{j,k} + \beta_j \cdot \sum_{i=1}^{n'} \frac{f_i l_i}{\lambda_{i,j}}. \tag{3.3}$$

3.4 Problem Formulation

We first consider the problem of scheduling a set of real-time jobs with fixed frequencies on a cloud computing platform with some heterogeneous servers and then present how to manage jobs with varying frequencies. We aim to minimize energy consumption while meeting jobs' deadlines. Thus, jobs can be grouped together so that each group shares the same VM.

3.4.1 Input

The provided heterogeneous servers are denoted as $\mathcal{S} = \{S_1, S_2, ..., S_m\}$, where the available computing resource of each server is denoted as C_j, and jobs that must be scheduled are denoted as $\mathcal{J} = \{J_1, J_2, ..., J_n\}$, where (f_i, l_i, d_i) denotes the ith job's frequency, computation load, and relative deadline.

3.4.2 Output

Because a job can be assigned to any VM on any server, we use $x_{i,j,k} = 1$, $(1 \le i \le n,\ 1 \le j \le m,\ 1 \le k \le o_j)$ to indicate that job J_i is assigned to the k-th VM of server S_j, and $x_{i,j,k} = 0$ otherwise. o_j is the number of VMs on server S_j. The allocated computing resource for the kth VM of server S_j, denoted as $V_{j,k}$, is denoted as $c_{j,k}$. Both $x_{i,j,k}$ and $c_{j,k}$ are decision variables.

3.4.3 Constraints

We assume that a job cannot be divisible to make the problem a combinatorial optimization problem. Thus, a job can be assigned to a single VM, and we have to guarantee that

$$\sum_{j=1}^{m} \sum_{k=1}^{o_j} x_{i,j,k} = 1, \quad 1 \le i \le n. \tag{3.4}$$

Constraint (3.4) does not exclude multiple jobs from being assigned to the same VM. For example, if we assign jobs J_1 and J_2 to the first machine of the first server, we obtain $x_{1,1,1} = x_{2,1,1} = 1$.

The next constraint is the computation resource limit, which states that the sum of allocated computing resources in each server should not exceed its limit:

$$\sum_{k=1}^{o_j} c_{j,k} \le C_j, \quad 1 \le j \le m. \tag{3.5}$$

If a VM contains multiple jobs, we use a nonpreemptive fixed-priority scheduling policy to schedule them. For this policy, we know that all jobs are schedulable only if their worst-case response time would not cause them to miss their deadlines. We assume that $J_1, J_2, ..., J_{n'}$ $J_{n'}$ are grouped together to share the same VM and have their priorities already ranked in descending order. According to Park [91], these jobs are schedulable if

$$\forall 1 \le i \le n' : \ \hat{\tau}^i + \sum_{J_j \in \hbar(J_i)} \lceil d_i \cdot f_j \rceil \cdot \tau_j \le d_i \tag{3.6}$$

where $\hat{\tau}^i = \max\{\tau_k | k > i\}$; τ_k is the execution time of job J_k; and $\hbar(J_i)$ denotes jobs whose priorities are not lower than J_i. In this study, we apply Audsley's optimal priority assignment algorithm [92], which assigns priorities from the lowest to the highest by iteratively checking (3.6).

3.4.4 Objective

The optimization goal in this study is to minimize the system power consumption, which is the sum of the power consumed by every VM on every server. From Section 3.3.3, we can derive the power consumed by a VM:

$$P_{j,k} = \alpha_j \cdot c_{j,k} + \beta_j \cdot \sum_{i=1}^{n} \frac{x_{i,j,k} \cdot f_i \cdot l_i}{\lambda_{i,j}}. \tag{3.7}$$

The optimization goal is the energy consumption over an interval of Δ:

$$\min \ \mathbb{E} = \sum_{j=1}^{m} \sum_{k=1}^{o_j} P_{j,k} \cdot \Delta. \tag{3.8}$$

For brevity, we can use the average power to represent the system's energy consumption because Δ is unchangeable. The optimization goal is then transferred into

$$\min \ \mathbb{P} = \frac{\mathbb{E}}{\Delta} = \sum_{j=1}^{m} \sum_{k=1}^{o_j} P_{j,k}. \tag{3.9}$$

The higher the energy efficiency, the lower the $\mathbb{P}$-value. As a result, we can represent energy efficiency with $\frac{1}{\mathbb{P}}$, and the optimization goal becomes

$$\max \ \frac{1}{\mathbb{P}} = \frac{1}{\sum_{j=1}^{m} \sum_{k=1}^{o_j} P_{j,k}}. \tag{3.10}$$

Constraints (3.4) and (3.5) are linear, while constraint (3.6) is nonlinear. Because $x_{i,j,k}$ is a binary variable and $c_{j,k}$ is an integer number representing the number of vCPUs allocated, the optimization problem under consideration is a nonlinear integer programming problem and is a complex combinatorial optimization problem with many unknown variables that is difficult to solve exactly. Although some intelligent optimization algorithms, such as a genetic algorithm and a PSO [93, 94], can be applied to find a good solution, these algorithms often take a long time to converge because they rely on time-consuming iterative search. In this chapter, we thus propose some efficient algorithms that can quickly find a suboptimal solution for this problem.

3.5 Scheduling Jobs in a Single Server

Before we present how to assign jobs and allocate computing resources to many heterogeneous servers, we narrow this problem to a single server in this section (i.e., all jobs are executed on a single server). For simplicity, we denote this server as S_1. Its available computing resources are C_1. $\mathcal{J} = \{J_1, J_2, ..., J_n\}$ are the jobs that must be assigned.

3.5.1 Power Analysis

The goal in this study is to minimize energy consumption. Because there is only 1 server available, $m = 1$ in (3.10), and the optimization goal becomes

$$\mathbb{P} = \sum_{k=1}^{o_1} P_{1,k} = \alpha_1 \cdot \sum_{k=1}^{o_1} c_{1,k} + \beta_1 \cdot \sum_{i=1}^{n} \sum_{k=1}^{o_1} \frac{x_{i,1,k} \cdot f_i \cdot l_i}{\lambda_{i,1}}, \tag{3.11}$$

where $\sum_{k=1}^{n} c_{1,k}$ is the number of allocated computing resources. Thus, the task is to find $c_{1,k}$ and $x_{i,1,k}$ such that P_S is minimized.

3.5.2 Problem Transformation

First, if there are too many jobs but insufficient computing resources, the server may be unable to accommodate all of them. Thus, there is no feasible solution to meet the deadline constraint. In this situation, scheduling more jobs is more important than reducing energy consumption. Thus, the first principle is to accommodate as many jobs as possible and then minimize energy consumption. We thus change the proposed optimization goal to achieve it.

$$\begin{aligned} \max\ \Omega = \gamma \cdot \left(\sum_{i=1}^{n} \sum_{k=1}^{o_1} x_{i,1,k}\right) + \frac{1}{\mathbb{P}} &= \gamma \cdot \left(\sum_{i=1}^{n} \sum_{k=1}^{o_1} x_{i,1,k}\right) \\ &+ \frac{1}{\alpha_1 \cdot \sum_{k=1}^{o_1} c_{1,k} + \beta_1 \cdot \sum_{i=1}^{n} \sum_{k=1}^{o_1} \frac{x_{i,1,k} \cdot f_i \cdot l_i}{\lambda_{i,1}}}, \end{aligned} \tag{3.12}$$

where γ is a scaling factor indicating the importance of completing more jobs; $\sum_{i=1}^{n} \sum_{k=1}^{o_1} x_{i,1,k}$ is the number of jobs placed; and γ is sufficiently large that increasing job placement is more important than minimizing energy consumption.

With the new optimization goal, we transfer the problem of placing jobs and allocating computing resources to an unconventional 0-1 knapsack problem that considers jobs as objects whose value depends on (3.12) and whose volume depends on (3.6). Computing resources are viewed as a bag with a capacity of C_1. Unlike a conventional 0-1 knapsack problem that does not consider the separation and volume allocation toward picked objects, the problem of interest in this study must separate computing resources (bag) into several VMs (small bags), and each VM must be allocated a certain number of computing resources (volume) such that its inside jobs (objects) can be done by their deadlines.

3.5.3 Dynamic Programming

Dynamic programming can be applied to find an optimal solution to the conventional 0-1 knapsack problem. We can also apply it to find a solution to the proposed problem, but this solution is only quasioptimal because the constraint is nonlinear and the optimization performance depends on the job assignment order. Before applying the approach, we must answer two related questions: what are the minimum computing resources required to meet a job's deadline, and how can we maximize Ω if a new job is assigned to a server?

3.5.3.1 Required Minimum Computing Resources

The required minimum computing resource denoted as $\check{c}_{1,i}$ for a new job, J_i, can be obtained by assuming that these computing resources are exclusively used to process the new job to meet its deadline. From (3.6), we can infer that

$$\check{c}_{1,i} = \min\left\{c_{1,i} \middle| \lceil d_i \cdot f_i \rceil \cdot \frac{l_i}{\lambda_{1,i} c_{1,i}} \leq d_i \right\}. \tag{3.13}$$

3.5.3.2 Maximizing Ω

The dynamic programming approach breaks the problem of allocating computing capacity C_1 down into simpler subproblems of allocating smaller capacity, and the optimal solution to each subproblem contributes to the optimal solution of the entire problem. We assume that jobs $J_1 - J_n$ are assigned to each small capacity individually. Typically, we discuss how to maximize Ω of (3.12) by placing a new job J_i on a server with a computing capacity of C_x.

We should first create a placement solution for J_1 to J_{i-1} with respect to a server with a capacity ranging from 1 to C_1. The value of placing jobs from J_1 to J_{i-1} into a server with a capacity of C_x is denoted by $\Omega(\mathbf{J^1_{i-1}}, C_x)$, where $1 \leq C_x \leq C_1$. The corresponding placement solution regarding VM creation and its assigned jobs is also known and is represented as

$$V_h = (\mathbf{J_h}, C_h), \tag{3.14}$$

where there are H VMs in total; V_h is the h-th VM, where $1 \leq h \leq H$; $\mathbf{J_h}$ is the job group in this VM, where $\bigcup_{h=1}^{H} \mathbf{J_h} = \mathbf{J^1_{i-1}}$; and C_h is the allocated computing resource (i.e., $\sum_{h=1}^{H} C_h = C_x$).

Then, there can be three cases for J_i's placement with resulting values denoted as $\Omega_1(\mathbf{J_i^1}, C_x)$, $\Omega_2(\mathbf{J_i^1}, C_x)$, and $\Omega_3(\mathbf{J_i^1}, C_x)$, respectively:

1. $C_x < \check{c}_{1,i}$: This value cannot meet J_i's deadline because the computing resources are not sufficient. Thus, J_i is abandoned, and

$$\Omega_1(\mathbf{J_i^1}, C_x) = \Omega(\mathbf{J_{i-1}^1}, C_x). \tag{3.15}$$

However, when $C_x \geq \check{c}_{1,i}$, we can choose to either create a new VM for J_i only or place it to the previously created VMs V_h.

2. $C_x \geq \check{c}_{1,i}$ and a new VM is created: In this case, a new VM is created to run J_i individually. There could be more than one option to create this VM; the best option is to maximize the proposed optimization goal, which is denoted as $\Omega_2(\mathbf{J_i^1}, C_x)$ in this case. $\Omega_2(\mathbf{J_i^1}, C_x)$ can be obtained by enumerating vCPUs for this new VM ranging from $\check{c}_{1,i}$ to C_x:

$$\Omega_2(\mathbf{J_i^1}, C_x) = \max\ \Omega(J_i, c_{1,i}) \oplus \Omega(\mathbf{J_{i-1}^1}, C_x - c_{1,i}), \tag{3.16}$$

where $\Omega(J_i, c_{1,i})$ indicates that a new VM is created with $c_{1,i}$ vCPUs to run J_i and $\check{c}_{1,i} \leq c_{1,i} \leq C_x$. $\Omega(\mathbf{J_{i-1}^1}, C_x - c_{1,i})$ and its corresponding VM creation and job assignments have been known before assigning J_i. In addition, $\Omega_2(\mathbf{J_i^1}, C_x)$ is not a linear sum of $\Omega(J_i, c_{1,i})$ and $\Omega(\mathbf{J_{i-1}^1}, C_x - c_{1,i})$ but a nonlinear function relied on (3.12). Thus, we use $\oplus$ to denote this calculation.

3. $C_x \geq \check{c}_{1,i}$ and J_i is placed into a previously created VM V_h: Before assigning J_i, we know that there are already H VMs that are assigned with $\mathbf{J_{i-1}^1}$. The new job J_i can be assigned to one of these VMs. We assume that this new job is assigned to VM V_h where $1 \leq h \leq H$. We have $\mathbf{J_h} = \mathbf{J_h} \cup J_i$. Then, we test whether all jobs in $\mathbf{J_h}$ can still meet their deadlines by (3.6); if yes, we use (3.12) to obtain $\Omega_3^h(\mathbf{J_i^1}, C_x)$, and otherwise, $\Omega_3^h(\mathbf{J_i^1}, C_x) = \Omega(\mathbf{J_{i-1}^1}, C_x)$. The final value is thus

$$\Omega_3(\mathbf{J_i^1}, C_x) = \max\ \Omega_3^h(\mathbf{J_i^1}, C_x),\ \forall 1 \leq h \leq H. \tag{3.17}$$

In the end, we can use a state-transition equation for the problem of placing J_i to maximize the proposed optimization goal:

$$\Omega(\mathbf{J_i^1}, C_x) = \begin{cases} \Omega_1(\mathbf{J_i^1}, C_x), & C_x < c_{1,i}^{\min} \\ \max(\Omega_2(\mathbf{J_i^1}, C_x), \Omega_3(\mathbf{J_i^1}, C_x)), & C_x \geq c_{1,i}^{\min} \\ 0, & i = 0 \end{cases}. \tag{3.18}$$

Then, by iteratively using (3.18) until $C_x = C_1$ and $i = n$, the final result of job placement and computing resource allocation can be determined, as shown in Algorithm 3.1. Because there are 2 loops in this algorithm, its time complexity is $O(n \cdot C_1)$.

Algorithm 3.1: Scheduling Jobs in a Single Servers

Require: Jobs J_1, ..., J_n, Server S_1
Ensure: Job Placement and Computing Resource Allocation

for $i = 1 \rightarrow n$ **do**
  obtain $\check{c}_{1,i}$ by (3.13);
  for $C_x = 1 \rightarrow C_1$ **do**
    if $C_x < \check{c}_{1,i}$ **then**
      Abandon job J_i;
      $\Omega(\mathbf{J}_\mathbf{i}^\mathbf{1}, C_x) = \Omega(\mathbf{J}_\mathbf{i-1}^\mathbf{1}, C_x)$
    else
      Obtain $\Omega_2(\mathbf{J}_\mathbf{i}^\mathbf{1}, C_x)$ and $\Omega_3(\mathbf{J}_\mathbf{i}^\mathbf{1}, C_x)$ by (3.16) and (3.17);
      if $\Omega_2(\mathbf{J}_\mathbf{i}^\mathbf{1}, C_x) > \Omega_3(\mathbf{J}_\mathbf{i}^\mathbf{1}, C_x)$ **then**
        Create a new virtual machine to job J_i and allocate the corresponding computing resource to it;
        $\Omega(\mathbf{J}_\mathbf{i}^\mathbf{1}, C_x) = \Omega_2(\mathbf{J}_\mathbf{i}^\mathbf{1}, C_x)$;
      else
        Place J_i on the previously created virtual machine;
        $\Omega(\mathbf{J}_\mathbf{i}^\mathbf{1}, C_x) = \Omega_3(\mathbf{J}_\mathbf{i}^\mathbf{1}, C_x)$;
      end if
    end if
  end for
end for

Table 3.1 Procedures of assigning three jobs to a server with three vCPUs.

C_x	1	2	3
J_1	$V_1(J_1, 1)$	$V_1(J_1, 2)$	$V_1(J_1, 3)$
J_2	$V_1(J_1, 1)$	$V_1(J_2, 2)$	$V_1(J_1, 1)$, $V_2(J_2, 2)$
J_3	$V_1(J_1, 1)$	$V_1(J_2, 2)$	$V_1(J_1, 1)$, $V_2(J_2 \cup J_3, 2)$

Example 3.1 *We can explain how this scheme works using a specific example. We assume that there are 3 jobs that must run in a server with 3 vCPUs. They are denoted as $J_1 - J_3$, whose required minimum vCPUs are 1, 2, and 1, respectively. In the first round, the schedule toward J_1 is decided by ranging C_x from 1 to 3. Results are shown in the second row of Table 3.1, where there is only one VM created for each C_x. Then, the assignment of J_2 depends on these results. Because J_2 needs 2 vCPUs to meet its real-time requirement, the result would be $V_1(J_1, 1)$ when $C_x = 1$. When $C_x = 2$, J_2 and J_1 cannot meet their constraints simultaneously. Thus, its result is $V_1(J_2, 2)$,*

where J_1 is abandoned. When $C_x = 3$, J_1 and J_2 can meet their constraints, and separating them into 2 VMs with 1 and 2 vCPUs, respectively, produces better performance than grouping them into a VM with 3 vCPUs. J_3 is assigned following this way. When $C_x \leq 2$, it is not possible to meet their constraints. However, when $C_x = 3$, there are only two cases: (1) create a new VM for J_3; and (2) assign it to either $V_1(J_1, 1)$ or $V_2(J_2, 2)$. In the first case, if a VM with 1 vCPU is created to run J_3, only 2 vCPUs remain to run J_1 and J_2. Thus, this case is not feasible because 2 vCPUs are insufficient to run J_1 and J_2. As a result, we examine the second case and conclude that the best solution is for J_2 and J_3 to share the same VM with 2 vCPUs.

3.6 Scheduling Jobs in Multiple Servers

The proposed method uses dynamic programming to solve the problem of interest on a single server. Jobs in this study are assumed to be static (i.e., their release frequencies are known and would not be changed dynamically). Next, we show how to schedule jobs across multiple servers to minimize energy consumption.

3.6.1 Server Energy Efficiency

Because the goal of this study is to reduce energy consumption, we try to use as few servers as possible to process jobs. How to choose a server to run jobs is critical because different servers have different energy efficiencies. We evaluate the server's energy efficiency by assuming that all jobs are placed on this server. For example, we know from (3.7) that the power of server S_j is

$$P_j = \alpha_j \sum_{k=1}^{o_j} \cdot c_{j,k} + \beta_j \cdot \sum_{i=1}^{n} \sum_{k=1}^{o_j} \frac{x_{i,j,k} \cdot f_i \cdot l_i}{\lambda_{i,j}}. \tag{3.19}$$

Because all jobs are placed at S_j, we have $\sum_{k=1}^{o_j} c_{j,k} = C_j$ and $\sum_{k=1}^{o_j} x_{i,j,k} = 1$. Thus, it can be concluded that:

$$\begin{aligned} P_j &= \alpha_j C_j + \beta_j \cdot \sum_{i=1}^{n} \frac{f_i \cdot l_i}{\lambda_{i,j}} \cdot \left(\sum_{k=1}^{o_j} x_{i,j,k}\right) \\ &= \alpha_j C_j + \beta_j \cdot \sum_{i=1}^{n} \frac{f_i \cdot l_i}{\lambda_{i,j}}. \end{aligned} \tag{3.20}$$

The smaller P_j, the higher the energy efficiency of S_j. Thus, $\frac{1}{P_j}$ represents the energy efficiency of S_j to process all jobs.

3.6.2 Job Placement in Multiple Servers

Servers can be sorted in descending order of energy efficiency using $\frac{1}{P_j}$. We assume that servers $\{S_1, S_2, ..., S_m\}$ have already been ranked in this order for generality. Thus, where $i > j$, S_i is more energy efficient than S_j. The servers from S_1 to S_m are then switched on one by one until all jobs have been successfully assigned. In particular, we only use S_1 in the first round to accommodate all jobs. If all jobs can be assigned to S_1 to meet their deadlines, the algorithm ends and returns the job placement result. Otherwise, the procedure goes to the second round, where S_2 is switched on, and then, S_1 and S_2 are used to accommodate jobs. If not, the game proceeds to the third round, in which S_3 is activated. This procedure repeats until all jobs are successfully assigned. If some jobs are not successfully assigned even after all servers have been switched on, the algorithm fails to find a feasible solution.

Now, we examine how to assign jobs to servers from S_1 to S_p in the p-th round, where $p \leq m$. From (3.20), we know that a larger $\lambda_{i,j}$ leads to a smaller P_j. $\lambda_{i,j}$ is the job execution efficiency, where a larger $\lambda_{i,j}$ reduces the job computation demand and increases the probability of meeting job J_i's deadline. Thus, the preference option of servers for J_i can be ranked from the highest to the lowest by the descending order of $\lambda_{i,j}$. In this study, we use $\mathcal{S}^i = \{S_1^i, S_2^i, ..., S_p^i\}$ to denote J_i's preferred server options that have been ranked in this order and use $\mathcal{J}^i = \{\mathcal{J}_1^i, \mathcal{J}_2^i, ..., \mathcal{J}_p^i\}$ to denote job sets of server S_i, where $\mathcal{J}_j^i$ denotes jobs that consider S_i as their jth preference option. Thus, we can use their preferred server options and develop a voluntary admission scheme that tries to assign each job to its preferred server.

As shown in Algorithm 3.2, when there are p servers that are switched on, the number of iterations for assigning jobs is p. In the first iteration, a server tries to admit jobs that consider it their first preference option (i.e., S_i tries to accommodate $\mathcal{J}_1^i$, $(i \leq m)$). Thus, the problem becomes scheduling jobs in every single server, and Algorithm 3.1 is used to solve this problem. After the first iteration, some jobs are successfully assigned, while others are not. Then, in the second iteration, each server has owned some jobs and begins to admit unassigned jobs that regard it as their second preferred option. This procedure continues till either admitting all jobs or the end of p rounds. If there are still some jobs unassigned after p rounds, the voluntary admission scheme fails, which leads to switching the next server on. Because the server is successively switched on and tested, the worst-case iteration round is $\frac{m(m-1)}{2}$. For every round, Algorithm 3.1 is applied to build a schedule. Thus, its time complexity is $O(m^2 \cdot n \cdot \hat{C})$, where $\hat{C} = \max_{j=1..m} C_j$.

Example 3.2 *We use an example to explain how a voluntary admission scheme works. We assume that there are four jobs that are denoted as J_1–J_4 that must be assigned to three servers denoted as S_1–S_3. For J_1, we have $\lambda_{1,1} = 1.1$, $\lambda_{1,2} = 0.8$, and $\lambda_{1,3} = 0.9$. Its preferred servers are thus ordered from high to low as S_1, S_3,*

Algorithm 3.2: Scheduling Jobs in Multiple Servers

Require: Jobs $J_1, \ldots, J_n$, Servers $S_1, \ldots, S_m$
Ensure: Job Placement and Computing Resource Allocation

```
Calculate P_j, (1 ≤ j ≤ m) by (3.20);
Sort servers to {S_1, ..., S_m} in ascending order of P_j;
S' = ∅;
for p = 1 → m do
    S' = S' ∪ S_p;
    Update S^i and J^i in S' according to λ_{i,j};
    for j = 1 → p do
        for i = 1 → p do
            Assign J_j^i to S_i by Algorithm 3.1;
            Update the job set in J^i to filter out assigned jobs;
        end for
    end for
    if All jobs are successfully assigned then
        Return result;
    end if
end for
```

and S_2. For J_2, we have $\lambda_{2,1} = 1.2$, $\lambda_{2,2} = 0.8$, and $\lambda_{2,3} = 1.0$. Its preferred servers are thus S_1, S_3, and S_2. For J_3, we have $\lambda_{3,1} = 1.0$, $\lambda_{3,2} = 1.2$, and $\lambda_{3,3} = 0.8$. Its preferred servers are thus S_2, S_1, and S_3. For J_4, we have $\lambda_{4,1} = 0.8$, $\lambda_{4,2} = 1.0$, and $\lambda_{4,3} = 1.1$. Its preferred servers are thus S_3, S_2, and S_1. As a result, we can obtain the first/second/third-priority job sets of each server, as presented in Figure 3.2a. Then, in the first iteration, J_1 and J_2 are assigned to S_1, J_3 is assigned to S_2 and J_4 is assigned to S_3 by Algorithm 3.1. Only J_1 and J_4 are successfully assigned. Based on their assignments, J_3 and J_2 that fail in the first iteration are assigned to S_1 and S_3 in the second iteration, where J_3 is assigned successfully. In the third iteration, J_2 is assigned to S_2, as shown in Figure 3.2b.

3.7 Online Workload-aware Scheduling

The request frequency for computing jobs from users is dynamic. A typical example is the cloud computing service for an intelligent transportation system. When the traffic is light, the requested computation is less frequent compared to the heavy traffic situation, and therefore, fewer servers are required. In contrast, more servers would be required during rush hours to provide sufficient computing capacity to meet the demand for frequent computation jobs. Thus, to save energy

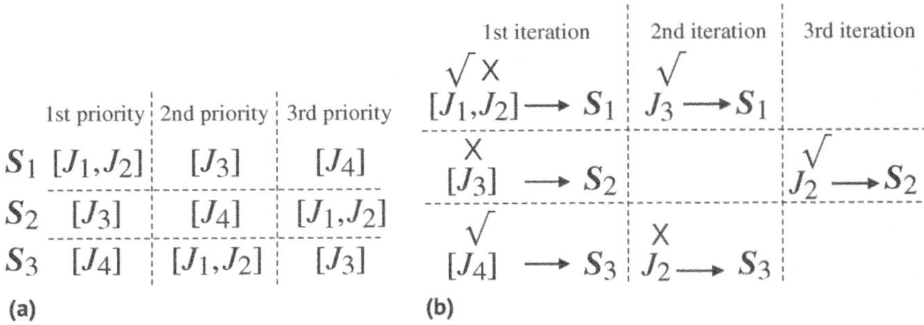

Figure 3.2 Illustration of voluntary admission scheme: (a) 1st/2nd/3rd-priority job sets of each server and (b) assigned jobs using voluntary admission scheme.

consumption, cloud computing servers should be dynamically activated or deactivated, depending on whether there are sufficient computing resources to meet all jobs' deadlines.

3.7.1 Job Frequency Profile

In reality, job frequency varies over time; thus, we use $f_i(t)$ to denote the frequency of job J_i at time t, where $f_i(t)$ can be obtained by collecting and analyzing job J_i's past data. Then, the scheduling policy toward jobs can be adjusted by relying on the $f_i(t)$ of each job. However, the creation and elimination of VMs incur a large additional computation and energy overhead, which makes it not worthwhile to change the schedule too often. Thus, we divide a day into many periods, and for each period, we use the job's maximum frequency as the frequency during this period:

$$\hat{f}_i^q = \max_{qT<t\leq(q+1)T} f_i(t), \ 1 \leq i \leq n, \tag{3.21}$$

where T is this period. Thus, jobs' frequency is upper-bounded by $\hat{f}_i^q$, and we can safely rely on $\hat{f}_i^q$, $1 \leq i \leq n$ to adjust the schedule periodically. An example is presented in Figure 3.3, where its period is 2 hours.

3.7.2 Energy-efficient Job Accommodation Scheme

We consider jobs' new frequencies in each period and propose an energy-efficient job accommodation scheme. Completely removing all previously created VMs and building new ones in each period is impractical because the provided service would must be suspended for a while due to the destruction and creation of VMs,

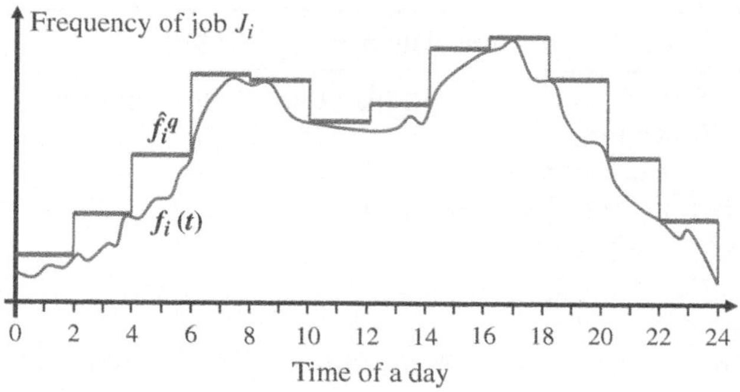

Figure 3.3 An illustration of job frequency profile.

and a suspended service may cause serious traffic problems. To ensure smoothness in the provided services, we propose using the following two principles: (1) creating new VMs only on new servers when the system workload increases; and (2) deactivating the energy-inefficient server and shifting its jobs to other servers when the system workload drops. The cloud computing capability can thus be increased or decreased without affecting QoS.

We now look at how to adjust a schedule when the system moves from the $(q-1)$th to qth period. We know that VMs in the $(q-1)$th period can manage jobs whose frequencies are $\hat{f}_i^{q-1}$. However, when jobs' frequencies become $\hat{f}_i^q$ at the qth period, the schedule must be adjusted and may be smaller than $\hat{f}_i^{q-1}$ or larger. For the first period, the job does not need to be changed because the previous schedule can meet its deadline. For the second one, we have

$$\hat{f}_i^q = \hat{f}_i^{q-1} + \hat{f}_i^q - \hat{f}_i^{q-1} = \hat{f}_i^{q-1} + \Delta\hat{f}_i^q. \tag{3.22}$$

In contrast with the previous constraint that states that jobs cannot be split, jobs with varying frequencies in this case are permitted to be split such that previously created VMs do not must be changed. Then, we can split job J_i into two jobs, where one is J_i with frequency $\hat{f}_i^{q-1}$ and the other is still J_i but with frequency $\Delta\hat{f}_i^q$. To distinguish them, J_i with $\Delta\hat{f}_i^q$ is denoted as J_i^Δ. Thus, previous VMs can meet the deadlines of jobs from J_1 to J_n, and we only need to consider how to schedule J_i^Δ $(1 \leq i \leq n)$.

We take a two-stage scheduling procedure to manage jobs J_i^Δ $(1 \leq i \leq n)$, where in the first stage, the activated servers try to accommodate them as much as possible without missing the deadlines of jobs from J_1 to J_n. If some jobs are left unaccommodated, in the second stage, new servers are activated to manage them. However, if all jobs have been accommodated, in the second stage, we test whether it is possible to shift jobs from energy-inefficient servers to energy-efficient ones. If possible, the former would be deactivated to reduce energy consumption.

Algorithm 3.3: Energy-efficient Job Accommodation Scheme Online

Require: Jobs $J_1, \ldots, J_n$, Servers $S_1, \ldots, S_m$, Schedule of $(q-1)$th period where there are p servers activated to serve jobs.
Ensure: Job Placement and Computing Resource Allocation
Split jobs to J_i and J_i^{Δ} $(1 \leq i \leq n)$ with new frequencies;
Update $\mathcal{S}^{\Delta_i} = \{S_1^{\Delta_i}, S_2^{\Delta_i}, \ldots, S_p^{\Delta_i}\}$ by $\lambda_{i,j}$;
for $j = 1 \rightarrow p$ **do**
  for $i = 1 \rightarrow n$ **do**
    if $J_i \in S_j^i$ **then** ▷ A virtual machine exists in S_j^i that can process J_i
      Determine the frequency f_i^j of J_i^{Δ} that can be accommodated by $S_j^{\Delta_i}$; ▷ This frequency is added to J_i and it should not miss their deadlines
      $\Delta \hat{f}_i^q = \Delta \hat{f}_i^q - f_i^j$; ▷ Reduce the frequency of J_i
    end if
  end for
end for
if there are jobs left not accommodated **then**
  Place them on servers ranging from S_{p+1} to S_m by Algorithm 3.2.
else
  for $j = p \rightarrow 1$ **do**
    Jobs from S_j are considered new jobs and are accommodated by servers S_1 to S_{j-1};
    if Success **then**
      Deactivate S_j and shift jobs from S_j to servers S_1 to S_{j-1};
    else
      Return result;
    end if
  end for
end if

These specific procedures are described in Algorithm 3.3. We assume that there are p servers that have been activated to serve jobs in the $(q-1)$th period. At the beginning, jobs are split into J_i and J_i^{Δ} $(1 \leq i \leq n)$, where jobs J_i are still processed by the schedule of the $(q-1)$th period, and jobs J_i^{Δ} are individually assigned to the activated servers. Servers that can accommodate J_i^{Δ} are sorted to $\mathcal{S}^{\Delta_i} = \{S_1^{\Delta_i}, S_2^{\Delta_i}, \ldots, S_p^{\Delta_i}\}$ by $\lambda_{i,j}$. Then, J_i^{Δ} is successively accommodated by servers of $\mathcal{S}^{\Delta_i}$. J_i^{Δ} can be accommodated by a server only if it has a VM to process J_i because new VMs on activated servers will not be created to provide a smooth service.

The binary search can be used to determine how much of the frequency J_i can be accommodated by server S_j. We denote this search as f_i^j. The added job J_i^{Δ} with

f_i^j should not miss deadlines of other jobs in this server. Then, $\Delta\hat{f}_i^q$ is deducted by f_i^j to relieve the burden of placing J_i^{Δ}. In the end, if there are still some jobs left, new servers ranging from S_{p+1} to S_m must be activated, where Algorithm 3.2 can be used to create new VMs and allocate computing resources for them. Otherwise, we consider whether it is possible to shift the jobs of some energy-inefficient servers to energy-efficient ones, where jobs in these servers are treated similarly to jobs J_i^{Δ}. Because Algorithm 3.2 may be called to schedule jobs that are not accommodated, its worst-case complexity is $O(m^2 \cdot n \cdot \hat{C})$, where $\hat{C} = \max_{j=1..m} C_j$.

Example 3.3 *We use a specific example to show how VMs are created dynamically to accommodate jobs with varying frequencies. There are 3 jobs that are denoted as* J_1–J_3, *and 4 servers that are denoted as* S_1–S_4. *At* $t = 0$, *jobs' frequencies are* $f_1 = 10Hz$, $f_2 = 8Hz$, *and* $f_3 = 15\,Hz$. *At* $t = T$, *their frequencies become* $f_1 = 12\,Hz$, $f_2 = 12\,Hz$, *and* $f_3 = 18\,Hz$. *At* $t = 2T$, *their frequencies become* $f_1 = 18\,Hz$, $f_2 = 15\,Hz$, *and* $f_3 = 20\,Hz$. *As shown in Figure 3.4,* J_1 *and* J_2 *are assigned to* S_1, *and* J_3 *is assigned to* S_2 *at* $t = 0$, *where* S_3 *and* S_4 *are switched off. Jobs' frequencies increase at* $t = T$. *Because* S_1 *can hold* J_1, J_2 *with* $f_1 = 12\,Hz$, $f_2 = 10\,Hz$ *and* S_2 *can hold* J_3 *with* $f_3 = 16$, S_3 *must be switched on to hold* J_2 *and* J_3 *with their additional frequencies. When* $t = 2T$, S_1–S_3 *try to accommodate* J_1–J_3 *as much as possible.* S_4 *must be switched on to hold* J_1–J_3 *because these jobs cannot be accommodated completely by* S_1–S_3.

VM creations and resource allocations are finished once a server is switched on. Because the maximum frequencies of jobs in each profile period are known prior to the schedule design, resource allocation in VMs and job assignments in a newly switched-on server can be completed ahead of time. For example, in Example 3.3, the setup of S_3 and S_4 can be started at $t = T - \varsigma$ and $t = 2T - \varsigma$, respectively, where ς is the required time to finish the configuration. Thus, no VMs would be created abruptly, and how to create VMs and assign jobs could be solved by Algorithms 3.1 and 3.2.

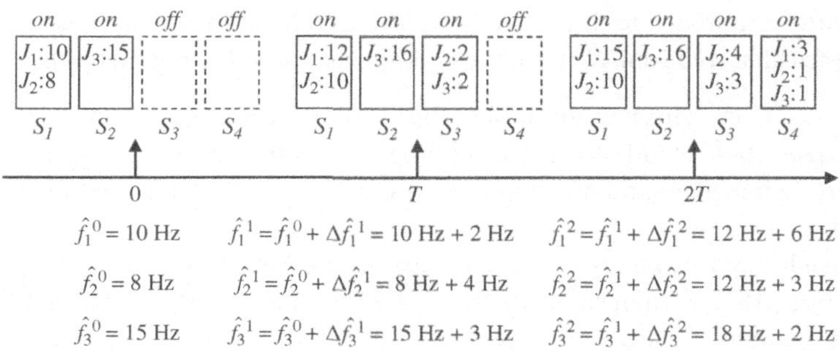

Figure 3.4 Illustration of job accommodation scheme.

To be more specific, we suppose that T is set to be 60 minutes, and the setup time of VMs in a newly switched-on server is 5 minutes. Then, S_3 can be started at $t = 55$ minutes, such that VMs of S_3 have been created and configured at $t = 60$ minutes. In this way, the creation and configuration of VMs would not affect the job scheduling in S_1 and S_2 during $t \in [0,\ T]$, and it would also not affect the job scheduling during $t \in [T,\ 2T]$. On the other hand, when the frequency of a job declines, there would be no jobs in a server, and the switched off of such a server has not impact on the job scheduling.

3.8 Performance Evaluation

3.8.1 Simulation Setup

The proposed approach adaptively schedules varying workloads on cloud computing servers. Thus, the simulation environment should include varying workloads and cloud computing servers. In this study, we setup a cloud computing environment that includes m servers, and each server has C_j virtual CPUs (e.g., $m = 5$, $C_j = 100,\ \forall 1 \leq j \leq m$). The static power efficiency α_j and dynamic power efficiency ranges β_j are $[0.4,\ 0.6]$ and $[1.8,\ 2.2]$, respectively. For a specific job J_i, its release frequency $f_i \in [0.05,\ 0.2]$, its load $l_i \in [5,\ 50]$, and its execution efficiency on server S_j is $\lambda_{i,j} \in [0.8,\ 1.2]$. In general, a job's relative deadline should be less than or equal to its release period (i.e., 1/(release frequency)). As a result, we set the relative deadlines for jobs as $[5,\ 20]$. These parameters are consistent with the following works Shi et al. [47] and Hu et al. [49]. The simulation is run on a desktop computer with an Intel® Core™ i7-7700K 4.2 GHz processor and 16 GB of RAM using the MATLAB simulator.

3.8.2 Compared Approaches

The problem considered in this study is an integer programming problem with nonlinear constraints. To solve this problem, people often turn to using some intelligent optimization approach to find a good solution or rely on some heuristics to quickly find a feasible solution. We have thus compared the following methods:

- M_0 (Proposed One): This method applies the idea of dynamic programming to assign arrival jobs to cloud servers. Depending on the number of arriving jobs, servers are switched on and off adaptively, and VMs are created or destroyed adaptively.
- M_1: For each job, this method calculates its required minimum computing resource by (3.13) and then creates a new VM with such resources for the job.
- M_2: This method creates only one VM with all the server's computing resources, and all jobs run on this VM.

- M_3: We apply a PSO to search for the best solution for the proposed studied problem. Two-segment encoders are used for server and VM selection. The inertia weight is 0.6, both acceleration coefficients are 2, and the iteration is 10000. There are 200 particles that are randomly initialized. These parameter values are chosen because they achieve the fastest convergence and highest objective in many tests.
- M_4: This method is similar to M_3. The only difference is that some of its initial particles are the results from M_0. In principle, if the initial particles are already good sufficient, PSO can often find better ones by testing more solutions nearby.

These approaches are chosen either because they are the most widely used approaches for solving such a problem or because they can find a solution in a short time. For all of them, we use three metrics to evaluate their performance: (1) the success rate of a job being completed; (2) the system's power or energy consumption per day; and (3) the computation time of searching for the solution of VM creation and job assignment.

3.8.3 Results

We compare the performance of these methods using three settings: (1) a single server with fixed-frequency jobs; (2) multiple servers with fixed-frequency jobs; and (3) multiple servers with changing-frequency jobs. Synthetic jobs with the aforementioned parameters are generated in each setting.

3.8.3.1 Results of a Single Server

We assume that there is only a single server with 100 virtual CPUs. The number of jobs varies from 10 to 50 at an increment of 10 and denotes the number of jobs in a job set. For each number of jobs, 100 job sets are generated and tested by these approaches. The average energy consumption, job assignment success rate, and average computation time for finding a schedule are all recorded and shown in Figure 3.5:

- Figure 3.5a shows that, among all approaches, M_0 and M_4 achieve the highest success rate, and their capability in assigning jobs is the same. This result shows that the schedule built by the proposed approach has fallen into a good local solution, and it is difficult to find a better one using PSO, even with good initial particles. M_1 and M_2's poor performance demonstrates that simple heuristics are ineffective because they ignore job interactions and response times. The result of M_3 shows that an intelligent optimization algorithm can improve the quality of solutions compared to simple strategies. It is, however, easy to fall into a poor local optimal solution and difficult to jump into a better one.

- Figure 3.5b shows that M_0 is effective at reducing the energy consumption per assigned job compared to its peers. Such improved performance becomes more apparent if there are more jobs to be assigned. M_1 and M_2 have poor performance for energy reduction because they do not take this aspect into consideration.
- Figure 3.5c shows that the computation time of the compared approaches spans from 10^{-3} to 10^3 seconds. Thus, the vertical axis is on a log-scale. M_1 and M_2 are fast because they involve few computations. However, the two PSO approaches require a long time to determine the final schedule, which can be 6 orders greater than the two strategies. Fortunately, the proposed approach can quickly find a good solution. Its computation time is approximately 1 second, which is three orders of magnitude less than that of PSO and is acceptable for many practical implementations.

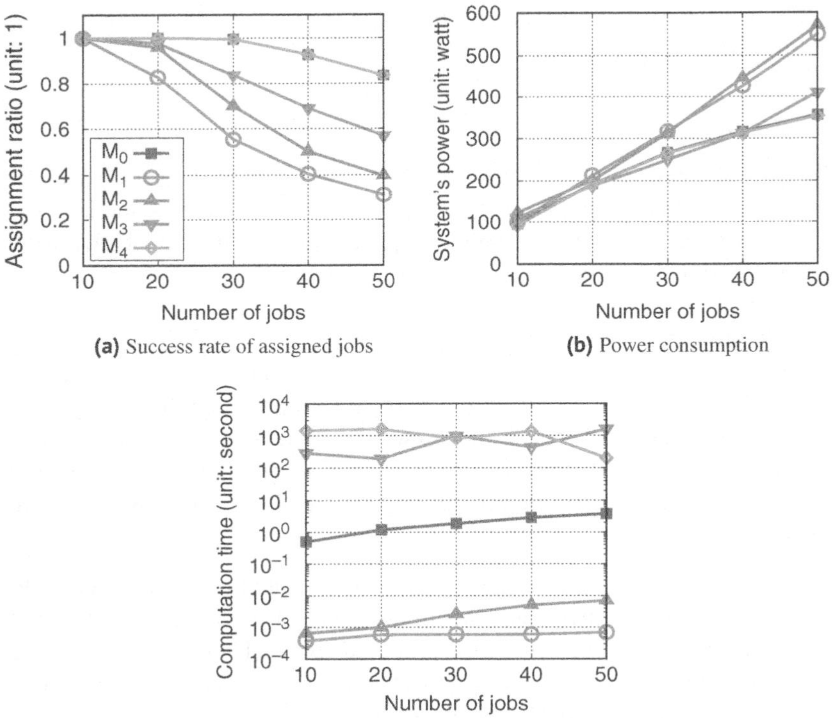

(a) Success rate of assigned jobs

(b) Power consumption

(c) Computation time per job set

Figure 3.5 Results of scheduling jobs with fixed frequency on a system with a single server, where all plots share the same legend as the first one.

Thus, the results show that, compared to its peers, the proposed approach requires a short time to find a high-quality solution with a high success rate and low energy consumption.

3.8.3.2 Results of Multiple Servers

We then investigate the cases with multiple servers. We assume that 100 virtual CPUs are uniformly distributed on 2, 4, 5, and 10 servers. There are 50 jobs that must be assigned to these servers. Results are shown in Figure 3.6. In general, creating multiple VMs on servers has limited effects on the scheduling performance of all compared approaches. In addition, the proposed approach outperforms its peers in terms of assignment ratio and power consumption per job. Its computation time is still approximately 1 second because there are 100 virtual CPUs in total distributed among several servers, which is analogous to a server that is separated

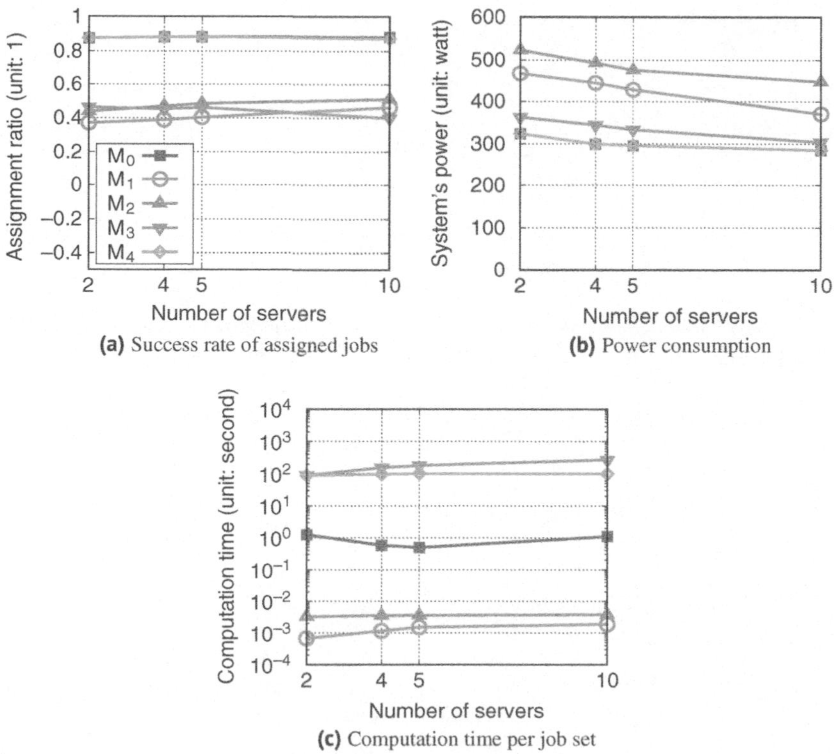

(a) Success rate of assigned jobs

(b) Power consumption

(c) Computation time per job set

Figure 3.6 Results of scheduling jobs with fixed frequency on a system with multiple servers, where the number of total vCPUs among servers is equal to 100. All plots share the same legend as the first one.

into many VMs. The results also demonstrate that the high performance of the proposed approach is not impaired by the increasing number of servers. Note that the reason for the nondecreasing power with respect to increasing number of servers is because the total virtual CPUs are equal among these different server settings.

Also, we examine the performance of various approaches on a system with many servers. We assume that there are servers ranging from 100 to 500, where each server holds 100 vCPUs. There are 5000 jobs that must be assigned to them. Results are shown in Figure 3.7. Figure 3.7a shows that M_0 has a higher success rate than that of M_1 and M_2. To completely schedule 5000 jobs, the average number of required servers is 106 for M_0, 269 for M_1, 197 for M_2 and 106 for M_4, which indicates that M_0 can save half the number of servers compared to M_1 and M_2. The assignment ratio is 0 for M_3, which means that M_3 cannot schedule jobs in this scenario. According to Figure 3.7b, M_0 consumes roughly half or two-thirds of the

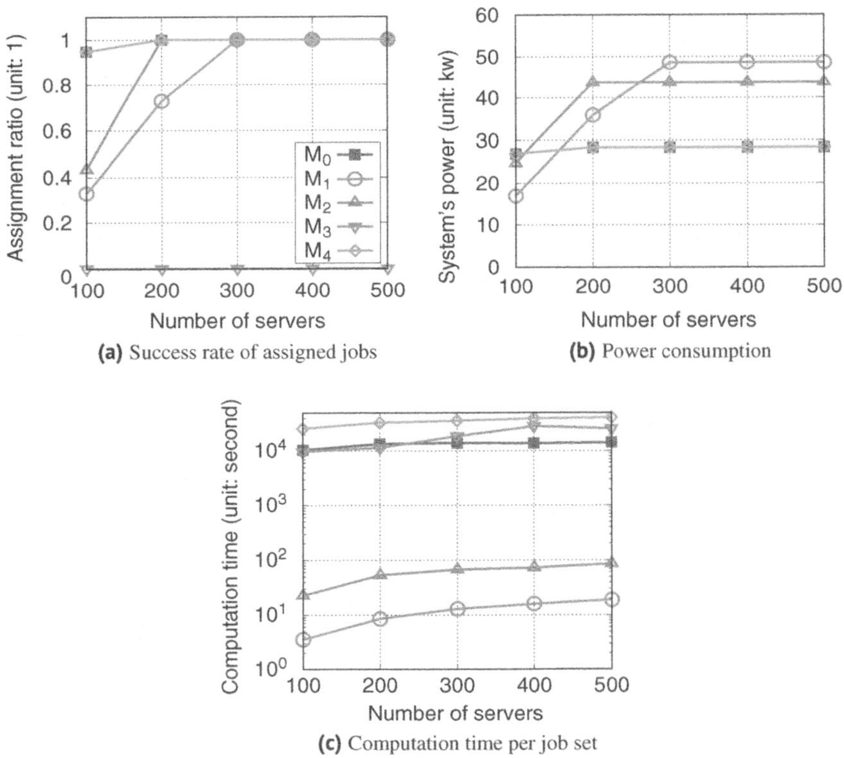

(a) Success rate of assigned jobs

(b) Power consumption

(c) Computation time per job set

Figure 3.7 Results of scheduling jobs with fixed frequency on a system with hundreds of servers, where all plots share the same legend as the first one.

power consumed by M_1 and M_2 because M_0 takes up half the number of servers as its peers. A peculiar point is that the system's power of M_0 is higher than that of M_1 and M_2 when the number of servers is 100. This is because M_0 has three times the number of assigned jobs as M_1 has and twice the number of jobs as M_2 has. More scheduled jobs in the system consume more power. Figure 3.7c shows that the computation time of M_0 can be 2 orders of magnitude higher than that of its peers. To find a schedule, M_0 needs approximately 10000 seconds. Considering that the schedule is designed offline, it should not be a major issue in some real-world use cases. Also, M_4 achieves the same assignment ratio and power consumption as M_0, implying that the proposed approach's solution is suboptimal and difficult to improve using an intelligent search algorithm such as particle swarm optimization.

3.8.3.3 Results of Dynamic Jobs

Finally, we evaluate the performance of the proposed job accommodation scheme to handle dynamically released jobs. We assume that there are 5 servers, where each server holds 100 virtual vCPUs. One hundred jobs are released following a trend of traffic flow in a day, as shown in Figure 3.3. For the other approaches except for M_0, jobs's maximum frequency for a day is assumed, such that the built schedule is capable of handling them without adjustment at runtime. For the proposed approach M_0, the profile period is set to be 0.5, 1, 2, 4, 6, and 24 hours, where the chosen period of 24 hours corresponds to the jobs' maximum frequency of a day. We test this approach 50 times and collect the energy consumption per day. Results are presented in a boxplot, as shown in Figure 3.8. The proposed approach with a profile period $T = 0.5$ hour achieves the best performance, and its performance decreases with an increasing profile period. An interesting result is that its performance with $T = 24$ hours is even better than its performance with $T = 4$ hours and $T = 6$ hours because the proposed approach can find a good schedule that fits jobs with a maximum frequency of a day. However, when $T = 4$ hours or $T = 6$ hours, the schedule built by the proposed approach is changed by the job accommodation scheme at the beginning of every period, and the changed schedule is not optimal or locally optimal, which leads to the problem that its performance may be inferior to the optimal schedule when $T = 24$ hours. The distinguishing advantage of the proposed job accommodation scheme is that it determines the service smoothly because the VMs used for processing future jobs can be created at the moment before entering the next period.

Note that our proposed scheduling algorithm decides when to switch on or off a server, how to create VMs, and how to assign jobs to these VMs. The bad effect of switching on/off a server and VM management has been alleviated by the energy-efficient job accommodation scheme in the proposed algorithm. The overhead of assigning jobs online is small because the assignment plan has

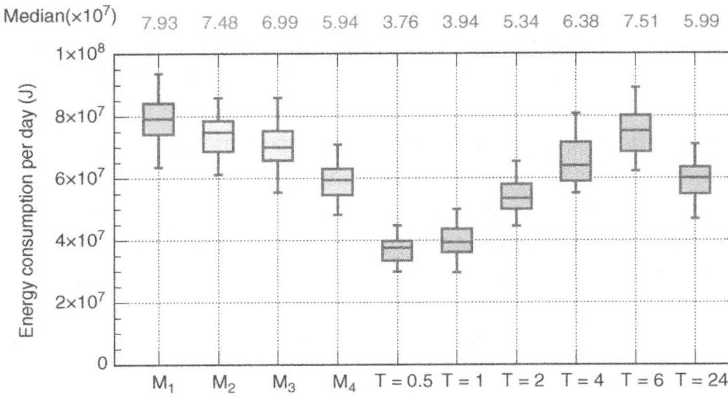

Figure 3.8 Results of scheduling dynamic jobs, where T stands for the profile period used in our proposed approach.

been decided in advance. Jobs in each VM are scheduled by a nonpreemptive fixed-priority scheduling policy, whose overhead is very small and ignorable in many cases, as demonstrated in many textbooks such as Lee and Seshia [95] and Kopetz [96].

3.9 Summary

Energy consumption is a major cost in maintaining cloud computing services, making energy-efficient job scheduling a critical challenge. This study explores the problem of scheduling real-time jobs in a cloud computing system to minimize energy consumption. Since the frequency of requested computation jobs fluctuates throughout the day based on traffic patterns, an adaptive scheduling approach is essential to handle these variations effectively. To address this challenge, we propose a workload-aware scheduling approach that dynamically switches cloud servers on and off based on real-time computation demand. The scheduling problem is formulated as a nonlinear integer programming problem, which is challenging to solve using exact or heuristic optimization methods. To overcome this difficulty, we transform the problem into an unconventional 0-1 knapsack problem, derive a corresponding state-transition equation, and apply dynamic programming to obtain a near-optimal solution efficiently. Additionally, we develop an energy-efficient job accommodation scheme that leverages the upper bound of job frequency to manage workload variations in real time. A key advantage of our approach is its ability to provide a smooth and flexible service without compromising performance. Experimental results demonstrate that the proposed method quickly identifies high-quality schedules and outperforms a PSO and two heuristic methods in both job execution success rate and energy savings.

4

Energy-minimized Scheduling of Real-time Dependent Tasks in Cloud

This chapter introduces an energy-efficient scheduling algorithm designed for processing user applications with real-time requirements in a cloud computing system. The problem is formulated as a nonlinear mixed-integer programming challenge. Initially, an optimal closed-form solution is derived to its relaxation problem, aiming to minimize energy consumption without considering real-time requirements. To ensure real-time requirements are met, a task placement adjustment strategy and a resource allocation strategy are presented to strike a favorable balance between energy consumption and task execution time. Additionally, two equivalent optimal resource allocation strategies are discussed once task placement is complete. Finally, the start time of task execution is adjusted again to further reduce application completion time.

4.1 Introduction

Cloud computing is an infrastructure-based and service-oriented computing model that offers on-demand computing capabilities to users [44, 97, 98]. With the help of modern virtualization techniques supporting flexible job allocation and dynamic resource management, cloud service users can simply submit their requests to the cloud computing system. Based on these user requests, the cloud system automatically provides the necessary hardware resources for processing, freeing users from the burden of setting up and maintaining a computing platform, and enabling them to focus more on their computing applications [99]. In this scenario, the central challenge for a cloud service provider is to allocate hardware infrastructures and schedule applications in a manner that minimizes their processing costs.

Intelligent Scheduling of Tasks for Cloud-Edge-Device Computing Systems, First Edition.

Published 2025 by John Wiley & Sons, Inc.

Energy consumption constitutes a significant portion of the costs in large-scale cloud computing systems at various levels of computational processes. For instance, the Tianhe-2 supercomputer, which held the title of the world's fastest computer in 2014 and 2015, consists of 16000 computing nodes and consumes 17808 kW of power [100]. High energy consumption not only increases operational costs but also adversely affects system performance, reducing reliability, and has environmental consequences, such as increased carbon emissions. Consequently, minimizing energy consumption has become a major concern for many cloud computing providers, motivating them to design and optimize their systems with energy efficiency in mind [101–105].

On the other hand, minimizing the completion time of user tasks is equally important. A shorter completion time allows users to obtain computed results quickly, saving their valuable time. From a cloud service provider's perspective, shorter completion times lead to higher system throughput and, consequently, increased profits. However, this objective of improving real-time processing capabilities often conflicts with the goal of minimizing energy consumption, as reducing task completion time may require additional hardware resources, resulting in higher energy usage. To address this conflict, an efficient scheduling algorithm is required to allocate and utilize cloud resources effectively.

This chapter addresses this challenging problem and focuses on scheduling a user application that consists of parallel and dependent tasks with data synchronization. Such applications can be generalized as Directed Acyclic Graphs (DAGs). In a DAG, nodes represent individual tasks, and directed edges represent inter-task data dependencies between pairs of tasks [106]. Many user applications can be categorized as DAG models, such as Fourier transformation [107], Gaussian elimination [108], and image processing applications [109, 110]. In a cloud computing platform, servers are composed of virtual machines, and each virtual machine processes individual tasks from user applications. The execution model in the cloud places each task in an application on a physical server, where it is processed in a virtual machine created for it. To achieve the dual objective of minimizing energy consumption while meeting real-time computing requirements, we must address the following three critical questions:

1. How to place tasks in a DAG application to servers?
2. When to execute each task to meet the task-dependency requirement?
3. How to allocate resources to the virtual machine created for each task?

Indeed, answering the above questions is challenging. Task scheduling with the objective of minimizing task completion time is a well-known NP-hard problem [111]. Similarly, our concerned problem, which aims to simultaneously reduce energy consumption and shorten response time, also falls into the category of NP-hard problems. Engineers face the difficult task of reconciling the conflicting requirements of minimizing energy consumption while achieving shorter response times, as these two objectives are tightly interwoven and complexly related. Intuitively, reducing energy consumption may result in longer response times for parallel workflows, making the problem a typical bicriteria optimization problem where both objectives need to be carefully balanced.

Currently, several scheduling approaches partially address the questions raised above. In Shi et al. [47], a scheduling algorithm is proposed to minimize job completion time while considering energy consumption constraints. However, the scheduled job in Shi et al. [47] consists of a set of independently parallel tasks without data synchronization, different from a DAG application's characteristics. Another method proposed in Zhao et al. [112] focuses on scheduling data-intensive applications with energy and deadline awareness, mainly concentrating on task assignments to virtual machines. Similarly, in Hosseinimotlagh et al. [113], a virtual machine scheduling algorithm is presented to optimize energy consumption based on a given quality of service (QoS) requirement. However, this approach assumes that virtual machines are pre-mapped to servers, whereas our problem involves determining both virtual machine placement and resource allocation. While several other scheduling approaches have been proposed for cloud computing systems [114–116], none of them specifically address the task scheduling problem for a DAG application, which involves deciding task placement, task execution start times, and resource allocation in virtual machines simultaneously. Moreover, many existing approaches, such as genetic algorithms (GAs) and particle swarm optimization [117–121], find scheduling solutions through time-consuming iterative searches, making them impractical for large-size parallel applications that require fast processing in a cloud environment.

Being aware of the aforementioned challenges, in this chapter, we present a scheduling algorithm that efficiently addresses the raised questions by utilizing a closed-form solution for the relaxation problem, which focuses on minimizing energy consumption without considering timing requirements. The main contributions of this chapter are as follows:

- First, we formulate the scheduling problem as a nonlinear mixed-integer programming problem. Leveraging the energy model, we derive an optimal closed-form solution for task placement on servers to minimize energy consumption.
- Second, to ensure data synchronization among tasks, we categorize and schedule tasks according to the application levels. Considering the real-time constraint, the task placement aimed at minimizing energy consumption may lead to an application's completion time exceeding its timing constraint. Therefore, we introduce an algorithm that strikes a balance between completion time and energy consumption by slightly increasing energy consumption to achieve a substantial reduction in completion time.

- Third, after determining task placement, we discover two equivalent optimal resource allocation strategies that minimize an application's completion time. Specifically, creating multiple virtual machines with optimal resource allocation to execute tasks in parallel is equivalent to providing resources to only one virtual machine to execute tasks sequentially. Leveraging this property, we developed an algorithm to efficiently adjust the start time of task execution in a backward manner, resulting in further reduction of an application's completion time.
- Finally, we evaluate the performance of our proposed algorithms through extensive simulations. The results demonstrate that our algorithms outperform a meta-heuristic GA in terms of computation time, energy consumption, and success rate in finding an optimal schedule.

4.2 Related Work

There have been numerous studies investigating the task scheduling problem in cloud computing. In this section, we provide a survey of some relevant research work that sheds light on our studied problem. These scheduling algorithms can generally be categorized into two types: intelligent optimization algorithms, such as GAs and ant colony optimization, and heuristic algorithms.

Intelligent optimization algorithms are often effective in finding good solutions, as they rely on iterative search processes [122, 123]. For example, in Shen et al. [66], a GA with two fitness functions is proposed to adaptively adjust the energy and performance targets before task assignments in a cloud. This enables users to meet their specific requirements. In another study [124], authors propose an improved ant colony algorithm to solve a bicriteria optimization problem, aiming to minimize both makespan and a user's expense. Some works combine multiple optimization techniques. In Gan et al. [125], an algorithm that integrates a GA and simulated annealing is proposed. The GA generates offspring, which are further optimized using simulated annealing. Additionally, a clonal selection algorithm has been adopted in Jena [126] to minimize energy consumption and task processing time, achieving a good balance between the two objectives. However, it's worth noting that these intelligent optimization algorithms typically demand significant computation to decide on a schedule. This may limit their applicability in cloud scenarios with fast timing response requirements.

Heuristics can often provide quick scheduling solutions as they rely on simple rules to make decisions. For instance, in Zhao et al. [112], a tree-to-tree task scheduling algorithm is proposed, where datasets and tasks are modeled as a binary tree to enhance the energy efficiency of a cloud system. To minimize energy consumption on a host, [113] introduces an optimal utilization level for executing a certain number of instructions. Based on this level, a virtual machine scheduling algorithm is proposed to regulate computing resource allocation. In

Xiao et al. [114], a set of heuristics is proposed to balance different types of workloads and improve the overall utilization of a system by executing tasks with high energy efficiency. Authors in Baker et al. [127] suggest using a bin-packing technique to select energy-efficient services from cross-continental clouds, reducing energy consumption. In Zhang and Zhou [128], a two-stage strategy is proposed, initially utilizing historical scheduling data to classify arriving tasks and then proactively creating virtual machines to minimize non-optimal task allocation in the cloud. With the widespread deployment of Internet of Things (IoT) devices, the offloading of requests from centers to edges has become crucial. In Al-khafajiy et al. [129], a fog computing framework is proposed to enable data processing by collaborating fog nodes, allowing IoT requests to be quickly served and improving QoS. However, these approaches either disregard real-time requirements of various applications or make assumptions about task placements and resource allocation, which may not be well-suited for solving our specific problem.

4.3 Problem Formulation

To schedule an application submitted to a cloud computing system, the task scheduling problem involves placing each task on a server and creating a virtual machine with an appropriate amount of computing resources to execute it. This problem can be formulated with inputs, outputs, an objective function, and related constraints.

4.3.1 Input

In a cloud computing system, the inputs consist of a user application and a platform comprising a set of heterogeneous servers.

4.3.1.1 User Applications

As presented in Figure 4.1, an application composed of a set of parallel and dependent tasks can be represented as a DAG model. Mathematically, it is $G(\mathcal{T}, E)$, where $\mathcal{T}$ is a set of tasks and E is a set of edges that represent task dependencies. Specifically, $\mathcal{T} = \{T_1, T_2, ..., T_n\}$, where T_i denotes the ith task. E is a $n \times n$ matrix where $E(i, j) = 1$ denotes the dependency constraint between T_i and T_j, i.e., T_j can start its execution only after T_i completes its execution. If there is no such dependency, $E(i, j) = 0$. For instance, $E(1, 2) = 1$, $E(1, 3) = 1$ because T_2 and T_3 can start its execution after the completion of T_1. $E(4, 5) = 0$ because there is no such dependency relationship between T_4 and T_5. We use l_i to represent the computing load of task T_i, i.e., it needs execution time of l_i on a virtual machine with unit computing capacity created from a unit-efficiency server.

Additionally, we define two special tasks in the DAG, namely the entry task and the exit task. The entry task is a task that has no predecessor task, while the

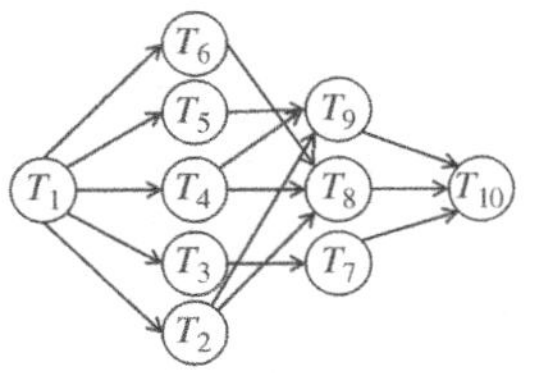

Figure 4.1 A DAG application.

exit task is one that has no successor task. If there is more than one task without any predecessor, we create a dummy task to serve as their predecessor. The same approach is used for multiple exit tasks, ensuring that there is only one entry task and one exit task in the DAG. The tasks are then labeled in sequence from the entry task to the exit task, such that $T_{\text{entry}} = T_1$ and $T_{\text{exit}} = T_n$.

4.3.1.2 Cloud Computing Platform

A cloud computing platform can be represented as a set of heterogeneous servers, denoted as $CCP = S_1, S_2, \ldots, S_m$, where S_j refers to the jth server in the platform. Specifically, we use C_j to represent the computing resource of server S_j. It is essential to note that due to server heterogeneity, the execution time of a task may vary on different servers [130]. To account for this heterogeneity, we introduce the concept of execution efficiency for each task, denoted as $\lambda_{i,j}$, representing the efficiency of executing task T_i on server S_j. Consequently, we can express this as follows:

$$e_i = \frac{l_i}{\lambda_{i,j}\varrho_i}, \tag{4.1}$$

where l_i is the task execution load, and e_i is the execution time of task T_i on a virtual machine allocated with ϱ_i computing capacity from server S_j.

4.3.2 Output

The outputs of scheduling an application in a cloud computing system include a task placement plan, a start time plan, and a resource allocation plan.

4.3.2.1 Task Placement Plan

The server assigned to execute a specific task is denoted by a task placement plan. For task T_i, we can use binary variables $x_{i,j}$ to denote its placement, where $x_{i,j} = 1$ denotes that T_i is placed on server S_j to execute, and $x_{i,j} = 0$ otherwise. Here, we should note that a task is non-divisible, which means that it can only be placed on one server at a time. The task placement plan can be represented by a matrix $\mathbf{X}$ with a size $n \times m$.

4.3.2.2 Start Time Plan

Due to the task dependency in an application, a task can start its execution only after all its predecessor tasks have been finished. Here, we use $\vec{s} = \{s_1, s_2, ..., s_n\}$ to denote their start time, where s_i denotes the time to start T_i's execution.

4.3.2.3 Resource Allocation Plan

A task is processed by a virtual machine, where a virtual machine is created from a server. A resource allocation plan denotes the number of computing resources allocated to each virtual machine. Here, we use $\mathcal{V} = \{V_1, V_2, ..., V_n\}$ to denote the set of virtual machines, where V_i is the virtual machine created for T_i. Correspondingly, we use $\vec{c} = \{\varrho_1, \varrho_2, ..., \varrho_n\}$ to denote a resource allocation plan in which ϱ_i is the number of computing resources allocated to V_i. In summary, an output schedule can be represented by $\mathcal{S} = \{\mathbf{X}, \vec{s}, \vec{c}\}$.

4.3.3 Objective

Before we present energy consumption minimization as an objective function, we will briefly introduce a power model commonly used in cloud computing.

We adopt a power model that is widely used in cloud computing energy analysis [65, 66, 99, 131–133]. On a virtual machine created for processing task T_i, its power consumption P_i is directly proportional to its resource utilization, i.e.,

$$P_i = \alpha_{i,j} \cdot \varrho_i, \tag{4.2}$$

where $\alpha_{i,j}$ is a specific power constant that only depends on a virtual machine itself. Then, the energy consumption E_i of the ith virtual machine is

$$E_i = P_i \cdot e_i = \alpha_{i,j} \cdot \varrho_i \cdot e_i = \frac{\alpha_{i,j} l_i}{\sum_{j=1}^{m} x_{i,j} \lambda_{i,j}}, \tag{4.3}$$

where $\sum_{j=1}^{m} x_{i,j}\lambda_{i,j}$ denotes the execution efficiency of task T_i on its allocated server.

Here, we use $\mathcal{E} = \{E_1, E_2, ..., E_n\}$ to denote the set of energy consumption of all created virtual machines, and the scheduling objective is to minimize the total energy consumption that can be presented as below:

$$\min \sum_{i=1}^{n} E_i. \tag{4.4}$$

4.3.4 Constraints

There are a variety of types of constraints when scheduling an application in a cloud computing platform.

4.3.4.1 Task Placement Constraints

Because a task is non-divisible, a task can only be allocated to 1 server at a time, i.e.,

$$x_{i,j} \in \{0, 1\} \text{ and } \sum_{j=1}^{m} x_{i,j} = 1, \; i = 1, \ldots, n, \; j = 1, \ldots, m. \tag{4.5}$$

4.3.4.2 Task-dependency Constraints

Due to the task dependency in an application, a task can start its execution only after all its predecessor tasks have completed their execution. Thus, we have

$$\begin{aligned} s_i &\le \max_{T_{i'} \in pred(T_i)} (s_{i'} + e_{i'}) \\ &= \max_{T_{i'} \in pred(T_i)} \left(s_{i'} + \frac{l_i}{\sum_{j=1}^{m} x_{i',j} \lambda_{i',j} \varrho_{i'}} \right), \end{aligned} \tag{4.6}$$

where $pred(T_i)$ represents the set of all predecessor tasks of task T_i, i.e., $pred(T_i) = \{T_{i'} | E(i', i) = 1, \;\; \forall T_{i'} \in \mathcal{T}\}$.

4.3.4.3 Real-time Constraint

Suppose that the first task (entry task) of an application starts its execution time at 0, i.e., $s_1 = 0$. The application's completion time is the moment of completing its exit task. Due to the timing constraint, we have

$$s_n + e_n = s_n + \frac{l_n}{\sum_{j=1}^{m} x_{n,j} \lambda_{n,j} \varrho_n} \le \mathcal{R}, \tag{4.7}$$

where $\mathcal{R}$ represents its real-time requirement.

4.3.4.4 Resource Availability Constraints

In a cloud computing platform, there is a specific number of computing resources available, and these resources have been specifically allocated to each server. The allocated resources to virtual machines on a server should not exceed its total quantity at any time. We observe that a computing resource would be added to a newly created virtual machine only when a task needs to start its execution. Therefore, the resource availability constraints only need to be checked at those moments, i.e., when a task is about to start its execution on a virtual machine. Thus, the resource availability constraints only need to be checked at those moments, i.e.,

$$A_{j,k} \cdot \sum_{T_i \in \mathcal{T}^j(t)} x_{i,j} \cdot \varrho_i \le B_{j,k},$$
$$k = 1, \ldots, R;\ j = 1, \ldots, m;\ t \in \{s_1, s_2, \ldots, s_n\}, \tag{4.8}$$

where $A_{j,k}$ is the resource coefficient in the kth type constraint; $B_{j,k}$ is the total number of the kth type constraints in jth server; $\mathcal{T}^j(t)$ is the set of tasks that are placed and executed on the jth server at time t.

From the above problem description, we can see that this scheduling problem is a complex nonlinear mixed-integer programming problem, which is very challenging to solve exactly. Moreover, using intelligent algorithms such as GA or differential evolution algorithm can be time-consuming to obtain a good solution. In this chapter, we propose a novel heuristic method that can quickly generate an energy-efficient schedule, even for large-scale scheduling problems.

Example 4.1 *For a DAG as presented in Figure 4.1, it is served in a cloud computing system with 3 servers, where its parameters are presented in Table 4.1. Suppose the real-time requirement is 9. We have to build a schedule in this system to minimize its energy consumption with real-time and resource constraints.*

Table 4.1 Parameters of the DAG and cloud computing platform in the example.

l_i

T_1	T_2	T_3	T_4	T_5	T_6	T_7	T_8	T_9	T_{10}
200	300	400	200	300	500	200	400	500	500

$\lambda_{i,j}$

	T_1	T_2	T_3	T_4	T_5	T_6	T_7	T_8	T_9	T_{10}
S_1	0.9	0.9	0.5	0.8	0.7	1.0	0.5	0.6	0.6	0.5
S_2	0.8	0.6	0.6	0.9	0.6	0.7	0.9	0.6	0.9	1.0
S_3	0.7	0.5	0.5	0.5	0.9	0.8	0.7	0.9	0.6	1.0

$\alpha_{i,j}$

	T_1	T_2	T_3	T_4	T_5	T_6	T_7	T_8	T_9	T_{10}
S_1	0.7	0.5	0.6	1.0	0.5	1.0	0.5	0.5	0.7	0.8
S_2	0.7	1.0	0.9	1.0	0.5	0.7	0.7	0.7	0.5	0.5
S_3	0.6	0.7	0.6	1.0	0.7	0.8	0.8	1.0	1.0	0.7

(Continued)

Table 4.1 (Continued)

$A_{j,k}$

k	1	2	3	4	5	6	7
S_1	200	300	300	300	500	300	300
S_2	200	300	300	500	500	300	500
S_3	400	300	200	400	300	200	200

$B_{j,k}$

k	1	2	3	4	5	6	7
S_1	0.2	0.8	0.8	1.0	0.3	0.7	0.2
S_2	0.9	0.8	0.1	0.5	0.9	0.6	1.0
S_3	0.4	0.7	0.4	0.9	0.5	0.3	1.0

4.4 Energy-efficient Scheduling Without Real-time Constraint

In this section, we will relax the problem to focus on minimizing energy consumption without considering real-time requirements. This relaxed scheduling solution will serve as a reference for the subsequent problem with a real-time requirement.

4.4.1 Energy Consumption-minimized Task Placement Plan

The energy consumption is the accumulated energy consumption of all tasks. Looking into (4.3) and (4.4), we can find out that the energy consumption of a task has the following properties.

Lemma 4.1 *The energy consumption of task T_i ($T_i \in \mathcal{T}$) only depends on its placement.*

Proof: The energy consumption of task T_i is E_i presented in (4.3), where l_i is a parameter that is related to T_i itself. Then E_i only depends on $\frac{\alpha_{i,j}}{\sum_{j=1}^{m} x_{i,j}\lambda_{i,j}}$, which means that its energy consumption only depends on the server that T_i is placed on.

Based on this lemma, we can further conclude Theorem 4.1.

Theorem 4.1 *The energy consumption for executing an application is minimized if each of its task is placed on a server as follows:*

$$x_{i,j'} = 1, \ \forall i = 1 \,..\, n, \tag{4.9}$$

where j' *is subject to* $\frac{\alpha_{i,j'}}{\lambda_{i,j'}} = \min_{j=1 \,..\, m}\{\frac{\alpha_{i,j}}{\lambda_{i,j}}\}$.

Proof: For task T_i, its energy consumption depends on $\frac{\alpha_{i,j}}{\sum_{j=1}^{m} x_{i,j}\lambda_{i,j}}$ only. Because $x_{i,j}$ is a binary value and $\sum_{j=1}^{m} x_{i,j} = 1$, we have

$$\frac{\alpha_{i,j}}{\sum_{j=1}^{m} x_{i,j}\lambda_{i,j}} \geq \min_{j=1 \,..\, m}\left\{\frac{\alpha_{i,j}}{\lambda_{i,j}}\right\} = \frac{\alpha_{i,j'}}{\lambda_{i,j'}}. \tag{4.10}$$

Thus, to minimize the value of $\frac{\alpha_{i,j}}{\sum_{j=1}^{m} x_{i,j}\lambda_{i,j}}$, $x_{i,j'}$ must be equal to 1. Because the energy consumption of each task is independent by Lemma 4.1, the total energy consumption is minimized based on (4.9).

From this theorem, we can decide the energy consumption-optimal task placement plan based on $\alpha_{i,j}$ and $\beta_{i,j}$ $(i \leq N, \ j \leq M)$.

4.4.2 Partition Scheduling

With a task placement plan in hand, our next step is to determine a start time plan and resource allocation plan for each task. However, due to task dependencies, a task can only start its execution after all its predecessors have been completed. To ensure this property, we designed a scheme to partition the schedule based on the application's DAG structure. This partitioning approach will help us efficiently schedule tasks while maintaining their dependencies.

Definition 4.1 In the DAG, we refer to a task as being in its lth level if the maximum number of edges from its entry task to it is $l - 1$.

In addition, we use $\mathcal{T}_l$ $(l \leq L)$ to denote the set of tasks in the lth level, and L represents the maximum level. With this definition, we can identify that tasks in the same level have no dependencies among them. As a result, they can be processed in parallel. By running tasks in the order of $\mathcal{T}_1$, $\mathcal{T}_2$, ..., $\mathcal{T}_L$, we ensure that task dependencies are satisfied because the processors of a task only remain

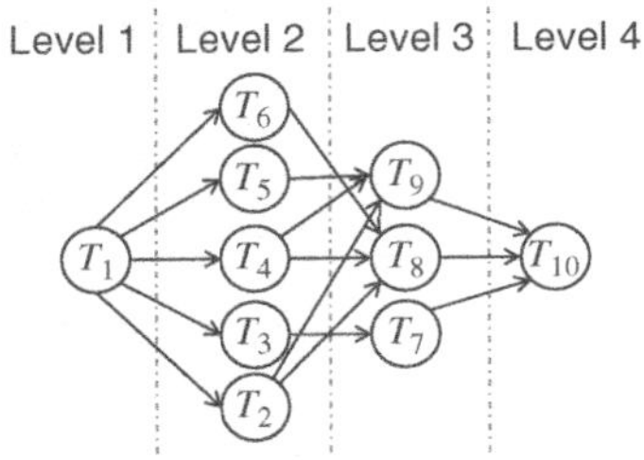

Figure 4.2 A DAG with 10 tasks divided into four levels.

in its upper levels. This scheme leads to a partitioned schedule, which simplifies the task execution order and enhances parallel processing. As presented in Figure 4.2, the DAG application of Figure 4.1 is divided into 4 levels, where $\mathcal{T}_1 = \{T_1\}$, $\mathcal{T}_2 = \{T_2, T_3, T_4, T_5, T_6\}$, $\mathcal{T}_3 = \{T_7, T_8, T_9\}$, and $\mathcal{T}_4 = \{T_{10}\}$.

Then, we analyze how to schedule tasks in the same level. In fact, there is an optimal resource allocation strategy to minimize their execution time. First, we define $\mathcal{T}_l^j$ representing tasks on the jth server and in the lth level. It can be decided based on Theorem 4.1.

Theorem 4.2 *To minimize the completion time of* $\mathcal{T}_l^j$, *the computing resource allocated to* T_i $(T_i \in \mathcal{T}_l^j)$ *should be*

$$\forall T_i \in \mathcal{T}_l^j,\ \varrho_i^* = \frac{l_i}{\lambda_{i,j} \sum\limits_{T_p \in \mathcal{T}_l^j} \frac{l_p}{\lambda_{p,j}}} \cdot \min_{k \in \{1...R\}} \left\{ \frac{B_{j,k}}{A_{j,k}} \right\}. \tag{4.11}$$

Proof: As there is no dependency in the same level, tasks in $\mathcal{T}_l^j$ can start their execution simultaneously, and the completion time of $\mathcal{T}_l^j$ depends on the maximum execution time of its tasks.

First, we denote that $\frac{B_{j,u}}{A_{j,u}} = \min_{k=1..R} \left\{ \frac{B_{j,k}}{A_{j,k}} \right\}$. We have

$$\begin{aligned} \varrho_i^* &= \frac{l_i}{\lambda_{i,j} \sum\limits_{T_p \in \mathcal{T}_l^j} \frac{l_p}{\lambda_{p,j}}} \cdot \min_{k=1..R} \left\{ \frac{B_{j,k}}{A_{j,k}} \right\} \\ &= \frac{l_i}{\lambda_{i,j} \sum\limits_{T_p \in \mathcal{T}_l^j} \frac{l_p}{\lambda_{p,j}}} \cdot \frac{B_{j,u}}{A_{j,u}} \end{aligned}$$

We then prove that with the resource allocation plan given in (4.11), all tasks in $\mathcal{T}_l^j$ have the same execution time, because for any two tasks T_i and $T_{i'}$ ($T_i \in \mathcal{T}_l^j$, $T_{i'} \in \mathcal{T}_l^j$, $i \neq i'$),

$$\begin{aligned} e_i^* &= \frac{l_i}{\lambda_{i,j}\varrho_i^*} = \frac{l_i}{\lambda_{i,j}} \cdot \frac{\lambda_{i,j}}{l_i} \cdot \sum_{T_p \in \mathcal{T}_l^j} \frac{l_p}{\lambda_{p,j}} \cdot \frac{A_{j,u}}{B_{j,u}}, \\ &= \frac{l_{i'}}{\lambda_{i',j}} \cdot \frac{\lambda_{i',j}}{l_{i'}} \cdot \sum_{T_p \in \mathcal{T}_l^j} \frac{l_p}{\lambda_{p,j}} \cdot \frac{A_{j,u}}{B_{j,u}} = e_{i'}^*. \end{aligned}$$

Last, we prove that ϱ_i^* is the optimal solution for minimizing the completion time of $\mathcal{T}_l^j$. We prove it by contradiction. We know that the completion time of $\mathcal{T}_l^j$ with ϱ_i^* is e_i^*. Now assume that instead of ϱ_i^*, another resource allocation $\varrho_i^\flat$ makes the completion time smaller, i.e.,

$$e_i^\flat = \frac{l_i}{\lambda_{i,j}\varrho_i^\flat} \leq \frac{l_i}{\lambda_{i,j}\varrho_i^*} = e_i^*.$$

Then, we have $\varrho_i^\flat > \varrho_i^*$. In this case, the total number of required resources ($\forall k \in [1..R]$) is

$$\begin{aligned} A_{j,k} \cdot \sum_{T_i \in \mathcal{T}_l^j} \varrho_i^\flat &> A_{j,k} \cdot \sum_{T_i \in \mathcal{T}_l^j} \varrho_i^* \\ &= A_{j,k} \cdot \sum_{T_i \in \mathcal{T}_l^j} \frac{l_i}{\lambda_{i,j} \sum_{T_p \in \mathcal{T}_l^j} \frac{l_p}{\lambda_{p,j}}} \cdot \min_{k=1..R} \{\frac{B_{j,k}}{A_{j,k}}\}. \end{aligned}$$

Considering the uth resource constraint, we have

$$A_{j,u} \cdot \sum_{T_i \in \mathcal{T}_l^j} \varrho_i^\flat > A_{j,u} \cdot \frac{\sum_{T_i \in \mathcal{T}_l^j} \frac{l_i}{\lambda_{p,j}}}{\sum_{T_p \in \mathcal{T}_l^j} \frac{l_p}{\lambda_{p,j}}} \cdot \frac{B_{j,u}}{A_{j,u}} = B_{j,u},$$

which violates the resource availability constraint. As a result, there does not exist a resource allocation that is better than that in (4.11).

Given a resource allocation plan, we can decide the execution time of each task. As the schedule is partitioned level by level, we have

$$\begin{aligned} s_i &= t_{\mathcal{T}_{l-1}} \\ t_{\mathcal{T}_l} &= t_{\mathcal{T}_{l-1}} + e_{\mathcal{T}_l}, \end{aligned}$$

where

$$e_{\mathcal{T}_l} = \max\{e_i | \forall T_i \in \mathcal{T}_l\},$$

and $t_{\mathcal{T}_l}$ denotes the moment of completing all tasks in $\mathcal{T}_l$ as $t_{\mathcal{T}_l}$.

The detailed scheduling procedure is presented in Algorithm 4.1. Here, we use a specific example to explicitly show the scheduling results.

Example 4.2 *After applying Algorithm 4.1 to schedule DAG of Figure 4.2, we have the schedule shown in Figure 4.3, where the execution of any task in $\mathcal{T}_l^j$ ($l \leq L$, $j \leq M$) starts and ends simultaneously due to their equal execution time. The application's completion time is 13.36, and the energy consumption is 2755. This schedule needs to be further adjusted due to the timing requirement.*

Algorithm 4.1: Energy Consumption-optimal Schedule Without Real-time Constraint

---

function ENERGYOPTISCHEDULE($G(\mathcal{T}, E)$, CCP)
  Decide $x_{i,j}$ ($\forall i = 1..n$) according to Theorem 4.1.
  Based on the task placement plan and DAG structure, classify tasks to $\mathcal{T}_l^j$, where $j \leq M$, $l \leq L$.
  for $l = 1..L$ **do**
    for $j = 1..M$ **do**
      $\forall T_i \in \mathcal{T}_l^j$, $s_i = t_{\mathcal{T}_{l-1}}$ and allocate the computing resource to T_i according to Theorem 4.2
    end for
    $t_{\mathcal{T}_l} = t_{\mathcal{T}_{l-1}} + \max\{e_i | \forall T_i \in \mathcal{T}_l\}$
  end for
  Return $\mathcal{S}$
end function

4.5 Scheduling with Real-time Constraint

Although Algorithm 4.1 effectively minimizes energy consumption, its schedule may not meet real-time requirements. Therefore, we need to develop an approach that considers timing constraints. Since the schedule generated by Algorithm 4.1 optimizes energy consumption but not completion time, our idea is to make adjustments to this schedule to reduce completion time while incurring minimal extra energy consumption.

In this section, we present an efficient strategy to scale down the completion time of the schedule obtained from Algorithm 4.1 by trading off energy savings. By applying this strategy, we aim to achieve a schedule that meets real-time requirements while still minimizing energy consumption as much as possible.

4.5.1 Task Placement Adjustment Strategy

Before making adjustments to task placement, we need to identify potential tasks whose placement changes can bring the most significant benefit to reducing completion time. When examining the schedule generated by Algorithm 4.1 (e.g., Figure 4.3), we observe that task execution times vary across different servers. Consequently, tasks with the maximum execution time in their respective levels should be considered for placement on alternative servers. This arrangement is crucial to reducing an application's completion time. Such tasks with the maximum execution time in each level are referred to as *bottleneck tasks*. For instance, in Figure 4.3, $\mathcal{T}_2^1$ and $\mathcal{T}_3^2$ are bottleneck tasks in levels 2 and 3, respectively.

Naturally, the best strategy is to reduce the completion time maximally at the least cost of energy consumption. Thus, we have to find an appropriate indicator to characterize task. Before we provide it, we formally define the following notations. Suppose that a task T_i in the lth level has been placed on the jth server, i.e., $T_i \in \mathcal{T}_l^j$. Assume that this task is also a bottleneck task. If it is placed on the j'th server ($j \neq j'$), the increment of energy consumption is denoted as $\Delta E_i^{j \to j'}$, and the decrement of $e_{\mathcal{T}_l}$ is denoted as $\Delta e_{\mathcal{T}_l}^{j \to j'}$.

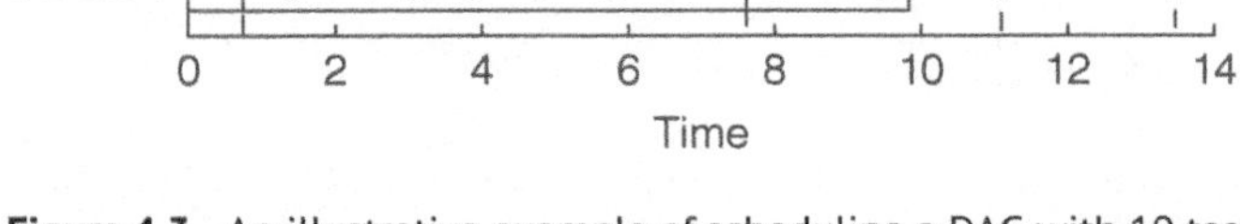

Figure 4.3 An illustrative example of scheduling a DAG with 10 tasks and four levels by Algorithm 4.1, where every task in $\mathcal{T}_l^j$ ($l \leq L$, $j \leq M$) has the same start and end time.

Definition 4.2 The energy-to-time factor for task T_i is defined as Γ_{t_i} that is calculated by

$$\Gamma_{t_i} = \begin{cases} \min\limits_{j' \neq j, j' \leq M} \left\{ \dfrac{\Delta E_i^{j \to j'}}{|\Delta e_{\mathcal{T}_l}^{j \to j'}|} \right\}, & \text{if } \Delta e_{\mathcal{T}_l}^{j \to j'} < 0 \\ +\infty, \text{ otherwise,} \end{cases} \tag{4.12}$$

where

$$\Delta E_i^{j \to j'} = E_i^{j'} - E_i^{j},$$
$$\Delta e_{\mathcal{T}_l}^{j \to j'} = e_{\mathcal{T}_l}^{j'} - e_{\mathcal{T}_l}^{j},$$

where $E_i^{j'}$ and $e_{\mathcal{T}_l}^{j'}$ denote the energy consumption and the execution time of T_i when T_i is placed on server j'.

We define Γ_{t_i} to be positive infinity when the adjustment does not shorten the execution time. In most cases, the smaller Γ_{t_i}, the greater ability T_i has to reduce completion time, which means that Γ_{t_i} reflects T_i's potential to reduce completion time. To better make task placement adjustment, we need to introduce the concept of a key bottleneck task in each level.

Definition 4.3 The key bottleneck task $T_{kb}^{\natural,l}$ in level l is the one whose energy-to-time factor is the smallest in its level, i.e.,

$$\Gamma_{kb}^{l} = \min\{\Gamma_{t_i} | \forall T_i \in \mathcal{T}_l\}. \tag{4.13}$$

Besides, we use the tuple $\{T_{kb}^{\natural,l}, y_{kb}^{l}, y_{kb}^{l*}, \Gamma_{kb}^{l}\}$ to represent the placement adjustment that moves the key bottleneck task $T_{kb}^{\natural,l}$ from server y_{kb}^{l} to server y_{kb}^{l*} to get Γ_{kb}^{l}. After calculating this tuple in each level, we can get a matrix denoted Ψ as follows:

$$\Psi = \begin{bmatrix} T_{kb}^{\natural,1} & y_{kb}^{1} & y_{kb}^{1*} & \Gamma_{kb}^{1} \\ T_{kb}^{\natural,2} & y_{kb}^{2} & y_{kb}^{2*} & \Gamma_{kb}^{2} \\ \cdots & \cdots & \cdots & \cdots \\ T_{kb}^{\natural,L} & y_{kb}^{L} & y_{kb}^{L*} & \Gamma_{kb}^{L} \end{bmatrix}.$$

Task placement is adjusted using the Ψ factor as outlined in Algorithm 4.2. Initially, the Ψ factor is calculated based on the schedule obtained from Algorithm 4.1. The Ψ factor reflects the energy-to-time trade-off for each task in the schedule. The algorithm then proceeds by selecting the task with the minimum energy-to-time factor and relocating it from its original server to a new server based on the Ψ factor. The schedule is updated accordingly. This process is repeated until the application's completion time meets the required timing constraints, or until there are no bottleneck tasks left that can further reduce the execution time. The goal of this approach is to adjust task placement strategically to achieve a balance between energy consumption and completion time. By identifying and relocating bottleneck tasks based on their Ψ values, the algorithm aims to efficiently reduce completion time with minimal additional energy consumption. If the timing requirements are met through these adjustments, the algorithm successfully terminates; otherwise, it continues until further improvements in completion time are no longer possible.

Example 4.3 *For the example shown in Figure 4.3, after applying Algorithm 4.2, we obtain a schedule as shown in Figure 4.4. In this adjusted schedule, the application's completion time has been shortened to 9.49, but the energy consumption has increased to 2864. As a result of the adjustments, three tasks have been migrated to new servers: T_3 is moved from server 1 to server 3, T_5 is moved from server 1 to server 2, and T_7 is moved from server 2 to server 3. However, despite these adjustments, the schedule still does not meet the required timing constraints and needs further refinement.*

Algorithm 4.2: Task Placement Adjustment Taking Real-time Constraint into Account

---

function PLACEMENTADJUSTMENTFUNCTION($\mathcal{S}$, $G(\mathcal{T}, E)$, CCP)
    With schedule from Algorithm 4.1, calculate Ψ by (4.12), (4.13)
    while true **do**
        From Ψ, pick up the key bottleneck task $T_{kb}^{\natural,p}$ with the minimum energy-to-time factor, i.e., $\Gamma_{t_{kb}^p} = \min\{\Gamma_{t_{kb}^i} | i = 1..L\}$
        Place the task $T_{kb}^{\natural,p}$ from $y_{t_{kb}^p}$ th server to $y^*_{t_{kb}^p}$ th server and re-allocate computing resource by (4.11)
        Update the schedule and pth row of Ψ
        if $t_{\mathcal{T}_L} \leq \mathcal{R}$ **then**
            Return $\mathcal{S}$
        else if $\min\{\Gamma_{t_{kb}^i} | i = 1..L\} = +\infty$ **then**
            Return Failure
        end if
    end while
end function

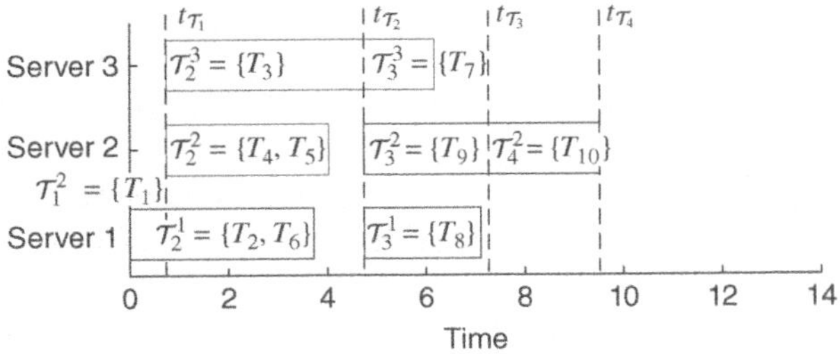

Figure 4.4 Scheduling results by Algorithm 4.2.

4.5.2 Start Time Adjustment

In our previous schedules, to ensure task-dependency constraints are met, task execution is partitioned based on DAG levels. While this approach guarantees task dependencies, it may not result in the most efficient schedule since some tasks are unnecessarily delayed. For example, T_9 can actually start right after the completion of $\mathcal{T}_2^2$, which would make the application's completion time shorter than that shown in Figure 4.4. In this section, we explore how to tightly schedule all tasks without the assumption that tasks on the same level must be grouped together to start simultaneously. By doing so, we aim to find a more efficient schedule that reduces the overall completion time of the application.

We have proven that the energy consumption depends only on the task placement plan, as stated in Lemma 4.1. The adjustments to task start time do not incur any energy cost, as their purpose is to shorten the completion time. Hence, following the schedule from Algorithm 4.2, we focus on adjusting task start times and computing resource allocation while keeping the task placement plan unchanged. We previously derived an optimal solution for computing resource allocation when tasks are grouped together to start their execution simultaneously. In fact, when tasks are ungrouped to start their execution sequentially, there is also an optimal solution for computing resource allocation. It can even be proven that these two optimal solutions achieve the same completion time.

Theorem 4.3 *Suppose that tasks in $\mathcal{T}_l^j$ start their execution sequentially. If the computing resource allocated to T_i ($T_i \in \mathcal{T}_l^j$) is*

$$\varrho_i^\sharp = \min_{k=1..R} \left\{ \frac{B_{j,k}}{A_{j,k}} \right\}, \tag{4.14}$$

the completion time equals that of allocating computing resource by (4.11) when tasks are simultaneously started.

Proof: The execution time of task T_i with $\varrho_i^\sharp$ is

$$e_i^\sharp = \frac{l_i}{\lambda_{i,j}\varrho_i^\sharp} = \frac{l_i}{\lambda_{i,j}\min\limits_{k=1..R}\left\{\frac{B_{j,k}}{A_{j,k}}\right\}}.$$

Because tasks in $\mathcal{T}_l^j$ start their execution sequentially, the completion time of $\mathcal{T}_l^j$ is

$$\begin{aligned}
e_{\mathcal{T}_l^j} &= \sum_{T_i \in \mathcal{T}_l^j} e_i^\sharp = \sum_{T_i \in \mathcal{T}_l^j} \frac{l_i}{\lambda_{i,j}\varrho_i^\sharp} = \sum_{T_i \in \mathcal{T}_l^j} \frac{l_i}{\lambda_{i,j}\min\limits_{k=1..R}\left\{\frac{B_{j,k}}{A_{j,k}}\right\}}, \\
&= \frac{l_i}{\lambda_{i,j}} \cdot \frac{\lambda_{i,j}}{l_i} \cdot \sum_{T_p \in \mathcal{T}_l^j} \frac{l_p}{\lambda_{p,j}} \cdot \frac{1}{\min\limits_{k=1..R}\left\{\frac{B_{j,k}}{A_{j,k}}\right\}} \\
&= \frac{l_i}{\lambda_{i,j}\varrho_i^*} = e_i^*
\end{aligned}$$

Therefore, we have proved that the resource allocation via (4.14) is equivalent to that via (4.11) in minimizing the completion time of $\mathcal{T}_l^j$.

With the resource allocation plan for tasks to start individually, we need to determine a task execution order. Based on the schedule from Algorithm 4.2, such order can be determined successively from the first level to the last one. Our idea is to start task execution as soon as possible. Therefore, we need to decide at which time a task can start its execution. The available start time for each task can be determined by considering the execution of its predecessor tasks and the available execution time on its allocated server. Then, task execution order is ranked in the ascending order of the calculated available start time, i.e., the earlier a task's execution can start, the higher priority it gets executed ahead of others. If the available start time of some tasks are the same, a random order is generated among them.

Algorithm 4.3 outlines the concrete procedure of task start time adjustment. It begins by initializing the available time of all servers to 0. Then, starting from the first level to the last one, the task execution order is determined based on the completion times of their predecessor tasks. Subsequently, the task start times are adjusted according to the new execution order. By following this algorithm, each task starts its execution individually as soon as its predecessor tasks are completed and the required computing resources are available on its allocated server. This ensures that tasks can be executed as efficiently as possible, leading to a shortened completion time for the application. Importantly, this adjustment is carried out without incurring any additional energy consumption.

Algorithm 4.3: Task Start Time Adjustment Algorithm

function TASKSTARTTIMEADJUSTMENT($\mathcal{S}$, $G(\mathcal{T}, E)$, CCP)
  Initialize server available time as $[avail_{S_1}, avail_{S_2}, ..., avail_{S_m}] = [0, 0, .., 0]$.
  for $l = 1..L$ **do**
    for $j = 1..m$ **do**
      for $T_i \in \mathcal{T}_l^j$ **do**
        Allocate the computing resource to T_i according to (4.14)
        $est_i = \max\left(avail_{S_j}, \max_{T_{i'} \in pred(T_i)}(s_{i'} + e_{i'})\right)$
      end for
      Rank the execution order of tasks in $\mathcal{T}_l^j$ in ascending order of est_i
      $\forall T_i \in \mathcal{T}_l^j, s_i = \max\left(est_i, \max_{T_{i'} \in hiPri(T_i)}(s_{i'} + e_{i'})\right)$
      Suppose $T_{i*} = highestPriority(\mathcal{T}_l^j)$, $avail_{S_j} = s_{i*} + e_{i*}$
    end for
  end for
  Return $\mathcal{S}$
end function

Example 4.4 *After applying this algorithm to the schedule in Figure 4.4, a new schedule is obtained, as shown in Figure 4.5. In this new schedule, every task starts its execution individually, and the application's completion time has been further reduced to 8.74 without any increase in energy consumption. This demonstrates the effectiveness of the task start time adjustment in optimizing the overall scheduling performance.*

4.5.3 Schedule Adjustment in a Backward Way

We have introduced task placement adjustment and start time adjustment to reduce an application's completion time. The former incurs an additional energy

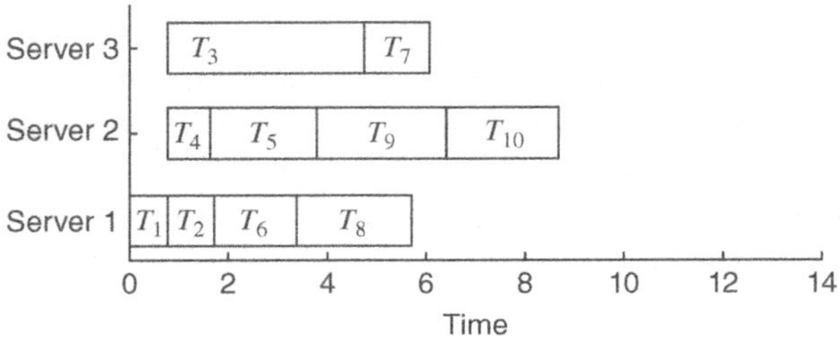

Figure 4.5 Scheduling results by Algorithm 4.3.

cost, whereas the latter does not. From this perspective, opting for the latter approach is more favorable. However, the latter method faces the issue of disrupting the level-based partition scheduling scheme, which makes the implementation of our task placement adjustment challenging.

To address this issue, our approach involves an aggressive adjustment of task placement using Algorithm 4.2 until either a real-time constraint is satisfied or there are no bottleneck tasks left to further reduce the completion time. When the real-time constraint is met, tasks are returned to their original servers one by one, following the reverse order of their placement as specified in Algorithm 4.2. Let's denote the task placement adjustment order in Algorithm 4.2 as $\{T_1^{\natural,p}, T_2^{\natural,p}, ..., T_Z^{\natural,p}\}$, where $T_1^{\natural,p}$ represents the first task whose placement was adjusted, and $T_Z^{\natural,p}$ represents the last one. Consequently, the tasks are returned to their servers in the order of $\{T_Z^{\natural,p}, ..., T_2^{\natural,p}, T_1^{\natural,p}\}$. Each time a task is returned, we assess whether the task start time adjustment described in Algorithm 4.3 results in a completion time smaller than the required one or not. This approach reduces energy costs since tasks placed on their previous servers consume less energy. If there are no bottleneck tasks remaining to further reduce the completion time after implementing Algorithm 4.2, we directly utilize the task start time adjustment algorithm (Algorithm 4.3) to shorten the completion time.

The step-by-step procedure is outlined in Algorithm 4.4. Initially, we have a schedule generated by Algorithm 4.2. If this schedule fails to meet the real-time constraint, the task start time is directly adjusted. Subsequently, the algorithm will either return a feasible schedule or a failure report, as indicated in Lines 15–20 of Algorithm 4.4. In the case where the schedule from Algorithm 4.2 already satisfies the real-time constraint, tasks are incrementally returned to their original servers. During this process, the schedule is regularly evaluated to determine if the task start time adjustment can still meet the timing requirement. If the timing requirement can be met, the tasks continue to be returned. However, if meeting the timing requirement becomes infeasible, the task-return process is halted, as illustrated in Lines 2–13 of Algorithm 4.4. The worst-case scenario for our task-return scheme is when no task can be returned without violating the timing requirement. In such a situation, the schedule remains unchanged from the one generated by Algorithm 4.2. Nevertheless, since the timing requirement has already been fulfilled by the schedule, we can always find an attainable schedule that meets the timing requirement by executing the code in Lines 2–13.

4.6 Performance Evaluation

In this section, we describe the simulation setup used to evaluate our proposed algorithm. We also present the compared approaches and the results obtained from the simulations.

Algorithm 4.4: Schedule Adjustment in a Backward Way

1: **function** SCHEDULEADJUSTMENTBACKWARD($\mathcal{S}$, G, CCP)
2:     **if** $t_{\mathcal{T}_L} \leq \mathcal{R}$ **then**
3:         **for** $i = Z..1$ **do**
4:             Return task $T_i^{\natural,p}$ to its previous server.
5:             $\mathcal{S} \leftarrow$ *TaskStartTimeAdjustment*($\mathcal{S}$, G, CCP)
6:             **if** $t_{\mathcal{T}_L} \leq \mathcal{R}$ **then**
7:                 Abandon the adjustment in Line 5.
8:             **else**
9:                 Abandon returning task $T_i^{\natural,p}$ in Line 4 and abandon the adjustment in Line 5.
10:                 $\mathcal{S} \leftarrow$ *TaskStartTimeAdjustment*($\mathcal{S}$, G, CCP)
11:                 **Return** $\mathcal{S}$
12:             **end if**
13:         **end for**
14:     **else**
15:         $\mathcal{S} \leftarrow$ *TaskStartTimeAdjustment*($\mathcal{S}$, G, CCP)
16:         **if** $t_{\mathcal{T}_L} \leq \mathcal{R}$ **then**
17:             **Return** $\mathcal{S}$
18:         **else**
19:             **Return Failure**
20:         **end if**
21:     **end if**
22: **end function**

4.6.1 Simulation Setup

The approaches presented in this chapter are designed to establish an energy-efficient schedule in a cloud computing platform for a specific application. As such, during simulations, it is essential to generate both the application and the cloud computing platform with predetermined hardware resources and performance parameters. For evaluation purposes, we have selected two real-case applications: Gaussian elimination and fast Fourier transform. These applications serve as representatives of concrete scenarios. Additionally, we incorporate the generation of random applications to enable a more comprehensive and generalized evaluation of the proposed approaches.

We suppose that a cloud computing platform is a data center with m servers and R resource types. A task load l_i in an application is a number uniformly generated from [0, 36] seconds. The task execution efficiency $\lambda_{i,j}$ is a random number in [0.1, 1], which is similar to the setup in Li and Wu [130]. The coefficient $A_{j,k}$ of the kth resource on server S_j, is a random number in [0.5, 1]. The number of the kth resource on server S_j, i.e., $B_{j,k}$, is a random number in [80, 100]. Similar to Shi et al. [47], we set the power model constant $\alpha_{i,j}$ of processing T_i to be a random number in $\{0.5, 0.6, 0.7, 0.8, 0.9, 1.0\}$. With the above parameters, we can decide the energy consumption-optimal schedule for any application by Algorithm 4.1. Suppose that the completion time with this schedule is $\mathfrak{R}$. We know that for any application whose real-time requirement $\mathcal{R}$ is greater than $\mathfrak{R}$, the schedule from Algorithm 4.1 is our solution for the energy minimization. In order to effectively evaluate the influence of real-time constraints on the performance of our proposed scheduling algorithms, we need to investigate the timing requirements that are smaller than $\mathfrak{R}$. Thus, we set $\mathcal{R} = \mu \cdot \mathfrak{R}$ where μ is a timing ratio that $\mu \in (0, 1)$.

4.6.2 Compared Approaches

To reduce an application's completion time, two distinct approaches are considered: relying solely on task placement adjustment or combining it with start time adjustment, as introduced in Section 4.5.3. These approaches are evaluated separately. To meet the real-time requirement, we employ a heuristic approach known as the enhancement heterogeneous earliest finish time (E-HEFT) method proposed in Samadi et al. [134]. E-HEFT aims to minimize the makespan of an application while achieving a well-balanced load distribution. Furthermore, we developed a GA to optimize the schedule with the primary objective of minimizing energy consumption. Since a time-optimal resource allocation plan has already been derived after task placement, the GA focuses on searching for an optimal task placement plan and start time plan. The hardware resources are allocated based on Theorem 4.2 once a task placement plan is determined.

- **TPA:** The approach that first applies the energy consumption-optimal schedule of Algorithm 4.1 to initially find a schedule, based on which the task placement adjustment of Algorithm 4.2 is applied to minimize the schedule under the real-time constraint.
- **TPA-STA:** On top of the schedule from TPA, this approach applies the schedule adjustment in a backward way as shown in Algorithm 4.4 to further reduce the energy consumption.
- **E-HEFT:** By using the upward rank value of Topcuoglu et al. [135] to sort a task allocation order, this approach successively allocates a task to a server and creates a virtual machine with full hardware resources to execute it. For each task, we calculate its completion time on each server and allocate it to a server that has the minimum completion time.
- **GA:** This approach applies GA to find a schedule. The task placement plan and start time plan are encoded in this algorithm. When a real-time constraint is not met, there is a big penalty such that the search abandons the populations that do not meet the timing requirement.

For all the compared approaches, we utilize three metrics to evaluate their performance. The first metric is energy consumption, which measures the amount of energy consumed during the execution of tasks. The second metric is the success rate of finding a schedule, which indicates the percentage of cases in which a feasible schedule satisfying the real-time constraint is achieved. Lastly, we consider the computation time required to find a schedule as the third metric, which measures the time taken by each approach to complete the scheduling process. These metrics collectively provide insights into the energy efficiency, reliability, and computational efficiency of the evaluated approaches.

4.6.3 Results

Gaussian elimination and fast Fourier transform (Figure 4.6) have been established as standard benchmarks to assess the scheduling performance in cloud computing systems, as highlighted in previous studies [135, 136]. In this evaluation, we begin by presenting the results obtained from testing these benchmarks. Subsequently, we proceed to display the evaluation results on synthetic applications. The synthetic applications consist of partially ordered task graphs, and they are generated using the approach outlined in Dick et al. [137]. These applications are purposely designed to simulate realistic workloads and provide a diverse set of scenarios for a comprehensive evaluation of the scheduling approaches.

4.6.3.1 Gaussian Elimination

Gaussian elimination consists of tasks arranged as depicted in Figure 4.6a. Due to the presence of only a single task in its odd level, this application exhibits low parallelism. Its size can be scaled by a factor ρ. The task count in this application,

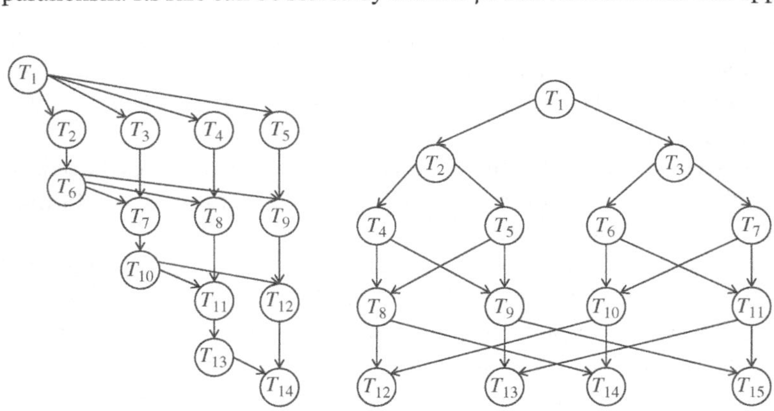

(a) Gaussian elimination with $\rho = 5$ **(b)** Fast Fourier transform with $\rho = 4$

Figure 4.6 Two real-case parallel workflows.

denoted by n, is given by $N = \frac{\rho^2 + \rho - 2}{2}$. The main focus of our investigation is to analyze the impact of the real-time requirement on the scheduling performance of all the compared approaches.

In our evaluation, we set the server count to $M = 24$ and the application size to $\rho = 24$. The timing ratio μ is varied from 0.5 to 0.95 at intervals of 0.05. With this setup, we have 299 tasks that need to be scheduled on 24 servers. To thoroughly assess the approaches, we generate 50 applications and compute the average energy consumption and computation time for evaluation. The success rate represents the percentage of applications for which feasible schedules have been successfully found among the 50 applications. This success rate helps gauge the reliability and efficiency of each approach in meeting the real-time constraints for different application scenarios.

The results are illustrated in Figure 4.7, where Figure 4.7a demonstrates that the TPA-STA approach achieves the lowest energy consumption. The energy consumption of TPA closely aligns with that of TPA-STA, and as the timing ratio

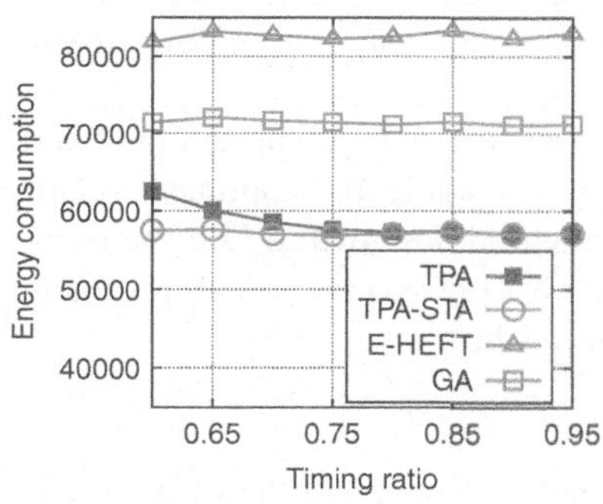

(a) Energy consumption w.r.t., timing ratio

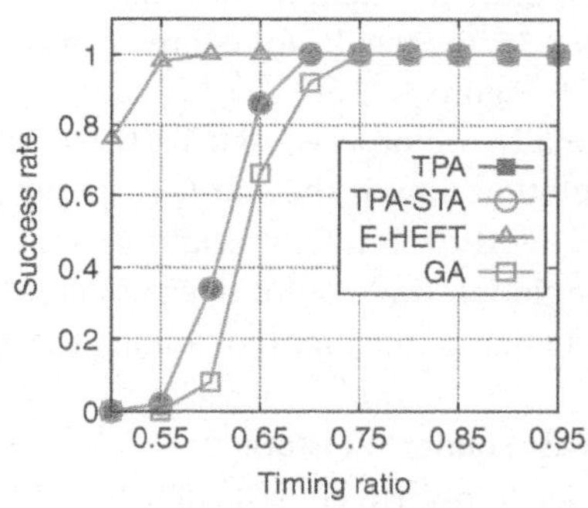

(b) Success rate w.r.t., timing ratio

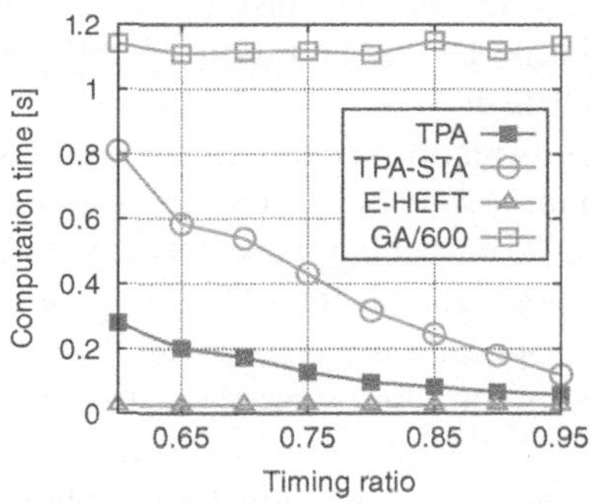

(c) Computation time w.r.t., timing ratio

Figure 4.7 Results of compared approaches on the Gaussian elimination application.

increases, the gap between these two approaches diminishes. This observation can be attributed to TPA's heavy reliance on paying additional energy costs to reduce the completion time of an application. When the real-time constraint significantly deviates from $\mathfrak{R}$, a larger energy cost is required to reduce the completion time.

Figure 4.7b displays that both TPA and TPA-STA attain the same success rate. This indicates that the task placement adjustment strategy is more effective than the start time adjustment strategy in reducing an application's completion time.

Regarding the computation time spent on finding a feasible schedule, Figure 4.7c shows that both TPA and TPA-STA can find solutions in less than 1 second. TPA-STA requires slightly more computation time compared to TPA because it incorporates the entire TPA process and involves additional computations for task start time adjustments. The computation time decreases with the increment of the timing ratio, as fewer tasks need to be relocated to other servers when the gap between $\mathfrak{R}$ and the timing constraint becomes smaller.

In contrast, GA performs the worst in all three metrics. Particularly, in the computation time metric, GA requires 600 times more time than TPA and TPA-STA to generate a schedule. It is noteworthy that, due to the low success rate when $\mu \leq 0.55$, the results for energy consumption and computation time are not included in Figure 4.7a,c.

Additionally, we observe that E-HEFT achieves a very high success rate, and its computation time is the shortest among the four compared approaches. This is because E-HEFT is a lightweight heuristic method designed to find the minimum completion time, but it does not consider energy savings, which results in the largest energy consumption among the approaches.

4.6.3.2 Fast Fourier Transform

Fast Fourier transform consists of tasks arranged as depicted in Figure 4.6b. The size of this application is determined by the parameter ρ. It comprises $2\rho - 1$ recursive call tasks and $\rho \log_2 \rho$ butterfly operation tasks, where $\rho = 2^k$ and $k \in \Join^+$. Due to the absence of sequential tasks between butterfly operation tasks, this application demonstrates high parallelism.

To investigate the effect of its real-time requirement on the scheduling performance, we set the server count to $M = 24$ and the application size to $\rho = 64$. The timing ratio is varied from 0.5 to 0.95 at intervals of 0.05. With this configuration, we have 511 tasks that need to be scheduled on 24 servers. Similar to the previous benchmark, we generate 50 applications and calculate their average energy consumption, average computation time, and success rate to evaluate the scheduling approaches.

The simulation results are displayed in Figure 4.8. We observe that the performances of TPA and TPA-STA are very similar, and both approaches significantly outperform GA in all three metrics. Notably, compared to the scheduling results

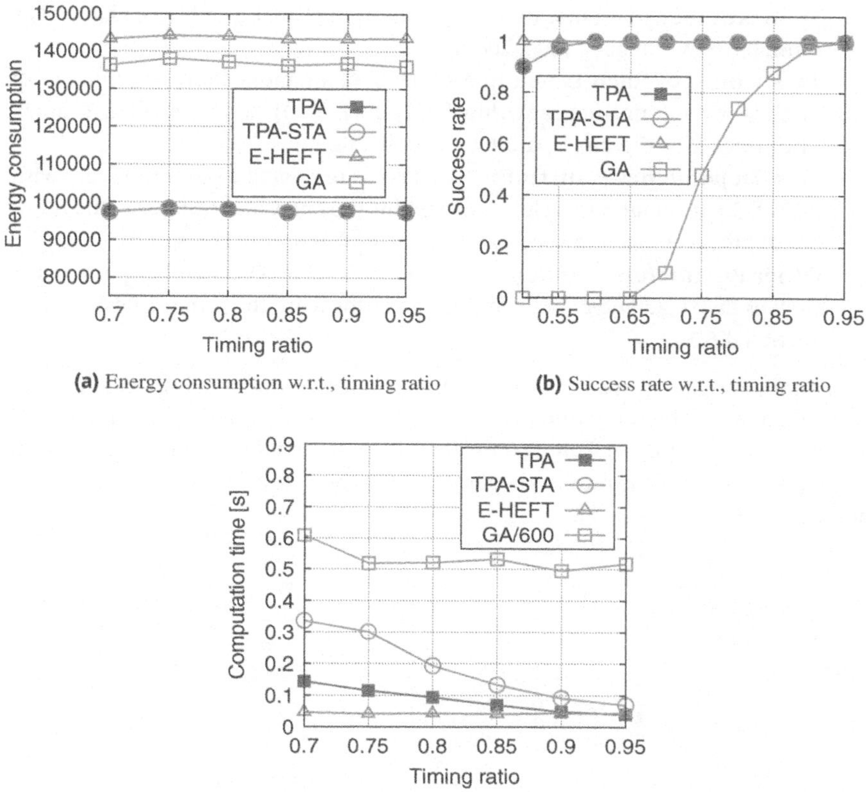

(a) Energy consumption w.r.t., timing ratio

(b) Success rate w.r.t., timing ratio

(c) Computation time w.r.t., timing ratio

Figure 4.8 Results of compared approaches on the fast Fourier transform application.

of Gaussian elimination, TPA and TPA-STA demonstrate a higher success rate in the scheduling of fast Fourier transform. This difference can be attributed to the fact that the structure of the fast Fourier transform is more parallel compared to Gaussian elimination, providing more task placement options that contribute to reducing the completion time. The higher parallelism allows for better utilization of resources and improved scheduling performance for fast Fourier transform.

4.6.3.3 Synthetic Applications

To validate our proposed scheduling techniques on general applications, we proceed by applying them to schedule randomly generated applications. The process of generating a random application follows a methodology similar to the approach presented in Dick et al. [137].

- **Total Number of Tasks:** In an application, the total number of tasks n is a number in the range of [500, 2000].
- **Task Count of Each Level:** In each level of an application, the number of tasks is a random integer within $[10K, 10(K+1)]$, where $K \in \{1, 2, ..., 9\}$. The larger K is, the more parallel an application has.
- **Task Dependency Constraint:** The task is restricted to communicate with tasks from its neighboring level. Except for the entry and exit tasks, the number of predecessors and successors of any task is an integer within [1, 6].
- **Other Parameters:** The number of servers is set to 50, and other parameters such as task load and cloud computing platform are the same as described in Section 4.6.3.2.

In our investigation, we primarily focus on understanding the impact of parameters n and K on the scheduling performance. By setting the timing ratio to 0.55 and $K = 9$, and varying n from 500 to 2000, we obtained the energy consumption per application, success rate, and computation time per application, as presented in Figure 4.9.

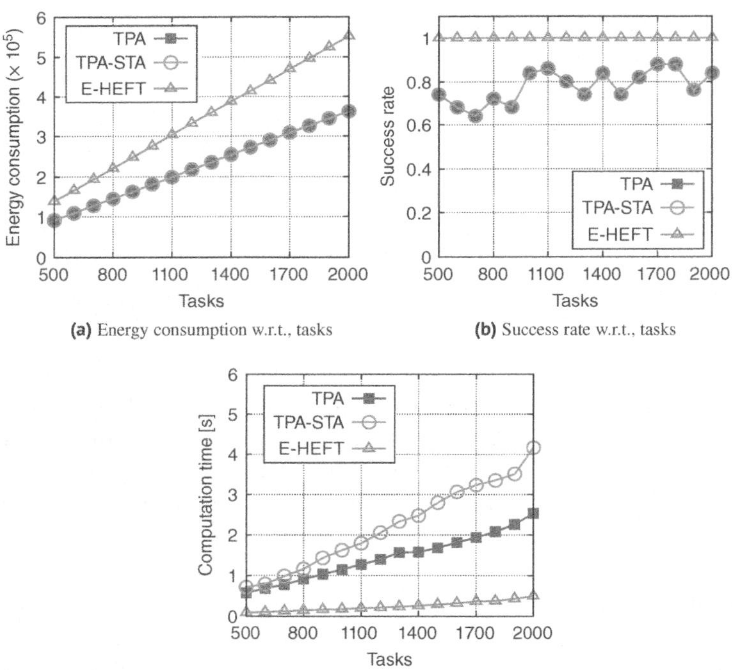

(a) Energy consumption w.r.t., tasks

(b) Success rate w.r.t., tasks

(c) Computation time w.r.t., tasks

Figure 4.9 Results of compared approaches on the synthetic application.

GA's results are not included since it faces difficulties in finding a schedule in this particular setting. However, we observe that the energy consumption of both TPA and TPA-STA increases at a slower rate compared to E-HEFT as n increases. This difference arises because TPA and TPA-STA select energy consumption-optimal servers for task execution, while E-HEFT prioritizes time-optimal servers, which tend to consume more energy.

Moreover, we find that n does not significantly impact the success rate of TPA and TPA-STA in finding a feasible schedule. This suggests that both approaches are relatively robust and effective in handling applications of varying sizes.

In contrast, the computation time of TPA and TPA-STA increases at a faster rate than that of E-HEFT as n grows. The reason behind this is the increasing number of levels in an application as n becomes larger. More levels result in more key bottleneck tasks that need to be addressed, leading to a higher computational burden for TPA and TPA-STA. On the other hand, E-HEFT does not rely on such levels for task scheduling, and its energy consumption only increases linearly with n, resulting in relatively lower computation times.

By setting the timing ratio to 0.55 and n to 2000, and varying K from 1 to 9, we explore the effect of task concurrency on the scheduling performance. As before, GA faces difficulties in finding a schedule in this setting; hence, its results are not presented.

The results, as depicted in Figure 4.10, show that TPA-STA exhibits a slight advantage over TPA in reducing energy consumption when K is small. This indicates that TPA-STA performs slightly better for applications with lower parallelism. This finding is consistent with the results from processing the Gaussian application, as shown in Figure 4.7a.

Regarding the success rate, we observe that larger K improves the success rate of both TPA and TPA-STA. This implies that TPA and TPA-STA are more effective at finding a schedule for applications with high task concurrency. This conclusion aligns with the comparison of the success rate between scheduling fast Fourier transform and Gaussian elimination.

Additionally, we find that the computation time of TPA and TPA-STA decreases as K increases. This reduction occurs because more tasks can be grouped into a level, resulting in a reduced number of levels. Conversely, the computation time of E-HEFT remains constant since n does not change, and E-HEFT does not rely on the concept of levels for task scheduling.

4.7 Summary

Finding a high-performance schedule for cloud computing is crucial for reducing the system's energy consumption. In this chapter, we have derived an energy consumption-optimal solution for task placement in parallel applications and a time-optimal resource allocation plan for independent tasks at the same level.

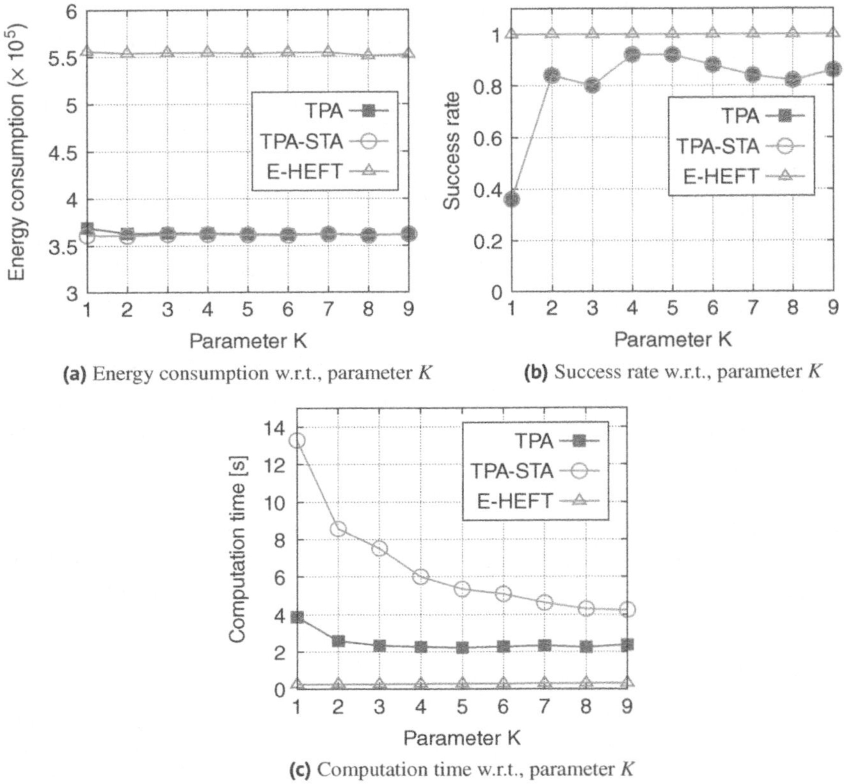

Figure 4.10 Results of compared approaches on the synthetic application.

Based on these closed-form solutions, we proposed a heuristic algorithm called TPA for adjusting task placements and a heuristic algorithm called TPA-STA for combining task placement adjustment with task start time adjustment in a backward manner. Experimental results have shown that our proposed approaches require significantly less computation time to find a good schedule for large-size parallel applications in the cloud compared to meta-heuristic GAs. This indicates that the presented approaches have immense potential in addressing cloud scheduling problems, particularly for large-scale parallel applications.

However, it is essential to note that our current work focuses solely on real-time requirements in scheduling, which might not be sufficient in practical scenarios. In future research, our aim is to design more applicable algorithms capable of incorporating constraints related to various performance indices, such as reliability and throughput. By advancing our approaches to encompass a broader range of constraints, we aim to make significant contributions to optimizing cloud computing scheduling processes, leading to more energy-efficient and high-performance cloud systems.

5

Workload-aware Scheduling of Real-time Dependent Tasks in Vehicular Edge Computing

Vehicular edge computing (VEC) [138] has emerged as a promising paradigm that offers lower service latency and higher bandwidth compared to traditional cloud computing. However, the geographically dispersed nature of edge computing resources and the dynamic mobility of vehicles present significant challenges to efficient service provisioning. This chapter introduces an adaptive scheduling approach designed to minimize energy consumption in VEC servers while handling dynamic real-time computing requests. To achieve this, we propose an auction-based bidding scheme that determines the optimal roadside unit (RSU) to process each computing request. In this scheme, requests are auctioned, and the RSU with the lowest energy consumption wins the bid. The decentralized nature of this model enhances its scalability and reduces implementation complexity. To process computing requests structured as directed acyclic graph (DAG) applications, we employ an upward rank-based method to decompose DAGs into individual tasks. A deadline-aware queue jump algorithm is then introduced to optimize task assignment within the server queues of a selected RSU. Additionally, a group scheduling (GS) scheme is developed to assign multiple applications collectively, improving overall scheduling efficiency. Extensive experiments are conducted to compare the proposed approach with various heuristic and state-of-the-art methods. The results demonstrate the effectiveness of our approach in reducing system energy consumption while ensuring a rapid response to computing requests.

5.1 Introduction

The rapid advancement of autonomous driving technologies has introduced numerous computation-intensive functionalities into vehicles, necessitating powerful hardware resources for real-time processing. However, the limited computing and storage capabilities of modern in-vehicle devices are increasingly

Intelligent Scheduling of Tasks for Cloud-Edge-Device Computing Systems, First Edition.

Published 2025 by John Wiley & Sons, Inc.

inadequate to meet the stringent requirements for low latency and high-quality service. VEC has emerged as a promising solution to this challenge. By extending cloud computing resources to the network edge, VEC not only enhances a vehicle's computational capacity but also improves data transmission rates and caching efficiency. Furthermore, the widespread deployment of 5G wireless communication provides robust support for building a more effective and responsive edge computing network.

While edge computing enhances service quality by providing powerful computing resources, such as large-scale servers, it also demands substantial electrical power. This not only increases operational costs but also contributes significantly to carbon emissions. To mitigate these negative effects, the power management of computing resources must be dynamically adjusted to minimize energy consumption while maintaining service efficiency. For instance, during peak traffic hours, when computation requests surge, most edge computing resources should be activated to ensure rapid processing. Conversely, during off-peak periods, when traffic is light, a significant portion of these resources can be switched off to conserve energy. Given that an edge computing system typically operates as a distributed network of computing servers, energy consumption arises from both static power leakage and dynamic switching activities. To address this, energy efficiency can be improved through techniques such as dynamic voltage and frequency scaling (DVFS), which adjusts processor frequency to reduce power usage, and dynamic power management (DPM), which transitions servers into energy-efficient modes when demand is low. While DVFS and DPM have been extensively studied over the past decades [139–141], few works have explored energy management in edge computing while accounting for the dynamic nature of user computation requests. In this chapter, we focus on adaptive power mode management for edge computing servers, optimizing energy efficiency based on real-time user demand.

Given the critical importance of energy efficiency and real-time performance, a wide range of scheduling techniques have been developed in distributed computing systems to optimize these two aspects. Most existing approaches focus on scheduling a fixed number of real-time applications. For instance, extensive research has been conducted on minimizing the energy consumption of individual real-time parallel applications [108, 142, 143]. However, these methods struggle to scale effectively when handling multiple concurrent applications. To address this, a dependency-aware task scheduling approach was proposed in Liu et al. [7] to minimize the average completion time of multiple applications. However, this approach does not account for energy consumption, leaving a significant gap in the literature. To the best of our knowledge, no existing scheduling framework is both adaptive and flexible enough to minimize the energy consumption of dynamic real-time applications in VEC systems.

In this chapter, we investigate this complex scheduling problem, which presents significant optimization challenges. It involves multiple critical aspects, including selecting the optimal servers, decomposing applications into tasks and assigning them efficiently, ensuring real-time execution, and dynamically managing server power modes to minimize energy consumption. Furthermore, given the dynamic nature of computation requests, adaptability is a key requirement for any scheduling approach. In general, when applications and servers are predefined, this problem can be formulated as a mixed-integer nonlinear programming (MINLP) problem, where energy consumption is the optimization objective and task dependencies and real-time constraints serve as constraints [49]. Solving this problem using exact methods is computationally infeasible due to its complexity. While intelligent algorithms such as particle swarm optimization (PSO) and genetic algorithms (GAs) can provide near-optimal solutions, their iterative nature makes them slow to converge, rendering them impractical for real-time dynamic scheduling. Given these challenges, we focus on developing heuristic algorithms that can achieve high efficiency while balancing multiple competing factors. However, this is far from being straightforward, as the interdependencies among task scheduling, real-time constraints, and energy optimization create complex trade-off issues. Effectively resolving them is crucial for achieving optimal scheduling performance.

Inspired by the divide-and-conquer approach commonly used in programming algorithms, we decompose the complex optimization problem into smaller, more manageable subproblems and design lightweight algorithms to efficiently solve each one. Specifically, we introduce and formulate the adaptive energy-minimized scheduling problem for dynamic real-time computation requests in VEC as a MINLP problem for the first time. To address this problem, we first develop a task execution model for edge computing servers and propose a decentralized auction-based bidding mechanism to allocate applications to the most energy-efficient RSU. For task execution, we utilize the upward rank value to prioritize task decomposition and introduce a deadline-aware queue-jump algorithm, which dynamically inserts each task into an optimal position within a servers ready queue. Additionally, we develop a GS scheme, where multiple applications are aggregated within a time slot, partitioned into groups, and then allocated to RSUs for improved efficiency. Experimental evaluations on synthetic automotive applications demonstrate that our proposed approach achieves significant energy savings compared to both the energy-aware processor merging algorithm from Xie et al. [108] and a GA.

5.2 Related Work

As an emerging and promising computing paradigm, VEC shifts computing and storage resources from centralized cloud infrastructure to the network edge, significantly reducing service latency and communication overhead. Performance optimization plays a crucial role in maintaining the efficiency and reliability of VEC systems, and numerous techniques have been proposed to enhance it from various perspectives. In this section, we review key research efforts on optimal scheduling, focusing on approaches that minimize application completion time and energy consumption while improving system adaptability to dynamic workloads.

Minimizing application completion time is a key focus in scheduling research. In Yao et al. [144], a Hadoop YARN scheduler called HaSTE is proposed to reduce the makespan of a given set of MapReduce jobs with precedence constraints. It achieves this by leveraging system information such as requested resources and task dependencies. For heterogeneous computing systems [145] present a multi-priority queue GA that prioritizes tasks and selects processors to minimize the makespan of a static DAG application. Security concerns in DAG-based task scheduling are addressed in Xiaoyong et al. [146], where the trust level of processing nodes is evaluated using differential equations. Meanwhile, Liu et al. [7] introduce a dependency-aware scheduling algorithm that ensures task completion within predefined time constraints through a prioritization scheme. A priority-based task scheduling algorithm (PBTSA) is proposed for multiaccess edge computing (MEC)-enabled Internet of Vehicles (IoV) networks to efficiently offload interdependent tasks and minimize processing delay [147]. By modeling tasks as a DAG and applying a reverse breadth-first search to prioritize subtasks, PBTSA achieves nearly a 10% reduction in delay compared to existing methods. The task scheduling and cache updating (TSCU) problem is addressed in Shen et al. [148], where tasks can be processed locally, via V2V, or V2I offloading. By formulating the problem as a mixed-integer nonlinear program and solving it with an improved discrete cuckoo search algorithm, the proposed method achieves up to a 12% improvement in offloading efficiency over benchmark approaches. However, a common limitation of these studies is that their scheduling approaches are designed for static job sets. They generate fixed schedules for predefined tasks and become ineffective in handling dynamic workloads, which are essential in real-world applications.

Energy consumption is another critical factor, often studied in conjunction with application completion time constraints. In Cui et al. [149], a trade-off between energy consumption and latency is explored to address the requirements of various Internet of Things (IoT) applications. The problem is formulated as a constrained multi-objective optimization, and a modified fast and elitist nondominated sorting genetic algorithm (NSGA) is used to identify the optimal solution. In Ning et al. [150], a heuristic algorithm is proposed that jointly considers task scheduling across mobile edge computing servers and the downlink energy consumption of RSUs. This approach aims to minimize the energy consumption of RSUs while adhering to task latency constraints. Similarly, Xie et al. [151] introduces a global scheduling scheme for cyber-physical cloud systems, aiming to minimize the energy consumption of multiple workflows that must be completed within their respective deadlines. Alternatively, in Xie et al. [152], the schedule length is minimized under energy consumption constraints. In Yang et al. [56], an iterative algorithm is proposed for an uplink non-orthogonal multiple access (NOMA)-based mobile-edge computing network, deriving closed-form solutions in each optimization step to minimize both energy consumption and end-to-end application delay. Despite their effectiveness, these approaches are not adaptive enough to handle dynamic scenarios, which limits their applicability in real-time systems.

Online task scheduling is essential for adapting to dynamic environments. In Cai et al. [153], an online DVFS scheme is proposed, which dynamically adjusts the CPU frequency based on the slack time from previously completed tasks. However, this scheme is based on offline designs, limiting its flexibility for tuning task execution in real-time. In [154], the Dedas algorithm is introduced to meet the maximum number of deadlines by jointly managing network bandwidth and computing resources. Recognizing that system performance can degrade due to task execution uncertainty, Xu et al. [155] present a dynamic resource provisioning method and a software-defined network-based edge computing framework to optimize both energy consumption and completion time using the NSGA-III algorithm. Game theory is also leveraged to balance dynamic workloads across servers [156] or enhance benefits for both cloud customers and service providers in multi-attribute cloud resource provisioning environments [157]. More recently, learning-based approaches have been proposed to develop online scheduling policies. For instance, in Wang et al. [158], an imitation learning model is introduced to schedule tasks online with near-optimal performance. However, these learning-based policies often require a large volume of samples to train, take considerable time to converge, and can sometimes exhibit instability, particularly when faced with significant changes in the operating environment compared to the trained samples.

5.3 Models and Problem Formulation

In this section, we introduce our studied models, including a vehicular computing model, an application model, an energy consumption model, and a response time model. In the end, we present our studied problem.

5.3.1 Vehicular Computing Model

As illustrated in Figure 5.1, there are three layers in the vehicular computing model. From bottom to top, they are the vehicle layer, edge layer, and cloud layer, where vehicles generate real-time applications that request the edge layer to process, and the cloud layer collects the information from the edge layer and manages their operations. Here, we suppose that applications from vehicles are processed by the edge server only. The road is segmented into m zones from L_1 to L_m, and in

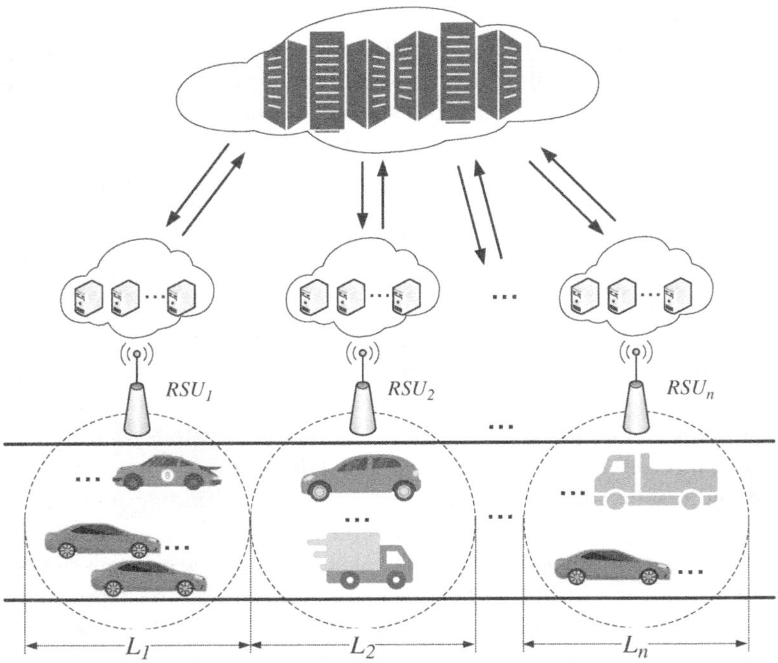

Figure 5.1 Vehicular edge computing architecture.

each segment there is a RSU with many servers to process applications from vehicles within this segment. The corresponding RSUs are denoted as Υ_1, Υ_2, ..., Υ_m, and servers belonging to RSU Υ_i are denoted as $\{S_1^i, S_2^i, ..., S_n^i\}$, where each RSU has the same amount of servers. The processing capability of a server S_j^i is denoted as f_j^i. In addition, the vehicles are moving on this road in two directions, which means they are in different zones at different times, depending on how fast they move.

5.3.2 Application Model

A vehicle-generated application can be represented as a DAG $G = \langle \mathcal{V}, \mathcal{E} \rangle$, where $\mathcal{V}$ is the set of its inside tasks and $\mathcal{E}$ is the set of these task dependencies. An example of DAG application G_i is presented in Figure 5.2, where T_j^i is used to denote the jth task of this application. A directed edge $e_{j,k}^i$ denotes the dependency and communication cost between tasks T_j^i and T_k^i, where $e_{j,k}^i > 0$ if T_j^i must be completed ahead of T_k^i, and $e_{j,k}^i = 0$ otherwise. The demanded computation of a task T_j^i is denoted as c_j^i. If this task is assigned to a server with processing capability f,

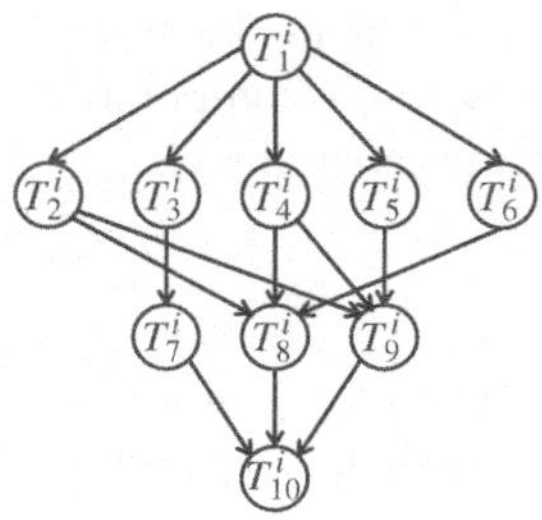

Figure 5.2 An example of DAG application.

its execution time would become $\frac{c_j^i}{f}$. The entry and exit tasks are two special tasks in a DAG application, where the former has no predecessor and the latter has no successor. Here, an entry task and an exit task are denoted as the first and the last tasks, respectively, i.e., $T_1 = T_{entry}$ and $T^i_{|V_i|} = T_{exit}$, where $|V_i|$ is the task count of application G_i. In addition, edge servers are supposed to be capable of processing certain types of applications, and each type of application has a relative deadline that should not be missed.

5.3.3 Power Model

The state-of-the-art DPM model [159, 160] is adopted in this chapter. The server has three power modes, i.e., *active, standby, and sleep modes.* When the server is in *active* mode, its power consumption is

$$P_a = P_s + P_d = P_s + \beta \cdot f^{\mu}, \tag{5.1}$$

where f is the processing capability of this server; β is a circuit-dependent constant; μ represents the dynamic power exponent and is commonly assumed to be greater than 2; P_s stands for its static power and P_d for the dynamic power. Tasks are processed only when server is in *active* mode. However, a server can switch to *sleep* mode anytime with the power P_σ. The switching from *active* mode to *sleep* mode (switch-on) and back (switch-off) needs extra energy, denoted by E_{off} and E_{on}, and takes time, denoted by t_{off} and t_{on}. Except for staying in *active* and *sleep* mode, when the server is not processing any task, it stays in *standby* mode with P_s power consumption. Here, we have $P_a > P_s > P_\sigma$. We also reasonably assume that the switching between *standby* and *active* has negligible overhead. Under this power model, there exists a minimum energy-efficient processing capability f_{ee} to process a specific task [161, 162], which is

$$f_{ee} = \sqrt[\mu]{\frac{P_s}{(\mu - 1)\beta}}.$$

Here, we suppose that the processing capability of any server in the system is larger than f_{ee}, i.e., $f_j^i > f_{ee}$ ($\forall 1 \leq i \leq m,\ 1 \leq j \leq n$). If the task's computation demand is c, the consumed energy in a server with processing capability f is

$$E = (P_s + \beta \cdot f^{\mu}) \cdot \frac{c}{f}.$$

Because E is a monotonically increasing function with f when $f \geq f_{ee}$, it is more energy-efficient to process this task in a server with lower processing capability.

Suppose that in an interval with length Δ, a server stays in active mode for Δ_a, standby mode for Δ_s, sleep mode for Δ_σ, and switch-on for n_{on} times and switch-off for n_{off} times. Then the energy consumption of this server during this interval is

$$E_\Delta = P_a\Delta_a + P_s\Delta_s + P_\sigma\Delta_\sigma + E_{on}n_{on} + E_{off}n_{off}, \tag{5.2}$$

where

$$\Delta = \Delta_a + \Delta_s + \Delta_\sigma + t_{on}n_{on} + t_{off}n_{off}.$$

5.3.4 Response Time Model

The response time is the time length from the time that an application G is generated to the time that application finishes its execution. In our edge computing model, the response time is composed of four parts, i.e., the vehicle movement time, data transmission time, wait time, and the application execution time. Suppose that a vehicle moves with a velocity v. At time t_0, it generates an application, which is scheduled to be processed at a roadside l distance away. Then the vehicle movement time $t_v = \frac{l}{v}$. This application has a data size of d that needs to be uploaded into the server via wireless communication. The transmission time is $t_d = \frac{d}{b}$ if the data transmission rate is b. After successfully transmitting, the application must wait for t_w before proceeding with its execution. The actual execution time spans from the start time of entry task execution to the end time of exit task execution. We use t_{entry}^{start} and t_{exit}^{end} to denote them, respectively. In this way, the response time RT of this application is represented by

$$\begin{aligned} RT = t_{exit}^{end} - t_0 &= t_v + t_d + t_w + t_{exit}^{end} - t_{entry}^{start} \\ &= \frac{l}{v} + \frac{d}{b} + t_w + t_{exit}^{end} - t_{entry}^{start}. \end{aligned}$$

5.3.5 Problem Formulation

Vehicles are moving along the road, and they generate applications at any time. Our aim is to schedule applications with servers in the RSU such that each application can finish its execution before its deadline. Here, we suppose that an application can be processed by one RSU only. Once tasks of an application have been assigned to servers, these assignments are not influenced by tasks from other applications. However, the task execution priority in a server can be changed. For a new application, our aim is to find appropriate RSU, assign the application's tasks to servers, decide tasks' execution priority, and manage the server mode such that the system energy consumption is minimized without violating the deadline requirement. In particular, if there are applications $G_1, G_2, \ldots, G_h$, whose release time and deadlines are within the interval $(0, \Delta)$, the studied problem is thus

$$\begin{aligned} \min \quad & \sum_{k=1}^{m}\sum_{j=1}^{n} E_{\Delta}(S_j^k) \\ \text{subject to}: \quad & RT_i \leq D_i, \forall i \leq h \end{aligned}, \tag{5.3}$$

where $E_{\Delta}(S_j^k)$ is the energy consumption of server S_j^k during this interval; RT_i and D_i denote the response time and deadline of G_i, respectively.

5.4 Decentralized Auction-bid Scheduling Scheme

We adopt the principle of auction-bid to schedule applications, i.e., whenever an application is generated, it is immediately allocated to one RSU, and its tasks are assigned to servers of this RSU. For this strategy, there are four questions to be answered: how to choose a RSU; how to assign tasks to servers; how to execute tasks on a server; and how to manage the power mode of a server.

5.4.1 Auction-bid Strategy

We propose an auction-bid scheme to choose the RSU for processing an application. In this strategy, every generated application is auctioned, and each RSU along the road submits its needed energy as a bid to handle this application. The application will be uploaded to the RSU with the lowest bid. For instance, suppose that an application G_i is generated at time t_0, the RSUs from Υ_1 to Υ_m submit the energy bid of $E^1(G_i)$ to $E^m(G_i)$, respectively. This application will be finally submitted to the RSU Υ_z whose energy bid meets $E^z(G_i) = \min_{k=1}^{m} E^k(G_i)$.

The energy bid of a RSU is estimated by assuming that the generated application is processed by it, and the energy consumed in its processing is considered as the bid. Here, we need to design an energy-efficient scheduling scheme such that it can minimize this bid and finish the application before its deadline. As shown in Figure 5.3, this scheme should generally include three steps, i.e., to decompose the application into a task priority queue, assign the task to servers, and decide the task execution priority of each server.

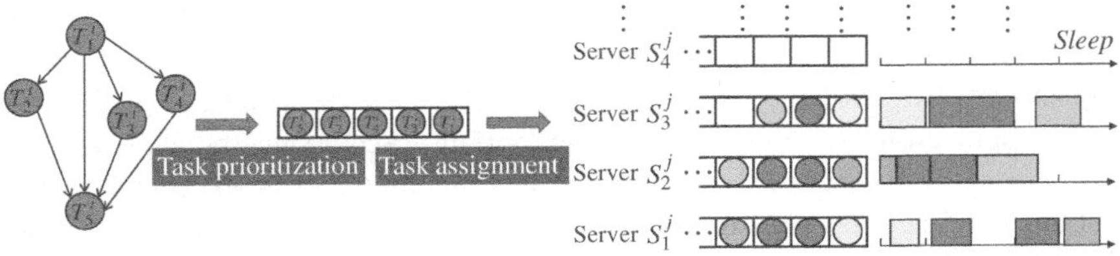

Figure 5.3 The application scheduling flowchart, where a DAG application is first decomposed to some individual tasks whose assignment order depends on their upward rank value, and then they are successively assigned to the server queue. Because the server queue has stored some previous tasks, the newly inserted tasks can be lifted to be ahead of others only if such a lift does not lead to a deadline miss. Tasks will be schedule automatically according to the server queue, as presented in the Gantt chart.

5.4.2 Task Prioritization

According to the task dependency in an application, the entry task is the first one to be processed, and the exit task is the last. For some other tasks that have no dependency constraints, their execution priorities are interchangeable. However, their influence on the application response time is not equal. In general, for the aim of minimizing the application response time, tasks with a longer task chain should be prioritized over tasks with a shorter task chain. Here, we take this influence into account by prioritizing tasks according to their upward rank values ($rank_u$). The upward rank value is from the *heterogeneous earliest finish time* algorithm [135] and has been demonstrated to be very effective in minimizing application response time. It is defined as

$$rank_u(T_j^i) = \bar{c}_j^i + \max_{T_k^i \in \mathrm{succ}(T_j^i)} \{e_{j,k}^i + rank_u(T_k^i)\},$$

where $\bar{c}_j^i$ is the average computation time of task T_j^i on all servers; $\mathrm{succ}(T_j^i)$ represents T_j^i's successor tasks. Task priorities are ordered in the descending order of $rank_u$, i.e., the greater $rank_u$ is, the higher its task's priority is.

5.4.3 Task Assignment and Execution

For the energy-saving aim, servers should stay in sleep mode as long as possible. Thus, our strategy is to use as few servers as possible to process arrival tasks so that there are more unused servers that can stay in the sleep mode. Without loss of generality, we assume that server processing capabilities $f_1^j, f_2^j, \ldots, f_n^j$ have been ordered in ascending order. From subsection 5.3.3, we know that the energy consumption of a server toward a specific task is accordingly ordered in ascending

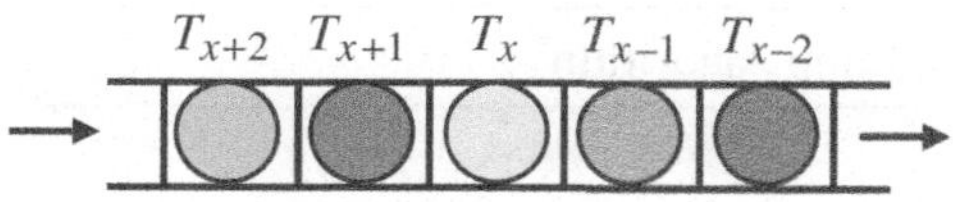

Figure 5.4 A task queue of a server.

order. Therefore, servers are switched to active mode successively from S_1^j to S_n^j, until all pending tasks can be finished before their deadlines.

Here, we take the assignment of tasks from G_i as an example to introduce our energy-minimized task execution scheme. We suppose that S_1^j, S_2^j, ..., S_q^j $(q \leq n)$ have been switched to active when G_i is going to be allocated to RSU Υ_j. Each server has a queue to store pending tasks. The stored tasks in a server queue are not permitted to migrate to other servers, but their execution priority can be adjusted. Once the task queues of all servers have been formed, their schedules will be automatically arranged. For example, if there is a task queue shown in Figure 5.4, we can deduce that the start time $ST(T_x)$ and finish time $FT(T_x)$ of task T_x in the queue have to meet the following condition:

$$\begin{aligned} ST(T_x) &= \max\left(FT(T_{x-1}), \max_{T_y \in pred(T_x)} \{FT(T_y) + e_{y,x}\}\right), \\ FT(T_x) &= ST(T_x) + c_x \end{aligned} \tag{5.4}$$

where $FT(T_{x-1})$ is the actual finish time of previous task in the same queue; $pred(T_x)$ denotes tasks that are predecessors of T_x; $e_{y,x}$ is the communication overhead between T_y and T_x; and c_x is the execution time of T_x on this server. The system is schedulable only if all applications finish before their deadlines, i.e., their exit tasks need to be finished before their deadlines.

With this schedulability test, we propose an approach named "deadline-aware queue jump" to find an appropriate server for each task and decide the task's execution priority. This approach assigns tasks successively in the ascending order of the upward rank value, and a task can only jump into an existing queue without breaking its relative task order. Thus, for a queue that has stored h tasks, from head to tail, there are $h + 1$ options for a new task to jump into. Intuitively, the new task should jump into a position that makes its finish time the earliest without violating the system's schedulability. We develop the deadline-aware queue jump algorithm following such a principle.

The algorithm is presented in Algorithm 5.1. At the beginning, we try to accommodate new tasks with the currently active server. If the system cannot be schedulable wherever a new task is assigned, a sleep server will be switched to active, and previous assigned tasks will be re-assigned to the newly active server. This scheme continues until all tasks have been assigned. If the system is still not schedulable after all servers have been switched to active, the algorithm fails.

Algorithm 5.1: Deadline-aware Queue Jump Algorithm

Input: G_i
Output: Task assignment of G_i

```
while G_i.task_priority_queue is NOT Empty do
    T_x ← G_i.task_priority_queue.dequeue();
    while there exists a sleep server do
        for each active server do
            for each queue position of this server do
                Insert T_x to this position;
                if system is schedulable then
                    Mark its position and finish time of T_x;
                    break;
                end if
            end for
        end for
        if system can be schedulable with T_x then
            T_x jumps into the position that has the earliest finish time among all servers;
        else
            Switch another server to active;
            Cancel the previous assignment;
        end if
    end while
    if T_x is not assigned successfully then
        Return Failure;
    end if
end while
```

5.4.4 Power Management

Except for the principle of switching the server successively from S_1^j to S_n^j to active, the server can be switched to sleep mode temporarily, depending on its runtime execution. For instance, there may be an idle gap between two successive executions. If this idle gap is large enough, the server should be switched to sleep for the purpose of saving energy, as presented in Figure 5.5. Such threshold of switching server to sleep is defined as the break-even time:

$$\Delta_{bet} = \max\left\{t_{on} + t_{off}, \frac{E_{on} + E_{off}}{P_s - P_\sigma}\right\},$$

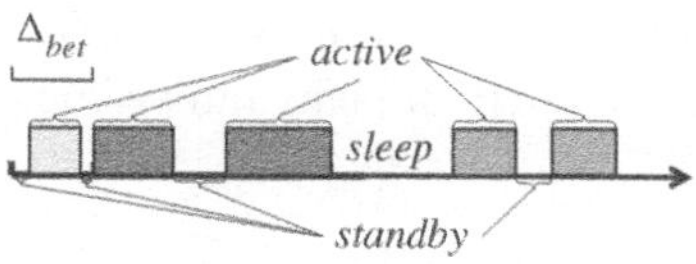

Figure 5.5 Power management depending on the idle gap.

where $t_{on} + t_{off}$ is the timing cost of switching, and $\frac{E_{on} + E_{off}}{P_s - P_\sigma}$ is the time length below which the energy consumption of standby mode is less than that of sleep mode.

In the end, the energy consumption can be calculated using the schedule before and after the assignment of G_i by (5.2). The energy consumption increment is used as the bid.

The auction-bid scheme works in a decentralized way where a RSU estimates its own energy consumption for every released computing request. Such an energy consumption estimation includes task prioritization, task assignment and execution in servers, and power management. Its complexity depends on task assignment and execution in servers because task prioritization can be decided by upward rank value in advance, and its power is automatically managed according to the break-even time. The worst case of Algorithm 5.1 is traversing every server and its task queue to assign a task. For an application with $|G_i|$ tasks, its worst-case assignment complexity would be $O(|G_i| \cdot m \cdot h)$, where m is the count of active servers and h is the task queue length.

5.5 GS Scheme

Unlike the first-come-first-serve scheduling scheme that decides a schedule for each released application immediately, the GS scheme collects a few applications together for the purpose of finding better schedules for them. In this section, we discuss how to design such a GS scheme.

5.5.1 Task Execution of Multiple Applications

If multiple applications are grouped together, tasks from different applications have different deadline requirements. The upward rank value is not suitable to prioritizing tasks any more, because such a value is not aware of tasks' deadline requirement. We thereby introduce a deadline to the upward rank value in order to explicitly show the task execution urgency. This new value is named "the laxity rank value." This value is defined for a task T_j^i from the application G_i as

$$rank_l(T_j^i) = D_i - rank_u(T_j^i),$$

where D_i and $rank_u(T_j^i)$ stand for the deadline G_i and upward rank value of T_j^i, respectively. Tasks are prioritized in the ascending order of their laxity rank value.

5.5.2 Application Group and Allocation

The next problem is how to group applications and how to allocate them to the RSU. We set a limit on the number of collected applications denoted as n_a. Because there are m RSU options to be allocated for each application, there will be m^{n_a} allocation options in total for n_a applications. It is impractical to find the optimal allocation by comparing the performance of every allocation option, especially when m or n_a is large. Inspired by the divide-and-conquer paradigm, we propose an approach called energy-based group allocation. This approach first finds the energy consumption of every RSU with respect to each individual application, and then groups and allocates applications with the aim of saving energy.

At the beginning, we compute how much energy a RSU needs for every single application. We use the symbol E_j^i to denote the energy cost of completing application G_j in the RSU Υ_i where $1 \leq i \leq m,\ 1 \leq j \leq n_a$. If a RSU fails to schedule an application (its deadline cannot be met in this RSU), we denote its energy cost as infinity. After this procedure, we can get an energy cost matrix that lists all energy cost values, such as the upper left matrix of Figure 5.6. Then, we group and allocate applications by updating this matrix.

In order to minimize energy consumption, applications should be grouped and allocated to the RSU that needs the least energy for their execution. In the first

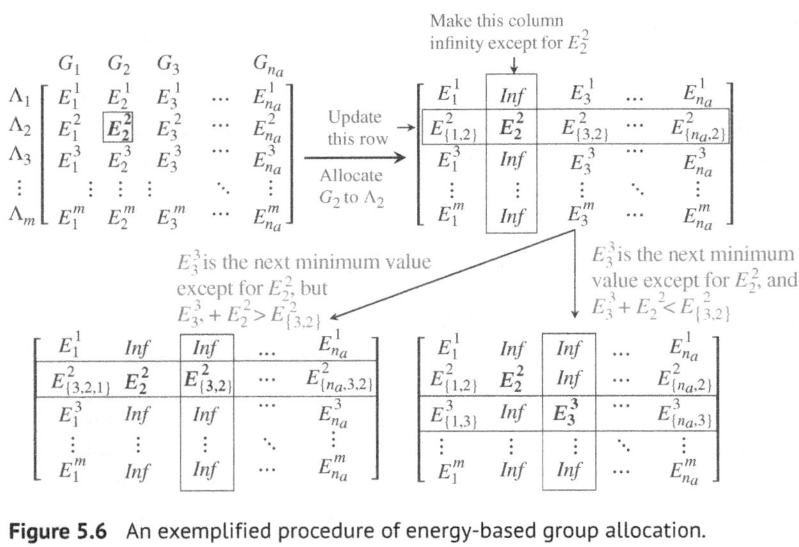

Figure 5.6 An exemplified procedure of energy-based group allocation.

round, we find out the minimum value from the energy cost matrix and allocate its application to its associated RSU. Subsequently, the corresponding row and column need to be updated. As an example in Figure 5.6, since E_2^2 is the minimum value in the initial energy cost matrix, application G_2 is allocated to RSU Υ_2, which makes G_2 not a candidate for allocation any more. It results in two changes to the matrix. On one hand, in order to eliminate other allocation options for G_2, we need to make values of the second column infinity except E_2^2. On the other hand, if other applications are going to be allocated to RSU Υ_2, they have to be grouped with G_2 for execution, and the second row is thus needed to be updated. Here, we use $E_{\{j,k\}}^i$ to denote the needed energy by grouping G_j and G_k together and allocating them to RSU Υ_i. If there are more than two applications grouped together, the subscript symbols such as j, k continue to grow. Analogously, in the second round, we find out the next minimum value. There can be three cases. In the first case, this value is on the same row as the value found in the first round. The two applications are grouped together and allocated to the same RSU. In the second case, although this value is on a different row, the sum of this value and the minimum value in the first round is greater than the energy cost of processing the two applications together in the RSU of the first round. In this case, the two associated applications should still be grouped together and allocated to the same RSU. In the third case, if the sum of this value and the minimum value in the first round is otherwise lower, the associated application of the second round is then allocated to its associated RSU. As an example in Figure 5.6, in the second round, if E_3^3 is the next minimum value and $E_3^3 + E_2^2 < E_{\{3,2\}}^2$, G_3 is then allocated to RSU Υ_3. The row and column corresponding to E_3^3 need to be updated in the same way as in the first round. But if $E_3^3 + E_2^2 > E_{\{3,2\}}^2$, G_3 and G_2 are then grouped together and allocated to RSU Υ_2. The row and column corresponding to $E_{\{3,2\}}^2$ also need to be updated. In this way, one application can be allocated in one round, and there would be n_a rounds in total for all applications.

The entire procedure of the energy-based group allocation algorithm is presented in Algorithm 5.2. At the beginning, the energy cost matrix is initialized. Then we find out the minimum value, and its associated application and allocated RSU in every round. If this application is grouped with other applications to get this minimum value, it is directly allocated to the RSU. However, if it is alone to get this value, we need to check whether a group with other applications is a better option. By comparing the energy costs of sole and group, we choose the allocation option that leads to the least energy cost increase. Compared to Algorithm 5.1, there are n_a applications that need to be assigned. A matrix is created for their assignment. At the p-th round, there are $n_a - p$ values in this matrix that need to be updated. Thus, the total update times is $n_a(n_a + 1)/2$. The worst-case complexity of Algorithm 5.2 is $O(n_a^2 \cdot |G_i| \cdot m \cdot h)$.

Algorithm 5.2: Energy-based Group Allocation Algorithm

Input: $G_1, G_2, \dots, G_{n_a}$
Output: Application group and allocation
1: Initialize the energy cost matrix;
2: **while** there exists an application not allocated **do**
3: Find next minimum value of the matrix, and denote its associated application as G^b and its RSU as Υ^b;
4: **if** G^b is grouped with other applications to get this value **then**
5: Allocate G^b to Υ^b and update the corresponding row and column of energy cost matrix;
6: **else**
7: Compare the energy cost of allocating G^b to another RSU with allocated applications;
8: Allocate G^b to the RSU that minimizes the total energy cost;
9: **end if**
10: **end while**

5.6 Evaluation

In this section, we evaluate the performance of our proposed energy-minimized scheduling approaches. In the following, we first present our simulation setup, including the simulation environment, compared approaches and performance metrics, and then we present the effect of several parameters, such as the application's release frequency, server count, and application's deadline.

5.6.1 Simulation Setup

In line with some relevant research works such as Dai et al. [163], Li [164], and Liu et al. [7], the road is set to a 1000-m double directional road where five RSUs are uniformly located along it. Each RSU has a certain number of heterogeneous servers, and the server's capability ranges from 1 to 5 GHz. Its power consumption in sleep mode and standby mode is 40 and 100 W, respectively. The circuit-dependent constant β is 80, and dynamic power exponent m is 2.2. Hence, the active power can be obtained by (5.1). The energy overhead of switching a server on and off is $E_{on} = 25\,\text{J}$ and $E_{off} = 15\,\text{J}$, and their time overhead is $t_{on} = 0.2\,\text{s}$ and $t_{off} = 0.1\,\text{s}$.

The number of vehicles moving on the road is in the range of [10, 30], and their motion speed is 100 km/h. Applications from vehicles are randomly generated following task trees in Dick et al. [137], where task count per application is in the range of [5, 20]. There are 10 types of DAG applications, and their released frequency is in the range [0.5, 5] Hz. The data size of an application is randomly drawn from [100, 500] kB, and the wireless communication bandwidth between RSU and vehicles is 5 MHz. The computation time of a task on a unit-capability server is within [0.1, 0.4] seconds, and the communication overhead between two tasks on two different servers is within [0.01, 0.1] seconds.

So far, there is not an approach that solves our studied problem exactly, so we need to make some appropriate supplements to similar approaches such that they can be applied to solve our problem. Our compared approaches include:

- **Nearest and HEFT Scheduling (N-HEFT):** Select the nearest RSU for the released application, and apply the heterogeneous earliest finish time algorithm [134] to successively schedule every application, where the later applications cannot interrupt the execution of former applications.
- **Auction-bid and Energy-aware Processor Merging (A-EAPM):** Select the RSU with the auction-bid scheme, and apply the energy-aware processor merging algorithm from Xie et al. [108] to successively assign tasks of each application, and turn off the server as many as possible, only if all applications can still meet their deadlines.
- **Auction-bid and Deadline-aware Queue Jump (A-DAQJ):** RSU is selected by the auction-bid scheme, and the application is scheduled with deadline-aware queue jump algorithm.
- **GS:** Group some applications together within a certain time length and use the energy-based group allocation algorithm to schedule them. Here, we can tune the group size and collection time length to optimize the system performance.
- **GA:** The GA is developed to optimize the schedule by iterative search. The schedule is encoded with two segments, where one maps a task to a server and the other indicates the task's assignment priority. The population size is set to 50, its cross rate is 0.8, and its mutation probability is 0.01. Its iteration is 2000, which is large to converge to a good result. Because this approach takes a long time to converge to a good solution, it is not practicable to be used online. Its results for static applications can be used as a reference to evaluate the performance of other approaches.

In general, two metrics are used to compare their performance, which are energy consumption, and the computation overhead of building a schedule for an application.

5.6.2 Performance Results

5.6.2.1 Static Scenario

We suppose that there are 10 different applications that need to be scheduled on a platform with 5 servers. Applications are released simultaneously, and they share

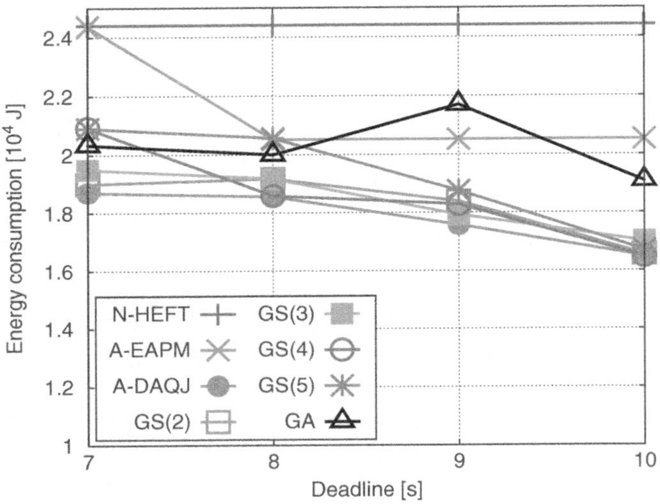

Figure 5.7 Energy of compared approaches, where GS(n_a) denotes that the number of collected applications in a group is limited to n_a.

the same deadlines that are set to 7, 8, 9, and 10 seconds, respectively. The energy consumption of these compared approaches is presented in Figure 5.7, where we observe that our proposed approach A-DAQJ achieves the lowest energy consumption to complete these applications. N-HEFT algorithm has the highest energy consumption, and it does not decline with the increasing deadline. This is because its primary purpose is to shorten the application completion time, and it is thus not aware of energy consumption. A-EAPM has a big energy consumption reduction when applications' deadlines increase from 7 to 8, because such a deadline increment leads to the turning off of a server. The GS has the least energy consumption when $n_a = 3$ or $n_a = 4$, which indicates an appropriate n_a is important for improving its scheduling performance. As a scheduling reference, GA is better than N-HEFT and A-EAPM but loses to A-DAQJ and GS. This shows that our proposed heuristics can converge to a good schedule very efficiently.

5.6.2.2 Dynamic Scenario

In real cases, traffic flow in rush hours can be several times more than those at midnight, which leads to the result that the frequency of computation requests is dynamic. In simulation, the frequency of computation requests is generated by following the traffic flow versus time of a day as indicated by Nasir et al. [46], where its minimal frequency is 0.1 Hz and its maximum frequency is 1 Hz. We collect the energy consumption results of 10 seconds per hour, as presented in Figure 5.8.

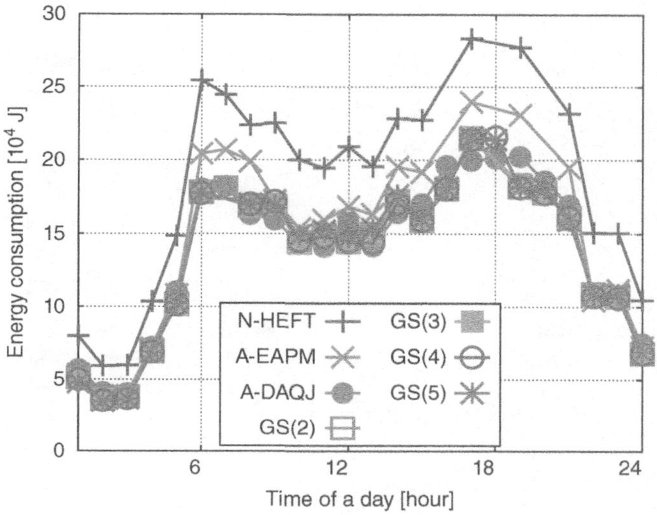

Figure 5.8 Energy of compared approaches, where GS(n_a) shares the same indication as Figure 5.7.

We observe that energy consumption peaks between 6 and 8 hours and between 17 and 19 hours, which corresponds to the day's rush hour. We observe that A-DAQJ and GS have lower energy consumption than N-HEFT and A-EAPM at any time of day. The result of GA is not presented because it does not fit for scheduling applications whose release frequency keeps changing.

5.6.2.3 Parameter Effect

We investigate the effects of application's release frequency, server count, and application's deadline on the scheduling performance of N-HEFT, A-EAPM, A-DAQJ, and GS grouping three applications to schedule. For every parameter configuration, we simulate the scheduling scenario of an interval with a 10 s time length for 100 times, and use the average energy consumption and computation time overhead as the final result. The success rate of successfully scheduled applications is also recorded. GA is not used here because its computation time is too long to perform in this setting.

- **Effect of Application's Release Frequency.** In this simulation, we vary the application's release frequency from 0.1 to 1 Hz by setting server count to 5. An application's deadline is the sum of all its tasks' execution time divided by the server count of a RSU. The results are presented in Figure 5.9, where we find that A-DAQJ needs less energy than N-HEFT and A-EAPM, and it also has a higher success rate than them with respect to various

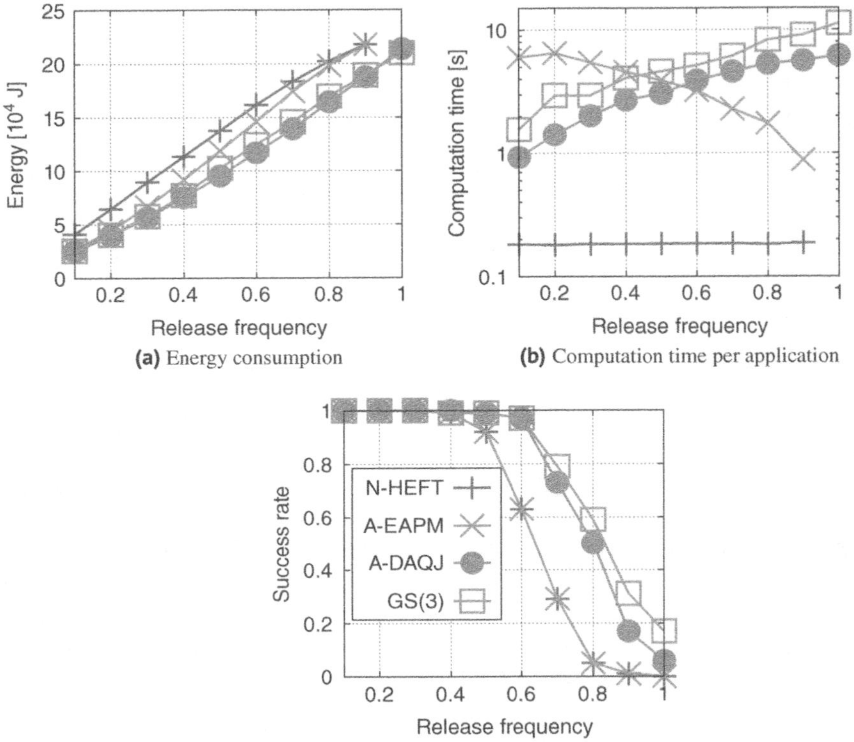

(a) Energy consumption

(b) Computation time per application

(c) Success rate

Figure 5.9 The performance of N-HEFT, A-EAPM, and A-DAQJ on synthetic automotive benchmark with varying application's frequency, where computation time is in log-scale.

applications' release frequency. In terms of computation overhead, A-DAQJ increases with the increasing release frequency, N-HEFT stays unchanged, and EAPM decreases. This illustrates that the performance of A-DAQJ becomes worse when applications are generated frequently. Besides, A-DAQJ achieves energy consumption close to GS, while A-DAQJ needs less computation time. On the other hand, GS has a higher success rate compared to other approaches.

- **Effect of Server Count.** In this simulation, we vary the server count from 4 to 10 by setting the application's release frequency to 0.5 Hz and setting its deadline the same as above. The results are presented in Figure 5.10, where we find that A-DAQJ and GS have constant energy consumption with varying server count. This is because the computation load is not changed with the server count, and extra servers are shut down to save energy. Besides, unlike

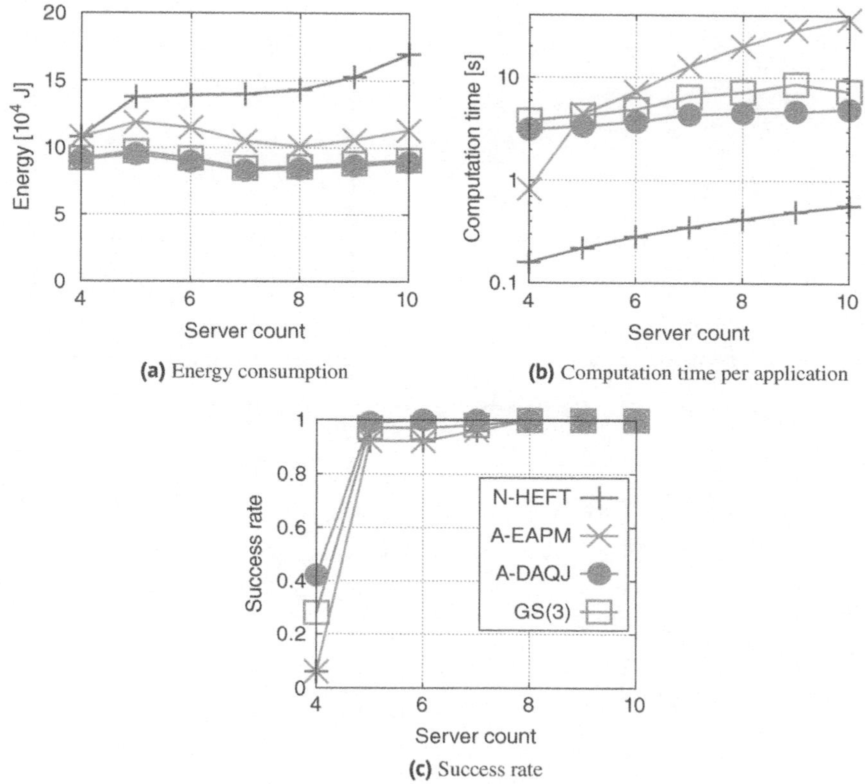

Figure 5.10 The performance of N-HEFT, A-EAPM, and A-DAQJ on synthetic automotive benchmark with varying server count on each RSU, where computation time is in log-scale.

N-HEFT and A-EAPM, whose computation overhead increases apparently with the server count, the computation overhead of A-DAQJ and GS increases minorly, due to the fact that their complexity is linearly increasing with the server count and the computation time in this figure is log-scaled. Last, Figure 5.10c shows that the success rate of A-DAQJ and GS is also higher than the other two approaches.

- **Effect of Application's Deadline.** In this simulation, we vary an application's deadline within 1∼5 folds of the sum of all its tasks' execution time divided by the server count of a RSU. The application's release frequency is set to 0.5 Hz, and the server count is set to 5. The results are presented in Figure 5.11, where we find that A-DAQJ and GS have the least energy

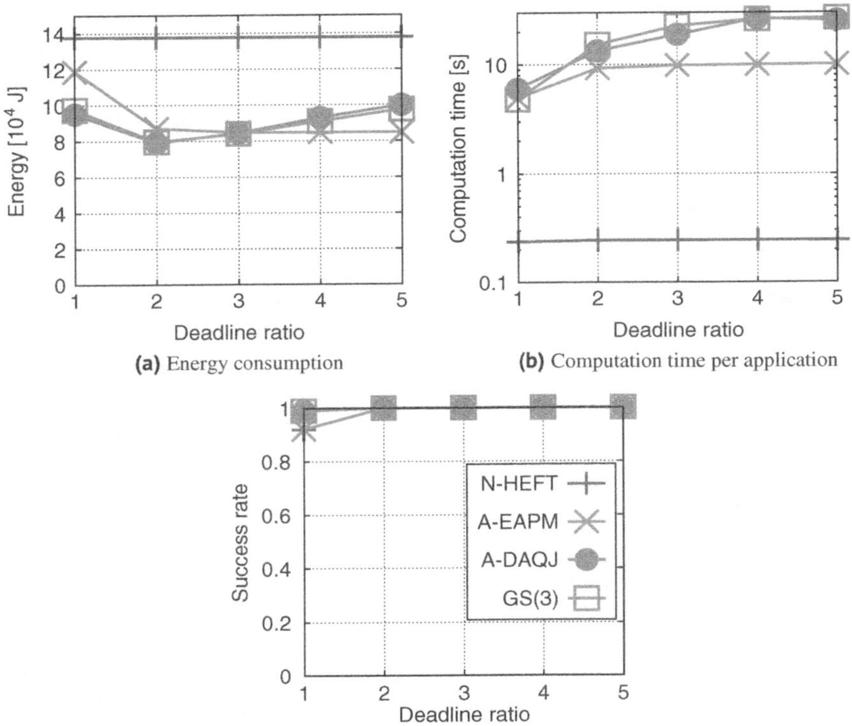

(a) Energy consumption

(b) Computation time per application

(c) Success rate

Figure 5.11 The performance of N-HEFT, A-EAPM, and A-DAQJ on synthetic automotive benchmark with varying deadline ratio, where computation time is in log-scale.

consumption when deadline ratio is below 3. However, they have a larger computation time overhead compared to A-EAPM and N-HEFT. The success rates are almost 1 with respect to every deadline ratio. This illustrates that the increasing deadline can relieve the ability of A-DAQJ and GS to save energy partly. When the deadline is large enough, there will be more tasks stacked in the task queue, which will make the scheduling overhead larger and larger.

In general, compared to N-HEFT and A-EAPM, our proposed approaches, A-DAQJ and GS, have good performance in terms of saving energy and keeping a high success rate on scheduling tasks. A-DAQJ and GS have shorter computation time than A-EAPM when there are fewer than 5 servers and applications are released less frequently.

5.7 Summary

This chapter addresses the challenge of utilizing computing servers deployed along the road to support a vehicle's requested applications. The problem is formulated as a combinatorial optimization problem with nonlinear constraints. A scheduling framework is proposed that decomposes an application into individual tasks and schedules each task using a task queue. To determine the most suitable server for each task, an auction-bid strategy is employed. The experimental results demonstrate the trade-offs among several parameters, including application release frequency, server count, and application deadlines, in minimizing energy consumption.

6

Scheduling Multiple-criticality Dependent Tasks in Vehicular Edge Computing System

This chapter addresses the design of an adaptive scheduling scheme for dynamic multi-criticality real-time applications in vehicular edge computing (VEC) systems. We formulate this scheduling problem as a mixed-integer nonlinear optimization problem and propose a workload-aware scheduling approach that ensures the schedulability of mixed-criticality applications while adaptively managing their execution based on runtime release frequencies. Specifically, we first present a response time analysis for multi-criticality applications in an edge computing system with heterogeneous computing servers. Next, we derive a state-transition equation that enables dynamic programming to construct an optimal schedule for a given criticality level. This approach is then extended to accommodate different criticality levels within the system. To enhance the quality of service for low-criticality applications, our strategy prioritizes their execution whenever possible, based on predicted frequencies. Extensive experimental results demonstrate the superiority of our proposed approach in improving the schedulability success rate and reducing the number of suspended applications during runtime.

6.1 Introduction

With the rapid advancement of autonomous driving and 5G mobile communication, a wide range of mobile services and applications have become integral to modern vehicles, including voice navigation, autonomous driving, vehicle following, and automated parking [165]. While these emerging in-vehicle services significantly enhance the driving experience, they also impose substantial demands on onboard computing, storage, and network communication resources. VEC [2, 166] has emerged as a promising solution, leveraging edge servers with high computational power to extend a vehicle's computing capabilities by deploying powerful

Intelligent Scheduling of Tasks for Cloud-Edge-Device Computing Systems, First Edition.

Published 2025 by John Wiley & Sons, Inc.

servers along the roadside. This enables vehicles to offload computation-intensive tasks to edge servers, reducing processing delays and ensuring low-latency performance [167].

While edge computing effectively addresses the challenge of limited computing resources in vehicles, efficiently scheduling offloaded computation tasks on edge servers remains crucial for optimizing system performance. In automotive systems, software applications vary in criticality levels, necessitating tailored scheduling strategies. Applications are categorized into three types based on their importance to vehicle safety: crucial applications, critical applications, and low-critical applications [168]. Crucial applications cannot be offloaded to edge servers, as their failure could lead to catastrophic consequences, and wireless communication may not be sufficiently reliable. In contrast, critical and low-critical applications, such as navigation and multimedia, can be offloaded due to their computational intensity and the tolerability of occasional failures. However, their quality of service must be carefully managed according to their criticality levels to ensure reliable performance.

A common approach to achieving this goal is to prioritize high-criticality applications over low-critical ones [169]. However, this method overlooks the urgency of individual applications, often leading to a significant degradation in service for low-critical applications. An alternative strategy for scheduling multi-criticality applications involves segmenting the system's runtime behavior into distinct modes. In each mode, only applications above a certain criticality threshold are allowed to execute, while lower-criticality applications are restricted [170–172]. Mode transitions are typically triggered by increases in an application's execution time or release frequency. This mode-based scheduling approach enables applications of varying criticality levels to share computing resources while ensuring that low-critical applications do not compromise the required quality of service for high-critical applications. In this chapter, we adopt a mode-switch scheduling scheme to provide differentiated service to applications based on their criticality levels.

Unlike traditional mixed-criticality systems (MCSs) that primarily focus on scheduling sporadic tasks in uniprocessor or multi-processor environments [19], this chapter explores the scheduling of sporadic directed acyclic graph (DAG) applications in an edge computing system with multiple servers. In this context, a DAG application must be decomposed into multiple tasks, which are then executed on virtual machines (VMs) created by the servers and allocated appropriate computing resources. Additionally, each application is subject to strict timing constraints, making the scheduling process more complex. This problem encompasses several interconnected challenges, including DAG decomposition, VM creation, task assignment, and resource allocation, making it significantly more intricate than traditional mixed-criticality scheduling.

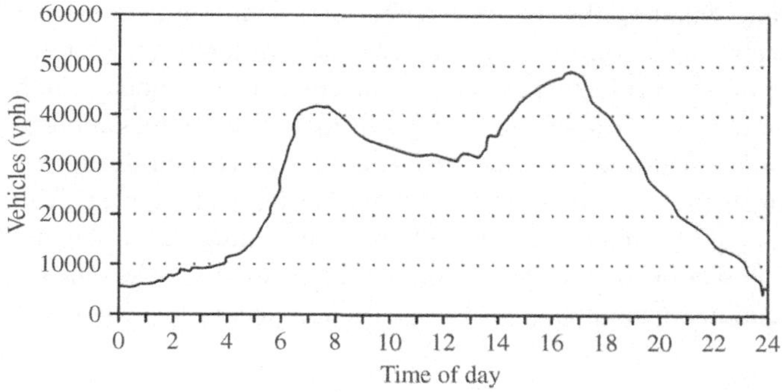

Figure 6.1 Typical traffic flow versus time of a day. [46]/CC BY 3.0.

One of the major challenges in scheduling applications in edge computing systems is the significant fluctuation in their release frequency throughout the day. As illustrated in Figure 6.1, the number of vehicles during peak hours can be 10 times higher than during off-peak periods, such as late at night. Consequently, computational demands during rush hours can be several times greater than those during quieter periods, making it difficult to design a scheduling strategy that effectively adapts to such dynamic variations. In edge computing systems, multiple heterogeneous servers often collaborate to process computational requests, with VMs serving as the fundamental processing units. The creation of VMs and the allocation of computing resources to them are crucial for scheduling efficiency and must be optimized based on the characteristics of incoming requests. Additionally, computational requests can be modeled as applications consisting of multiple tasks structured as a DAG [63, 173]. A scheduling algorithm must not only decompose these applications into individual tasks but also assign each task to an appropriate VM, a process that is generally NP-hard. An effective scheduling strategy should achieve three key objectives: (1) meet real-time application requirements as reliably as possible, (2) provide differentiated quality-of-service based on application criticality levels, and (3) dynamically adapt to fluctuations in request frequency throughout the day.

In this chapter, we achieve these three objectives by developing a workload-aware approach for adaptively scheduling multi-criticality real-time applications in VEC systems. We formally formulate the scheduling problem as an integer nonlinear optimization problem. However, solving it exactly is impractical due to the large number of variables and the absence of a closed-form equation for calculating application response times. To address this, we present a novel response time analysis for applications running on edge computing systems with heterogeneous computing servers. Building on this, we derive a state-transition equation for resource allocation, enabling the use of dynamic programming to construct an optimal schedule for a specific criticality level. To ensure differentiated service for applications with varying criticality, we adopt a mixed-criticality mode-switch scheduling scheme and introduce a scheduling algorithm that guarantees applications remain schedulable within each mode, ensuring they meet their deadlines. Furthermore, to mitigate the negative impact of fluctuating application release frequencies on scheduling performance, we propose an online management scheme based on frequency prediction. This approach enhances the quality of service for low-criticality applications, maximizing their execution opportunities whenever possible.

6.2 Related Work

VEC bridges automotive systems with edge computing networks, enabling more efficient resource utilization. Traditionally, automotive developers have relied solely on onboard computing resources to execute vehicle functionalities, and various scheduling strategies have been proposed to optimize system performance within this constraint [174, 175]. However, with the rapid advancement of autonomous driving technologies, the growing computational demands of modern vehicles have led researchers to explore external computing resources, such as edge servers, to supplement onboard capabilities. In this chapter, we review related work from both perspectives.

Automotive systems are safety-critical by nature, with functionalities categorized into different safety-integrity levels [176]. Such systems are commonly referred to as MCSs [19]. Existing scheduling approaches for mixed-criticality applications in vehicles primarily focus on utilizing onboard computing resources. For example, an adaptive dynamic scheduling approach proposed in Xie et al. [171] optimizes resource allocation and task assignment to minimize deadline misses in an automotive cyber-physical system. However, it does not guarantee mixed-criticality schedulability at runtime. In Nager et al. [177], a dynamic priority communication scheduling method based on a multi-core architecture is introduced, which effectively manages mixed-criticality data and adapts to bandwidth fluctuations in shared communication networks. Additionally, Cinque et al. [178] provides a preliminary investigation into the certification capabilities of Jailhouse, a widely used open-source partitioning hypervisor. To bridge the gap between mixed-criticality scheduling theory and real-world implementation, Jiang et al. [179] propose a generic industrial MCS architecture called practical-MCS, designed to enhance system predictability. Experimental results indicate that while practical-MCS improves system reliability, industrial requirements introduce additional overhead and performance trade-offs.

The resource allocation problem in edge computing focuses on efficiently and effectively distributing resources to support computation offloading and task processing. Many studies address this challenge by integrating resource allocation with task execution. VM technology has become a critical component for resource allocation in edge computing environments. For example, an energy-efficient VM placement framework is proposed in Alharbi et al. [180], where a mixed-integer linear programming model is developed to minimize the system's energy consumption. Similarly, Wang et al. [181] employ mixed-integer linear programming to design a VM placement strategy aimed at minimizing hardware consumption. When designing schedules, both system reliability and energy efficiency are often considered together [79]. To enhance users' quality of service, a fast service migration method is proposed in Lu et al. [182] to enable dynamic remote loading of applications, improving the startup and migration speed of VM-based edge services. Additionally, Hao et al. [183] introduce a formal concept analysis approach that reinterprets the VM scheduling problem as a task optimization challenge. In Li and Wang [184], an energy-aware edge server placement algorithm is proposed to reduce overall energy consumption while maintaining acceptable latency. Moreover, the industry has pioneered several general-edge computing frameworks, such as OpenStack [185] and Kubernetes [186], which have significantly contributed to advancing edge computing practices.

To the best of our knowledge, no effective scheduling approach currently exists to handle mixed-criticality functionalities in edge computing environments. In this chapter, we aim to offer a powerful method to do so.

6.3 Problem Formulation

As shown in Figure 6.2, edge servers are deployed along the roadway to receive and process computation requests from vehicles. In this context, we address the scheduling problem of multiple-criticality real-time DAG applications that are frequently released in a VEC system. The primary goal of the scheduling process is to meet the real-time requirements of these applications while ensuring that they remain schedulable according to their respective criticality levels.

6.3.1 Input

In particular, the provided heterogeneous servers associated to a roadside unit in the VEC system are denoted as $\{S_1, S_2, ..., S_m\}$. Here, we assume that computing resources, including processors, memory, and bandwidth in a server, are divided into many identical parts, and each part is represented by a virtual CPU (vCPU). Then the available computing resources of each server is the number of vCPUs that are denoted as C_{S_p} $(1 \leq p \leq m)$. Applications that need to be scheduled are denoted as $\mathcal{G} = \{G_1, G_2, ..., G_n\}$. Each DAG application G_i is associated with

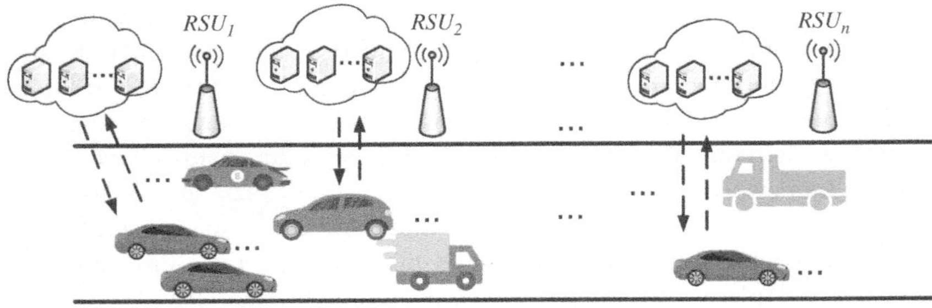

Figure 6.2 An illustrative diagram of a vehicular edge computing system.

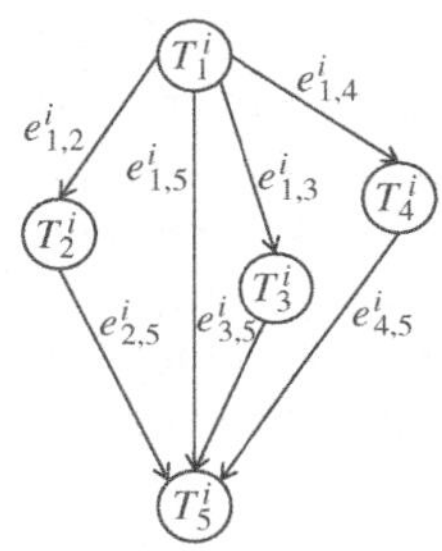

$$\Xi_i = \{T_1^i, T_2^i, T_3^i, T_4^i, T_5^i\}$$

$$E_i = \begin{bmatrix} 0 & 6 & 7 & 5 & 3 \\ 0 & 0 & 0 & 0 & 2 \\ 0 & 0 & 0 & 0 & 8 \\ 0 & 0 & 0 & 0 & 9 \\ 0 & 0 & 0 & 0 & 0 \end{bmatrix} \text{(ms)}$$

$$L_i = \{23, 31, 16, 19, 27\}\text{(ms)}$$

$$C_i = 3$$

$$F_i = \{10, 15, 20\}\text{(Hz)}$$

$$D_i = 50 \text{ ms}$$

Figure 6.3 An example of DAG application.

$(\Xi_i, E_i, L_i, C_i, F_i, D_i)$ that denotes its inside tasks, edges, task computation load, criticality level, level frequencies, and deadline, respectively. In particular, $T_j^i \in \Xi_i$ denotes its jth task, and $e_{j,k}^i \in E_i$ denotes the dependency and communication cost between task T_j^i and task T_k^i, where $e_{j,k}^i > 0$ if T_j^i must be completed ahead of T_k^i, and $e_{j,k}^i = 0$ if not. The communication cost needs to be taken into account only when tasks are assigned to different servers. For instance, $e_{1,2}^i = 6$ ms and $e_{4,5}^i = 9$ ms in Figure 6.3. The computation load of a task T_j^i is denoted as l_j^i. If this task is processed on a VM with computation resource c_s, its execution time would become $et_j^i = \frac{l_j^i}{c_s}$. Here, an entry task and an exit task are denoted as the first and the last tasks, respectively, i.e., $T_1 = T_{entry}$ and $T_{|\Xi_i|}^i = T_{exit}^i$, where $|\Xi_i|$ is the task count of application G_i. C_i denotes G_i's criticality level, and F_i denotes its level frequencies. $F_i = \{f_1^i, \ldots, f_{C_i}^i\}$, where f_k^i represents the frequency corresponding to kth level and $f_k^i < f_{k+1}^i$. For example, if $C_i = 3$, F_i includes three frequencies $\{f_1^i, f_2^i, f_3^i\}$ where $f_1^i < f_2^i < f_3^i$. In this work, we assume that the highest criticality level is 4. Besides, the last symbol D_i denotes G_i's relative deadline.

6.3.2 Output

Because a task can be potentially assigned to a VM of any server, we use $x_{p,q}^{i,j} = 1$, $(1 \le i \le n,\ 1 \le j \le |\Xi_i|,\ 1 \le p \le m,\ 1 \le q \le C_{S_p})$ to denote the case that task T_j^i is assigned to the qth VM of server S_p, and $x_{p,q}^{i,j} = 0$ denotes the opposite case. Computation resources are represented by vCPUs. Note that the computation resource of server S_p is C_{S_p}. Thus, there are at most C_{S_p} VMs that can be created, where a VM must be allocated with at least one vCPU. For the qth VM of server S_p denoted as $VM_{p,q}$, the count of allocated virtual CPU is denoted as $c_{p,q}$. In a VM, the scheduling policy is the non-preemptive fixed-priority scheduling that always executes the currently active task with the highest priority. In addition, once a task is running, it is not permitted to be preempted. The scheduling problem is to decide $x_{p,q}^{i,j}$, $c_{p,q}$ and a task's execution priority such that the below constraints are met.

6.3.3 Constraints

Because a task is not divisible, it can be assigned to a single VM only. Thus, we have to guarantee that

$$\sum_{p=1}^{m} \sum_{q=1}^{|C_{S_p}|} x_{p,q}^{i,j} = 1, \ 1 \le i \le n, \ 1 \le j \le |\Xi_i|. \tag{6.1}$$

It should be noted that constraint (6.1) does not exclude the case that several tasks can be assigned to the same VM. For instance, if job T_1^1 and job T_2^1 are assigned to the first VM of the first server, we have $x_{1,1}^{1,1} = x_{1,1}^{1,2} = 1$.

In order to maintain the sequence execution constraint of a DAG application, a task can start to be processed only after all its predecessor tasks have been finished. Besides, if two tasks are assigned to different servers, their communication cost needs to be taken into consideration. We know that $\sum_{q=1}^{|C_{S_p}|} x_{p,q}^{i,j} = 1$ if T_j^i is assigned to server S_p. Thus, if T_j^i and T_k^i are assigned to S_p, we have

$$\sum_{q=1}^{|C_{S_p}|} x_{p,q}^{i,j} \cdot \sum_{q=1}^{|C_{S_p}|} x_{p,q}^{i,k} = 1.$$

We use ft_j^i and st_k^i to denote the finish time and start time of processing T_j^i and T_k^i, respectively. Hence, this sequence execution constraint can be maintained by requiring

$$st_k^i \ge ft_j^i + e_{j,k}^i \cdot \left(1 - \sum_{q=1}^{|C_{S_p}|} x_{p,q}^{i,j} \cdot \sum_{q=1}^{|C_{S_p}|} x_{p,q}^{i,k}\right), \tag{6.2}$$

Table 6.1 Standard mixed-criticality scheduling procedures.

Mode	Applications	Frequency domain
Level-1	All applications	Below f_1^i
Level-2	Applications whose $C_i \geq 2$	Between f_1^i and f_2^i
Level-3	Applications whose $C_i \geq 3$	Between f_2^i and f_3^i
Level-4	Applications whose $C_i \geq 4$	Between f_3^i and f_4^i

where $e_{j,k}^i > 0$ and $1 \leq i \leq n,\ 1 \leq j \leq |\Xi_i|,\ 1 \leq p \leq m$. This constraint presents that, if T_k^i is a predecessor task of T_j^i, the start execution time of T_k^i must be after finishing T_j^i together with their communication.

Another constraint comes from the computing resource limit, i.e., the sum of allocated computing resources in each server should not be above its limit, i.e.,

$$\sum_{q=1}^{c_{S_p}} c_{p,q} \leq C_{S_p},\ \ 1 \leq p \leq m. \tag{6.3}$$

From many previous studies, such as Baruah et al. [187], Burns and Davis [19], Burns et al. [20], Hu et al. [13], a standard scheduling scheme to handle multiple-criticality tasks is to divide the scheduling process into several modes, depending on tasks' execution time or their released periods. In our studied model, the highest criticality level of an application is 4. The system scheduling procedure is presented in Table 6.1, where the first column denotes the system mode, the second column denotes the applications whose response time needs to be guaranteed, and the third column denotes their frequency domain. For example, at level-2 mode, applications whose $C_i \geq 2$ need to meet their deadlines, and applications whose $C_i = 1$ are thus abandoned. In this mode, there is at least one application whose frequency is between f_1^i and f_2^i. The system of this mode is schedulable if all applications whose $C_i \geq 2$ meet their deadlines. The system is called *mixed-criticality schedulable* if it is schedulable in each mode. In a VM, there may be several tasks. We adopt the non-preemptive fixed-priority policy to schedule them, and the last constraint is to guarantee the *mixed-criticality schedulability*.

6.4 Response Time Analysis

The response time analysis for DAG applications is necessary to test whether they can finish their execution before their deadlines. This is also a complicated problem because a DAG application can be separated into many tasks, and each task can be assigned to any VM on any server. Its response time should take DAG structure and the response time of each task into consideration. In this section, we present how to analyze the worst-case response time of DAG applications in an edge computing system with the aim of testing their schedulability.

6.4.1 Task's Response Time in a VM

We first analyze the response time of a task in a VM with several other tasks. Without any loss, we suppose that there are tasks denoted as T_1, T_2, ... , $T_{n'}$ whose priorities are ranked in descending order in a VM. Furthermore, we enforce the constraint that T_i belongs to an application that is distinct from all other tasks' applications. This constraint excludes the execution interference of tasks from the same application as T_i, because we take such interference into account in the application's response time analysis, as discussed in Section 6.4.2. The response time of T_i refers to the time length that spans from its release to its end. According to Park [91], its response time rt_i in a system with a non-preemptive execution scheme is

$$\begin{aligned} rt_i &= et_{max} + rt'_i \\ et_{max} &= max\{et_k \mid k > i\} \\ rt'_i &= et_i + \sum_{j=1}^{i-1} \lceil rt'_i \cdot f_j \rceil \cdot et_j \end{aligned} \tag{6.4}$$

where $et_{\max}$ denotes the maximum interference from lower-priority tasks; et_j $(j \leq i-1)$ denotes the execution time of task T_j in this VM; $\sum_{j=1}^{i-1} \lceil rt'_i \cdot f_j \rceil \cdot et_j$ is the execution interference from higher-priority tasks; rt'_i is the response time of T_i without taking the interference of lower-priority tasks' execution. Because the scheduling procedure in a VM is non-preemptive, the response time of T_i should combine the interference from its higher-priority tasks and the maximum interference from its lower-priority tasks.

6.4.2 Application's Response Time

We then analyze the response time of a DAG application G_i, and use st^i_j, rt^i_j, ft^i_j to denote the task T^i_j's release time, response time, and finish time, respectively. For the simplicity of analysis, we assume that T^i_j has a higher priority than T^i_k $(k > j)$ to get execution if they are in the same VM. According to the sequence execution constraint, a task can be released only after all its predecessor tasks have been finished, i.e., it needs to meet the constraint of (6.2). Besides, if there are several tasks from G_i that are assigned to the same VM, the task can be started only after tasks with higher priorities have finished. Thus, it can be concluded that

$$\begin{aligned} st^i_k &= \max\left(ft^{ib}_z, st^{ib}_k\right) \\ ft^i_k &= st^i_k + rt^i_k \end{aligned}, \tag{6.5}$$

where

$$ft_z^{ib} = \max\left(ft_z^i \cdot \sum_{p=1}^{m}\sum_{q=1}^{|Cs_p|}(x_{p,q}^{i,k} \cdot x_{p,q}^{i,z})\right), \ \forall z \le k$$
$$st_k^{ib} = \max\left(ft_j^i + e_{j,k}^i \cdot (1 - \sum_{q=1}^{|Cs_p|} x_{p,q}^{i,j} \cdot \sum_{q=1}^{|Cs_p|} x_{p,q}^{i,k})\right), \ \forall e_{j,k}^i > 0. \quad (6.6)$$

We know that $e_{j,k}^i > 0$ denotes that T_j^i is a predecessor of T_k^i, and $\sum_{p=1}^{m}\sum_{q=1}^{|Cs_p|}(x_{p,q}^{i,k} \cdot x_{p,q}^{i,z}) = 1$ only if both T_k^i and T_z^i are assigned to the same VM. Thus, ft_z^{ib} is the largest finish time of tasks that are predecessors of T_k^i and are assigned to the same VM as T_k^i. For T_k^i's predecessor tasks that are not assigned to the same VM, the communication cost needs to be taken into account, as presented in st_k^{ib}. By using (6.5) together with (6.4) for tasks from T_1^i to $T_{|\Xi_i|}^i$ successively, we can get the finish time of $T_{|\Xi_i|}^i$, which is the response time of this application.

6.5 Scheduling at Level-1 Mode

The scheduling problem is how to assign tasks of applications to VMs and how to allocate the computing resources to these VMs such that all applications can be mixed-criticality schedulable, i.e., they can meet their deadlines at different level-criticality modes. In this section, we only discuss how to schedule tasks in level-1 mode.

6.5.1 Application Decomposition

An application can be decomposed into many tasks. Here, we use the upward rank value from the heterogeneous earliest finish time algorithm [135] to decompose an application and decide the task execution sequence. Heterogeneous earliest finish time has been proven to minimize the DAG application's response time very effectively by using such an upward rank value, and has been extended to solve some other related problems [188]. This value is defined as

$$rank_u(T_j^i) = l_j^i + \max_{e_{j,k}^i > 0}\{e_{j,k}^i + rank_u(l_k^i)\},$$

where $e_{j,k}^i > 0$ denotes that T_k^i is a successor task of T_j^i. Task execution sequence is ordered in the descending order of tasks' $rank_u$, i.e., the greater $rank_u$ is, the higher the execution priority of its corresponding task is. Without loss of generality, we suppose that T_j^i $(i = 1 \to n,\ j = 1 \to |\Xi_i|)$ has already been ranked in this order.

6.5.2 State-transition Equation

There are n DAG applications that must be assigned to VMs of edge computing servers in level-1 mode. This is a complicated combinatorial optimization problem that involves three subproblems: how to create VMs on each server; how to assign tasks to VMs; and how to prioritize tasks in the same virtual machine. Checking every combination is practically impossible. Here, we transfer this problem into a knapsack problem where servers are bags and tasks are items. Compared to the classic 0-1 knapsack problem, our studied problem is more complicated because each server needs to be divided into many VMs, and constraints of response time need to be taken into account. Inspired by the divide-and-conquer idea, we derive a state-transition equation that makes the dynamic programming approach applicable to solving this problem.

We assign applications from G_1 to G_n successively. Thus, together with information of upward rank value, tasks are successively assigned in the order of T_j^i ($\forall i \in [1..n]$, $j = 1 \rightarrow |\Xi_i|$). On the other side, we use $(y_1, y_2, \dots, y_m)$ to denote the available vCPUs of each server for VM creation, where $1 \leq y_k \leq C_{S_k}$, $1 \leq k \leq m$. In order to derive this state-transition equation, we let the available vCPUs increase monotonously, i.e., at first y_1 increases from 1 to C_{S_1} by keeping others to be 0. Then with $y_1 = C_{S_1}$, y_2 increases from 1 to C_{S_2} by keeping y_3 to y_m to be 0. Such increment scheme is also applied to available vCPUs from y_3 to y_m successively. In this way, we can denote available vCPUs as $(C_{S_1}, C_{S_2}, \dots, C_{S_{p-1}}, y_p, 0, \dots, 0)$ where $1 \leq p \leq m$, and there are totally $\sum_{p=1}^{m} C_{S_p}$ situations of available vCPUs.

For each task, we check its assignment option in each situation of available vCPUs. For example, in the first situation with available vCPUs (1, 0, … , 0), the first task $v1_1$ is assigned to a VM with only a single vCPU in the first server. Analogously, in the second situation with available virtual CPUs (2, 0, … , 0), it is assigned to a VM with 2 vCPUs in the first server. Because it is not possible to allocate vCPUs from one server to another, it is assigned to a VM with 1 vCPU in the second server in the $(C_{S_1} + 1)$th situation. In the end, we know the schedule result of T_1^1 in every situation, and use $\mathcal{S}_1^1(z)$ to denote its schedule result in the zth situation where $1 \leq z \leq \sum_{p=1}^{m} C_{S_p}$. Based on schedules of $\mathcal{S}_1^1(z)$, we consider how to schedule the next task T_2^1.

In a general sense, we suppose that the schedule results of tasks from T_1^1 to T_{j-1}^i have been known with respect to each situation, i.e., $\mathcal{S}_{j-1}^i(z)$ has been built. Then, we start to schedule T_j^i. We discuss how to build its schedule in the h-th situation corresponding to available vCPUs of $(C_{S_1}, C_{S_2}, \dots, C_{S_{p-1}}, y_p, 0, \dots, 0)$ where $h = \sum_{k=1}^{p-1} C_{S_k} + y_p$. There are three cases to handle T_j^i.

Algorithm 6.1: Dynamic Programming Approach

Input: Applications $G_1, \dots, G_n$, Servers $S_1, \dots, S_m$
Output: Schedule $\mathcal{S}^n_{|V_n|}$

for $i = 1 \rightarrow n$ **do**
  for $j = 1 \rightarrow |\Xi_i|$ **do**
    for $h = 1 \rightarrow \sum_{p=1}^{m} C_{S_p}$ **do**
      if $i = 1 \& j = 1$ **then**
        Get $\mathcal{S}^1_1(h)$ by creating a virtual machine for it. ▷ Details are presented in above subsection
      else
        Get $\mathcal{S}^i_{j,C1}(h)$ with $ft^i_{j,C1}$, and $\mathcal{S}^i_{j,C2}(h)$ with $ft^i_{j,C2}$.
        if $ft^i_{j,C1} < ft^i_{j,C2}$ **then**
          Create a new virtual machine with $z^\sharp_p$ virtual CPU for T^i_j.
        else if $ft^i_{j,C1} \geq ft^i_{j,C2}$ **then**
          Assign T^i_j to an existing virtual machine.
        else if $\mathcal{S}^i_{j,C1}(h)$ and $\mathcal{S}^i_{j,C2}(h)$ not found **then**
          Fail.
        end if
      end if
    end for
  end for
end for

1. Case 1: create a new VM for T^i_j. Because the available vCPUs in the p-th server is y_p, the new VM can be allocated with z_p vCPUs where $1 \leq z_p \leq y_p$, and the schedule result of tasks from T^i_1 to T^i_{j-1} is thus $\mathcal{S}^i_{j-1}(h - z_p)$. From all these possible schedules, we choose the one that minimizes the response time of G_i's tasks from T^i_1 to T^i_j, while not making other applications miss their deadlines. This can be achieved through the response time analysis presented in Section 6.4. If T^i_j is assigned to a new VM with $z^\sharp_p$ vCPUs, the schedule of other tasks is $\mathcal{S}^i_{j-1}(h - z^\sharp_p)$. This final schedule is denoted as $\mathcal{S}^i_{j,C1}(h)$, and the finish time of T^i_j is denoted as $ft^i_{j,C1}$.
2. Case 2: assign T^i_j to existing VMs of p-th server. Suppose that there are U VMs in the p-th server in schedule $\mathcal{S}^i_{j-1}(h)$, and each VM is denoted as VM^i_u where $1 \leq u \leq U$. Then T^i_j can be assigned to any one of them. Besides, when

T_j^i is assigned to VM_u^i that may have been assigned other tasks, its execution priority also needs to be decided. For this reason, we check every possible assignment of VM and check every execution priority in each VM. In the end, we can get T_j^i's VM assignment and its execution priority that minimizes the response time of G_i's tasks from T_1^i to T_j^i, while not making other applications miss their deadlines. This final schedule is denoted as $\mathcal{S}_{j,C2}^i(h)$, and the finish time of T_j^i is denoted as $ft_{j,C2}^i$.

3. Case 3: failure. If it is not possible to guarantee that other applications from G_1 to G_{i-1} meet their deadlines by either creating a new VM for T_j^i or assigning it to existing VMs, the scheduling approach fails and the final schedule is an empty set, i.e., $\mathcal{S}_j^i = \emptyset$.

Through the analysis of the above three cases, we can derive a state-transition equation as below:

$$\mathcal{S}_j^i(h) = \begin{cases} \mathcal{S}_{j,C1}^i(h), & ft_{j,C1}^i < ft_{j,C2}^i \\ \mathcal{S}_{j,C2}^i(h), & ft_{j,C1}^i \geq ft_{j,C2}^i \\ \emptyset, & \mathcal{S}_{j,C1}^i(h) \text{ and } \mathcal{S}_{j,C2}^i(h) \text{ not built} \end{cases}, \tag{6.7}$$

where both $\mathcal{S}_{j,C1}^i(h)$ and $\mathcal{S}_{j,C2}^i(h)$ only rely on h, T_j^i, and $\mathcal{S}_{j-1}^i$. For this reason, (6.7) can be represented as a function of $\mathcal{S}_j^i(h) = g(\mathcal{S}_{j-1}^i, T_j^i, h)$ where $\mathcal{S}_{j-1}^i = \mathcal{S}_{j-1}^i(1) \cup \mathcal{S}_{j-1}^i(2) \cup \cdots \cup \mathcal{S}_{j-1}^i(\sum_{p=1}^{m} C_{S_p})$.

6.5.3 Dynamic Programming

With the state-transition function $\mathcal{S}_j^i(h) = g(\mathcal{S}_{j-1}^i, T_j^i, h)$, we develop a dynamic programming approach to solving this problem, as presented in Algorithm 6.1. Tasks decomposed from applications are successively assigned. The first task T_1^1 is a special task whose previous schedule is empty. Hence, a new VM must be created for it in every situation, as discussed in Section 6.5.2. Except this task, other tasks can always refer to the previous schedule result to build a new schedule by relying on the state-transition equation of (6.7). In the end, we can get $\mathcal{S}_{|V_n|}^n$ that presents all possible schedules to successively assign all tasks, while not missing their deadlines. If there are too many tasks and limited computing resources, the dynamic programming approach may not be able to find a feasible solution. There are three `for` loops in Algorithm 6.1, and its complexity is thus $O(n \cdot |\Xi_i| \cdot \sum_{p=1}^{m} C_{S_p})$ in general.

6.6 Mixed-criticality Scheduling

We have shown how to use the dynamic programming approach to guarantee schedulability in level-1 mode. In this section, we extend this approach to different level-criticality modes by switching the system level when applications' frequencies change, and then develop an online management scheme to flexibly run applications with the aim of meeting their deadlines as much as possible.

6.6.1 Mixed-criticality Schedulability Test

The lowest and highest criticality levels are 1 and 4. Hence, applications can be classified into four sets based on their criticality levels, where $\mathcal{G}^k$ $(1 \leq k \leq 4)$ denotes applications whose criticality levels are k. We thus have $\mathcal{G} = \mathcal{G}^1 \cup \mathcal{G}^2 \cup \mathcal{G}^3 \cup \mathcal{G}^4$. We now assign applications from $\mathcal{G}^4$ to $\mathcal{G}^1$ successively.

Algorithm 6.2: Finding Mixed-criticality Schedule

Input: Applications $G_1, \ldots, G_n$, Servers $S_1, \ldots, S_m$
Output: Schedules $\mathcal{S}_{L4}, \mathcal{S}_{L3}, \mathcal{S}_{L2}, \mathcal{S}_{L1}$

1: Classify $\mathcal{G}$ to $\mathcal{G}^4, \mathcal{G}^3, \mathcal{G}^2, \mathcal{G}^1$ based on their criticality levels
2: **Test Schedulability at Level-4 Mode:** Apply Algorithm 6.1 to assign $\mathcal{G}^4$ where $\forall G_i \in \mathcal{G}^4$, its release frequency is assumed to be f_4^i. The final schedule is denoted as $\mathcal{S}_{L4}$.
3: **Test Schedulability at Level-3 Mode:** Based on $\mathcal{S}_{L4}$, apply Algorithm 6.1 to assign $\mathcal{G}^3$ where $\forall G_i \in \mathcal{G}^4 \cup \mathcal{G}^3$, its release frequency is assumed to be f_3^i. The final schedule is denoted as $\mathcal{S}_{L3}$.
4: **Test Schedulability at Level-2 Mode:** Based on $\mathcal{S}_{L3}$, apply Algorithm 6.1 to assign $\mathcal{G}^2$ where $\forall G_i \in \mathcal{G}^4 \cup \mathcal{G}^3 \cup \mathcal{G}^2$, its release frequency is assumed to be f_2^i. The final schedule is denoted as $\mathcal{S}_{L2}$.
5: **Test Schedulability at Level-1 Mode:** Based on $\mathcal{S}_{L2}$, apply Algorithm 6.1 to assign $\mathcal{G}^1$ where $\forall G_i \in \mathcal{G}^4 \cup \mathcal{G}^3 \cup \mathcal{G}^2 \cup \mathcal{G}^1$, its release frequency is assumed to be f_1^i. The final schedule is denoted as $\mathcal{S}_{L1}$.

The detailed operations are presented in Algorithm 6.2. At first, we assign applications of $\mathcal{G}^4$, where $\forall G_i \in \mathcal{G}^4$, its release frequency is f_4^i. By dynamic programming approach, we can assign them to edge computing servers and get a schedule result denoted as $\mathcal{S}_{L4}$. This schedule guarantees that applications whose $C_i = 4$ can be schedulable if their release frequencies are f_4^i. Then, based on this schedule result, we start to test the schedulability at level-3 mode by assigning applications of $\mathcal{G}^3$ where $\forall G_i \in \mathcal{G}^4 \cup \mathcal{G}^3$ and their release frequencies are f_3^i. Such procedures continue until schedules $\mathcal{S}_{L4}, \mathcal{S}_{L3}, \mathcal{S}_{L2}, \mathcal{S}_{L1}$ have been built. Note that, at each level-criticality mode, applications' release frequencies have been assumed to match their levels. If schedules $\mathcal{S}_{L4}, \mathcal{S}_{L3}, \mathcal{S}_{L2}, \mathcal{S}_{L1}$ can be built successfully, the system is mixed-criticality schedulable. It should be noted that the mixed-criticality scheduling scheme in Algorithm 6.2 can be extended to cover more criticality levels by setting more mode switches. Compared to Algorithm 6.1, the assignment order of applications has been renewed, while other procedures are the same. Hence, its complexity is the same as Algorithm 6.1, i.e., $O(n \cdot |\Xi_i| \cdot \sum_{p=1}^{m} C_{S_p})$.

6.6.2 Online Management by Frequency Prediction

We have built schedules that can be mixed-criticality schedulable. However, it is a pessimistic management scheme to abandon all low-criticality applications when the frequency of high-criticality applications increases, because not all high-criticality applications are released at their maximum and the system may have extra capacity to permit execution of some low-criticality applications. We now discuss how to flexibly manage the execution of applications with the aim of meeting their deadlines as much as possible while still complying with the principle of guaranteeing high-criticality applications over low-criticality applications.

This scheme relies on the frequency prediction. We use $f_i(t)$ to denote the frequency of G_i at time t, and use $f_i^{\max}(t)$ to denote its maximum frequency from qT to $(q+1)T$, i.e.,

$$f_i^{\max}(qT) = \max f_i(t),\ qT < t \le (q+1)T,\ 1 \le i \le n,$$

where T denotes a time interval. Such prediction can be achieved by collecting and analyzing the history data of application frequency.

With $f_i^{\max}(qT)$ at $t = qT$ $(q \ge 1)$, we can manage our schedules by continuously abandoning the lowest-criticality applications until all remained applications can meet their deadlines. As presented in Algorithm 6.3, whenever $t = qT$, the schedule needs to be adjusted. Before the adjustment, we assume that all applications can be schedulable with $\mathcal{S}_{L1}$, i.e., $\mathcal{S}_{qT} = \mathcal{S}_{L1}$. Then, with the new frequency $f_i^{\max}(qT)$, $(1 \le i \le n)$, we test whether $\mathcal{S}_{qT}$ is still schedulable by the responsible time analysis. If not, the lowest-criticality application from $\mathcal{S}_{qT}$ is abandoned. This procedure continues until $\mathcal{S}_{qT}$ is schedulable, in which way the system always guarantees high-criticality applications over low-criticality applications. In addition, the system can make its full use of its computing resources to schedule applications. The worst case that could happen to this procedure is to abandon all applications. Therefore, the complexity of Algorithm 16 is $O(n)$.

Algorithm 6.3: Online Management by Frequency Prediction

```
Input: Applications G_1, ..., G_n, Servers S_1, ..., S_m, Schedule 𝒮_L1
Output: Schedule 𝒮_qT
if t = qT, (q ∈ ℕ+) then
    Update f_i^max(qT), (1 ≤ i ≤ n)
    𝒮_qT = 𝒮_L1
    while applications in 𝒮_qT are not schedulable do
        Find the lowest-criticality application G′ in 𝒮_qT
        Abandon G′ in 𝒮_qT and update 𝒮_qT
    end while
end if
```

6.7 Performance Evaluation

We perform simulation experiments to evaluate the performance of our proposed approach. A VEC environment is set up, where there are m servers and each server has C_{S_p} vCPUs, e.g., $m = 5$, $C_{S_p} = 100$, $\forall 1 \leq p \leq m$. The computing services provided to customers are modeled as DAGs that are generated by the following task trees in [29], where task count per application is in the range [5, 20]. We suppose that the system provides 10 types of computing services. The computation time of a task on a single vCPU is within [0.1, 0.4] seconds, and the communication overhead between two tasks on two different VMs is within [0.01, 0.1] seconds.

6.7.1 Compared Approaches

Except for our proposed approaches, we also introduce some classic heuristics and particle swarm optimization for a comparison purpose. In summary, the compared approaches include:

- M_0 (Proposed One): This approach refers to the proposed use of dynamic programming to create VMs and assign tasks of DAG applications to them.
- M_1: Instead of creating multiple VMs on a server, this approach creates a single VM with the whole computing resources of a server.
- M_2: A particle swarm optimizer (PSO) has been developed to search for a solution to our formulated problem. Here, the option of server and the creation of VMs are encoded. We configure the acceleration coefficient to 2, the inertia weight to 0.6, the iteration to 10000, and the initial particles to 200.
- M_3: In contrast with M_2 that initializes particles randomly, this approach takes some results from M_0 as initial particles. Because solutions of M_0 have already been optimized to certain extent, PSO can often find better ones after more optimization iterations.

Three metrics are defined to evaluate the performance of compared approaches, which are the success rate of successfully scheduling a set of applications; the computation time of finding out a feasible schedule; and the number of applications suspended online. The first one is statistical data by conducting experiments on a lot of applications. The second one refers to the average time expense needed by an approach to find a schedule that can meet all the application's requirements. The last one refers to the system's capability to save applications online, because the system may be overwhelmed every now and then by the dynamically released applications.

6.7.2 Results

We compare their performance by varying vCPUs, varying the application's release frequency, and varying the ratio of applications with different criticalities (Figure 6.4) on a single server and multiple servers, respectively. System performance online is evaluated by conforming the application's frequency to follow the trend of traffic flow versus time of day.

6.7.2.1 Results of a Single Server

We suppose that there is only a single server. First, we investigate the effect of the system's vCPUs on the performance of compared approaches. By varying vCPUs from 50 to 200 and setting the scope of the application's release frequency to [0.25, 10] Hz, the success rate of compared approaches is presented in Figure 6.4a. We observe that our proposed approach and PSO with scheduled results from our proposed approach have the same success rate, which is higher than the other two approaches. This illustrates that our proposed approach finds a good solution to our studied problem, and this solution is hard to improve by iterative search in its nearby space. A PSO without good initial particles is hard to find a solution, unless there are abundant vCPUs in the system. Additionally, we find that the success rate increases with increasing vCPUs. This is reasonable because more vCPUs imply greater DAG application scheduling capability.

The average computation time of compared approaches to finding a schedule is presented in Figure 6.5, where its vertical axis is log-scaled. It shows that the computation time of our proposed approach increases from around 10 seconds at vCPUs = 50 to 100 seconds at vCPUs = 200. PSO approaches need computation that is 10 times more than our proposed approaches. M_1 requires the least amount of computation because it considers it to be the only option, which is to create a VM with a full computation resource to schedule applications.

Second, we investigate the influence of applications' release frequency on the scheduling performance of compared approaches. From small to large, there are five scopes of frequency (Hz): [0.25, 0.5], [0.5, 1], [1, 2], [2, 5], and [5, 10]. The count

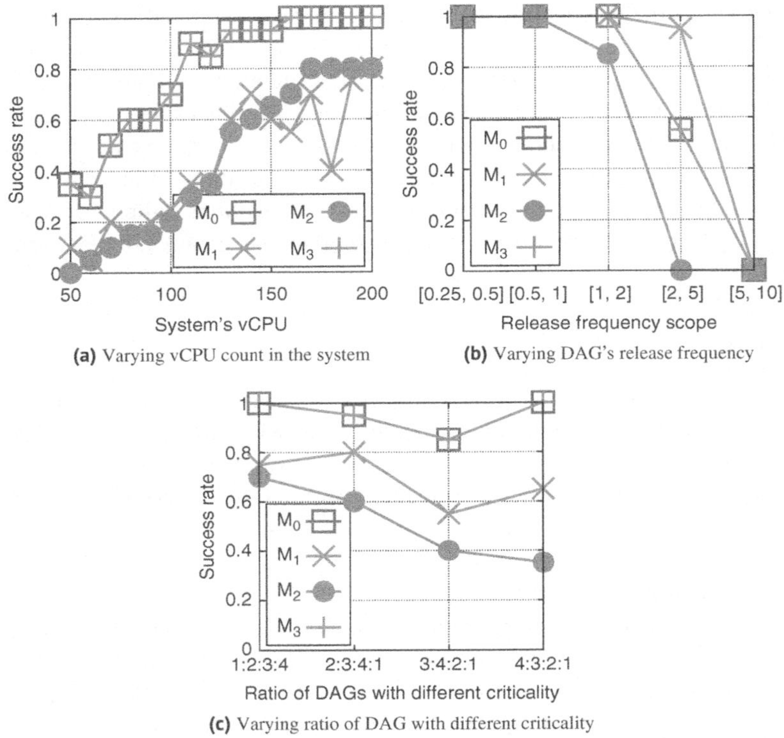

(a) Varying vCPU count in the system

(b) Varying DAG's release frequency

(c) Varying ratio of DAG with different criticality

Figure 6.4 The success rate of compared approaches with varying system's configurations.

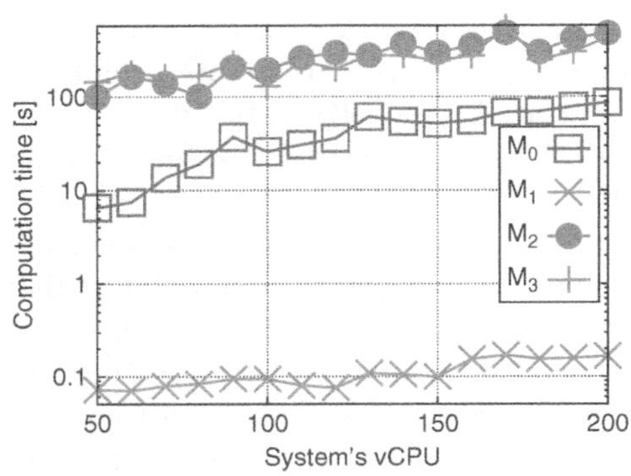

Figure 6.5 Computation time of compared approaches to decide a schedule with varying count of vCPU in the system.

of the system's vCPUs is set to 150. The success rate of compared approaches is presented in Figure 6.4b, where all approaches tend to become incapable of finding a successful schedule. This is because the system's limited hardware resources are not enough to meet the increasing workload. Nevertheless, our proposed approach still outperforms other approaches.

Last, we investigate the influence of the ratio of applications with different criticalities on the scheduling performance of compared approaches. We set the count of vCPUs to 150 and the scope of applications release frequency to [0.25, 10] Hz. We use a4:a3:a2:a1 to denote the ratio of applications whose criticality is 4, 3, 2, and 1, respectively. We investigate four ratios, i.e., 1:2:3:4, 2:3:4:1, 3:4:2:1, and 4:3:2:1. The result of the success rate is presented in Figure 6.4c, where it shows that approaches tend to lose some success rate with the increasing portion of high-criticality applications. This is because high-criticality applications need more levels of schedulability guarantee, which demands more hardware resources.

6.7.2.2 Results of Multiple Servers

We suppose that there are multiple servers, where the sum of vCPUs is set to 150. To investigate the influence of servers on the scheduling performance, the count of servers varies from 1 to 15, and they all have the same number of vCPUs. For example, if there are m servers, each server will have $\lceil \frac{150}{m} \rceil$ vCPUs, which means that 150 vCPUs are evenly distributed and rounded up. The average success rate of finding a schedule is presented in Figure 6.6. It shows that our proposed approach performs better than the others when there are few servers. Its performance decreases with the increase in server count in the system.

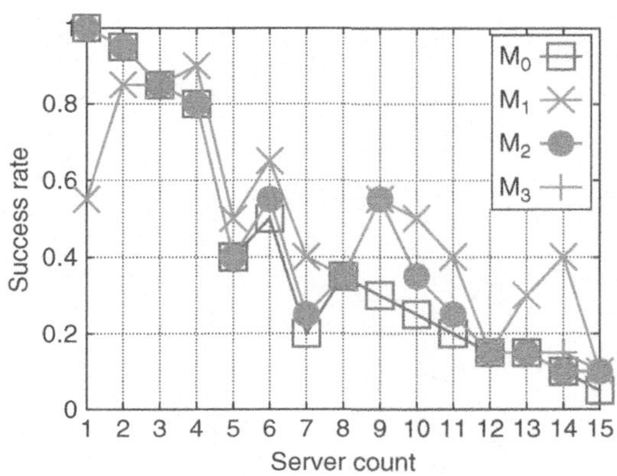

Figure 6.6 Success rate of compared approaches to decide a schedule with varying server count in the system.

6.7.2.3 Results of Dynamic Applications

Last, we evaluate the performance of our proposed scheduling approach to handle the dynamically released applications. Suppose that there are 3 servers, each holding 50 vCPUs. There are 10 DAG applications whose release frequencies conform to a trend of traffic flow in a day. For the other approaches except for M_0, applications' maximum frequency of a day is assumed, such that the built schedule is capable of handling them by following the designed mode-switch scheme offline. For our proposed approach M_0 that manages the schedule online by frequency prediction, applications are successively abandoned until success by Algorithm 6.3. The profiled period is set to 0.5, 1, 2, 3, 4, 6, 8, 12, and 24 hours, where the profiled period of 24 hours corresponds to the application's maximum frequency of a day. These profiled periods are chosen in order to divide 24 hours evenly, and they are enough to detect the influence of profiled periods on the scheduling performance. The average number of abandoned applications per hour is collected and presented in Figure 6.7. In general, all approaches tend to abandon more applications with the increasing profiled period. This is because the gap between applications' average frequency and their maximum frequency becomes larger when the profiled period increases. Scheduling approaches will make more conservative decisions to abandon more low-critical applications in order to protect high-critical applications. Even so, we find that our proposed online management strategy works very well, which reduces the number of abandoned applications by half compared to other approaches.

We also investigate the computation time overhead whenever the scheduler needs to be updated online. As shown in Figure 6.8, the computation time is very small, which is less than 0.002 seconds in most cases. This illustrates that our

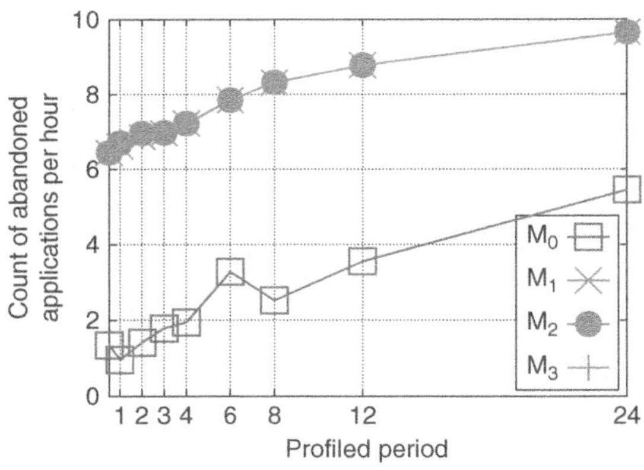

Figure 6.7 Number of abandoned applications of compared approaches with varying profiled period.

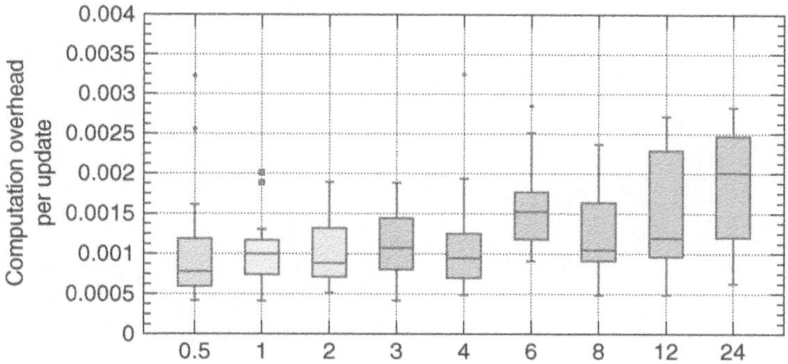

Figure 6.8 Computation time overhead per update with varying profiled period.

proposed online strategy has a minor impact on its online scheduling. Additionally, we find that the computation time increases slightly with an increasing profiled period. This is because more applications are abandoned when the profiled period becomes large, and the decision to abandon applications thus incurs more computation.

6.8 Summary

Vehicle systems typically host a range of applications with varying criticality levels. This chapter addresses the challenge of effectively utilizing VEC resources to support dynamic applications. We present an analysis of the response time of DAG applications when VMs are allocated for task processing. A state-transition equation is derived for task assignment to VMs on a server, and a dynamic programming algorithm is proposed to tackle the scheduling of static applications in a VEC environment. To accommodate varying criticality levels, we integrate a common mixed-criticality mode-switch scheme into our approach, ensuring that applications are served according to their criticality. Additionally, we develop an online management strategy to maximize the scheduling of low-critical applications. Experimental results demonstrate that our approach outperforms heuristic and PSO methods in terms of application scheduling success rates and computational efficiency.

7

Real-world Applications of Scheduling Technologies

7.1 Introduction

In an increasingly connected world, scheduling technologies are essential to orchestrating the operations of distributed, heterogeneous, and resource-constrained systems. Cloud-edge-device computing frameworks have enabled real-time intelligence across domains such as transportation, manufacturing, healthcare, and autonomous mobility. This chapter delves into real-world applications where effective task scheduling enhances performance, ensures timely responses, optimizes resource use, and improves user experience.

By aligning computational tasks with available resources across cloud, edge, and device layers, modern systems can adapt to dynamic workloads, maintain service continuity, and achieve high reliability. The following sections explore practical examples of scheduling technologies in action across various sectors.

7.2 Traffic Management

In smart cities, effective task scheduling directly impacts the quality of life by ensuring efficient use of resources and reducing environmental impact. Urban systems must handle vast, dynamic data from various sources such as traffic sensors, surveillance cameras, and public utility meters.

Edge devices located at intersections collect real-time data from traffic cameras and vehicle detection sensors. This data is processed locally to assess vehicle flow, congestion levels, and pedestrian activity. Scheduling algorithms then determine optimal timing for traffic lights based on real-time inputs, often leveraging machine learning models that reside in the cloud for long-term optimization.

To minimize unnecessary waiting at red lights and enhance overall traffic efficiency, Taipei has implemented an AI-powered intelligent traffic signal

Intelligent Scheduling of Tasks for Cloud-Edge-Device Computing Systems, First Edition.

Published 2025 by John Wiley & Sons, Inc.

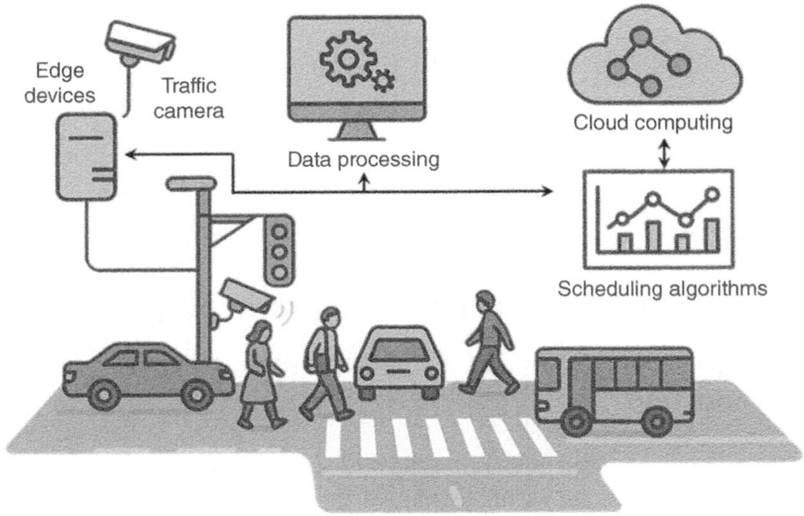

Figure 7.1 Traffic signal control scenario based on real-time data from traffic cameras and vehicle detection sensors.

control system, as illustrated in Figure 7.1 [189]. This system combines intersection surveillance cameras, industrial-grade edge AI computing devices, and advanced AI algorithms to dynamically adjust signal timings based on real-time vehicle and pedestrian flow. The goal is to alleviate long-standing congestion issues and streamline traffic movement.

The system architecture operates as follows: Artificial intelligence (AI)-enabled cameras installed at intersections continuously monitor vehicle and pedestrian activity in all directions. The live video feeds are transmitted to roadside edge devices, where AI algorithms process the footage to detect and locate vehicles and pedestrians. Based on this real-time analysis, the system calculates the optimal duration for green lights and activates an adaptive signal control mechanism that dynamically adjusts the traffic signals.

The decision-making logic of the system is centered around three key scenarios:

1. When the main road has a green light and pedestrians or vehicles are detected crossing, the system ensures a minimum green time for the cross street to allow safe passage.
2. When a side street has a green light and traffic is detected, the green duration can be extended accordingly.
3. If no vehicles or pedestrians are detected on the side street, the system skips the green phase for that direction and reallocates the time to the main road.

During the development of the system, special attention was given to training the AI model to perform reliably under high-contrast conditions, including nighttime, bright daylight, and rainy weather, to enhance recognition accuracy and minimize the risk of misidentification.

7.3 Smart Agriculture with Internet of Things

Agricultural systems are increasingly integrating Internet of Things (IoT) devices and data-driven technologies to enhance operational efficiency, sustainability, and overall productivity. A key component in this transformation is computational task scheduling, which coordinates the processing of sensor data, the control of field devices, and the execution of long-term analytics in a timely and resource-efficient manner.

In a typical smart farm, a wide array of IoT devices are deployed, including soil moisture sensors, weather monitoring stations, drone-based crop imaging systems, and automated irrigation controllers. These devices generate a continuous stream of data that must be processed at different layers of a computational hierarchy – device, edge, and cloud.

For example, as presented in Figure 7.2, in a scenario where soil moisture sensors detect the real-time hydration levels of different plots, the raw data is first processed at the device level to filter noise and detect anomalies. Next, edge computing units (such as a local gateway or edge server) analyze the aggregated data

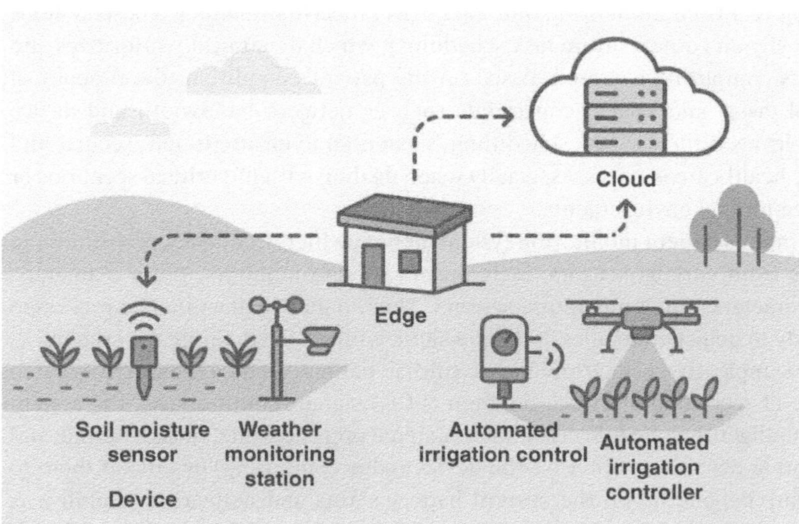

Figure 7.2 Smart agriculture with IoT devices.

from nearby sensors to make localized irrigation decisions, triggering water valves only in areas that require moisture. Meanwhile, the same data is periodically sent to the cloud, where more computationally intensive tasks like seasonal yield prediction and historical trend analysis are performed using machine learning models.

Without intelligent computation scheduling, such a system can become inefficient. For instance, if edge devices are overloaded with data or if cloud analytics are delayed, irrigation decisions might not reflect the real-time needs of the crops. This can result in over- or under-watering, leading to resource waste or reduced crop yields. Additionally, delayed or missed insights from cloud-based analytics can affect decisions on planting schedules, fertilizer use, or pest control strategies.

Computation task scheduling dynamically allocates processing tasks across devices, edge nodes, and cloud servers based on urgency, resource availability, and data relevance. This balancing act ensures that real-time tasks like irrigation are handled promptly at the edge, while long-term insights like productivity forecasts are derived from cumulative data in the cloud. As a result, smart agriculture systems have become more responsive, resource-efficient, and data-driven, contributing to both economic viability and environmental sustainability.

7.4 Healthcare Monitoring Systems

In modern healthcare, the integration of wearable sensors, mobile health applications, and hospital information systems has revolutionized patient care by enabling real-time monitoring and data-driven decision-making. These systems rely heavily on context-aware task scheduling, which dynamically prioritizes and allocates computing resources based on the patient's condition, the urgency of medical tasks, and system constraints such as network bandwidth and device battery levels. Efficient task scheduling is essential to ensure timely, secure, and reliable healthcare services, especially when dealing with life-critical scenarios or resource-limited environments.

Continuous patient monitoring systems generate high-frequency, real-time data streams from various sensors, including heart rate monitors, pulse oximeters, accelerometers, and temperature sensors. These data streams must be processed promptly to detect anomalies and issue alerts without overloading the system.

For example, in a scenario where a cardiac patient wears a smart chest patch capable of recording electrocardiogram (ECG) signals continuously, the system must intelligently schedule tasks, such as signal preprocessing, noise filtering, and arrhythmia detection, either on the device (edge computing) or offload them to the cloud, depending on the current battery status and network availability. A failure to properly prioritize these tasks could result in the delayed detection of life-threatening conditions such as atrial fibrillation.

7.5 Summary

The real-world applications explored in this chapter underscore the pivotal role of scheduling technologies in orchestrating complex, distributed systems across a variety of domains. Whether optimizing traffic flow in smart cities, enhancing precision and efficiency in agriculture, or enabling timely and accurate responses in healthcare monitoring, intelligent task scheduling serves as the backbone of modern digital ecosystems.

Each case study illustrates how dynamic and context-aware scheduling ensures that critical tasks are executed at the right place and time, balancing real-time responsiveness with long-term computational needs. In traffic management, edge-enabled scheduling reduces congestion and improves commuter experience. In agriculture, it supports sustainable practices through precise, demand-driven irrigation. In healthcare, it safeguards patient well-being by ensuring prompt detection and response to physiological changes.

As computational demands continue to grow alongside the proliferation of IoT and AI technologies, effective scheduling strategies will remain central to system performance, scalability, and resilience. The examples presented here demonstrate not only the feasibility but also the transformative potential of scheduling technologies when thoughtfully integrated into real-world applications. Future advancements will likely focus on making these systems more autonomous, adaptive, and context-sensitive – further bridging the gap between digital intelligence and everyday operations.

8

Summary and Future Research

8.1 Summary

This book presents a holistic overview of task scheduling techniques in cloud-edge-device computing systems, with a particular focus on real-time, energy-efficient, and workload-aware scheduling. It covers both theoretical foundations and practical implementation strategies across diverse computing environments, including cloud infrastructures, vehicular edge networks, and Internet of Things (IoT) systems.

Key topics include task and system modeling, schedulability analysis, hybrid scheduling algorithms, energy-aware optimization, and mixed-criticality management. The book also explores offline and online scheduling approaches, balancing computational performance with power efficiency and system responsiveness.

In addition to foundational concepts and algorithmic frameworks, the book highlights emerging trends and practical applications in domains such as autonomous vehicles, smart agriculture, traffic management, and healthcare monitoring. Through this comprehensive treatment, readers are equipped with the knowledge to design and evaluate scheduling solutions for dynamic, distributed, and resource-constrained computing environments.

8.2 Future Research

The rapid evolution of distributed computing environments calls for continued exploration in several key areas of task scheduling and resource management:

1. **AI-driven Scheduling Algorithms:** Future work can further integrate machine learning and reinforcement learning techniques to dynamically

Intelligent Scheduling of Tasks for Cloud-Edge-Device Computing Systems, First Edition.
Biao Hu et al.
Published 2025 by John Wiley & Sons, Inc.

predict workload trends, resource availability, and fault scenarios, enabling smarter, adaptive scheduling.

2. **Scheduling in Federated and Collaborative Edge Environments:** As federated learning and cross-domain data sharing grow, new models are needed to coordinate task execution across trust boundaries while preserving latency, security, and privacy.
3. **Security-aware Scheduling:** Integrating cybersecurity constraints into scheduling decisions will be vital, particularly in sensitive applications such as healthcare and autonomous transportation.
4. **Sustainable and Green Scheduling Models:** Climate-conscious computing calls for task schedulers that prioritize carbon footprint minimization, integrating renewable energy availability and carbon pricing models into real-time decisions.
5. **Human-in-the-loop Scheduling Systems:** As edge computing intersects with human decision-making (e.g., in smart cities or industrial IoT), co-adaptive scheduling systems that account for human behaviors and preferences can enhance robustness and user satisfaction.
6. **Standardized Benchmarking and Validation Frameworks:** There is a growing need for shared datasets, simulation tools, and benchmarking platforms to evaluate scheduling algorithms consistently across research and industrial domains.

As cloud-edge-device ecosystems become more intelligent, distributed, and context-aware, future research must align not only with performance and efficiency goals but also with trust, adaptability, and sustainability objectives. This convergence presents exciting opportunities for interdisciplinary innovation in both academia and industry.

References

1 Jing Bi, Haitao Yuan, Shuaifei Duanmu, MengChu Zhou, and Abdullah Abusorrah. Energy-optimized partial computation offloading in mobile-edge computing with genetic simulated-annealing-based particle swarm optimization. *IEEE Internet of Things Journal*, 8(5): 3774–3785, 2020.

2 Lion Silva, Naercio Magaia, Breno Sousa, Anna Kobusińska, António Casimiro, Constandinos X. Mavromoustakis, George Mastorakis, and Victor Hugo C. De Albuquerque. Computing paradigms in emerging vehicular environments: A review. *IEEE/CAA Journal of Automatica Sinica*, 8(3): 491–511, 2021.

3 Peter Arthurs, Lee Gillam, Paul Krause, Ning Wang, Kaushik Halder, and Alexandros Mouzakitis. A taxonomy and survey of edge cloud computing for intelligent transportation systems and connected vehicles. *IEEE Transactions on Intelligent Transportation Systems*, 23(7): 6206–6221, 2022.

4 Zhiyuan Jiang, Sheng Zhou, Xueying Guo, and Zhisheng Niu. Task replication for deadline-constrained vehicular cloud computing: Optimal policy, performance analysis, and implications on road traffic. *IEEE Internet of Things Journal*, 5(1): 93–107, 2017.

5 Ashwin Ashok, Peter Steenkiste, and Fan Bai. Vehicular cloud computing through dynamic computation offloading. *Computer Communications*, 120: 125–137, 2018.

6 Zhenyu Zhou, Pengju Liu, Junhao Feng, Yan Zhang, Shahid Mumtaz, and Jonathan Rodriguez. Computation resource allocation and task assignment optimization in vehicular fog computing: A contract-matching approach. *IEEE Transactions on Vehicular Technology*, 68(4): 3113–3125, 2019b.

7 Yujiong Liu, Shangguang Wang, Qinglin Zhao, Shiyu Du, Ao Zhou, Xiao Ma, and Fangchun Yang. Dependency-aware task scheduling in vehicular edge computing. *IEEE Internet of Things Journal*, 7(6): 4961–4971, 2020b.

Intelligent Scheduling of Tasks for Cloud-Edge-Device Computing Systems, First Edition.

Published 2025 by John Wiley & Sons, Inc.

8 Taesik Kim, Hong Min, Eunsoo Choi, and Jinman Jung. Optimal job partitioning and allocation for vehicular cloud computing. *Future Generation Computer Systems*, 108: 82–96, 2020.

9 Benoît Chretien, Lydie Nouvelière, Naïma Ait Oufroukh, Sébastien Glaser, Saïd Mammar, Mengchu Zhou, and Matthias Korte. A vehicle simulator for an efficient electronic and electrical architecture design. *IEEE Transactions on Intelligent Transportation Systems*, 14(4): 1967–1982, 2013.

10 Simon Fürst, Jürgen Mössinger, Stefan Bunzel, Thomas Weber, Frank Kirschke-Biller, Peter Heitkämper, Gerulf Kinkelin, Kenji Nishikawa, and Klaus Lange. Autosar–A worldwide standard is on the road. In *14th International VDI Congress Electronic Systems for Vehicles, Baden-Baden*, volume 62, page 5, 2009.

11 Robert I. Davis and Alan Burns. A survey of hard real-time scheduling for multiprocessor systems. *ACM Computing Surveys*, 43(4): 1–44, 2011.

12 Eugenia Ana Capota, Cristina Sorina Stangaciu, Mihai Victor Micea, and Daniel-Ioan Curiac. Towards mixed criticality task scheduling in cyber physical systems: Challenges and perspectives. *Journal of Systems and Software*, 156: 204–216, 2019.

13 Biao Hu, Lothar Thiele, Pengcheng Huang, Kai Huang, Christoph Griesbeck, and Alois Knoll. FFOB: Efficient online mode-switch procrastination in mixed-criticality systems. *Real-Time Systems*, 55(3): 471–513, 2019.

14 Georgios Karagiannis, Onur Altintas, Eylem Ekici, Geert Heijenk, Boangoat Jarupan, Kenneth Lin, and Timothy Weil. Vehicular networking: A survey and tutorial on requirements, architectures, challenges, standards and solutions. *IEEE Communications Surveys & Tutorials*, 13(4): 584–616, 2011.

15 Pranav Kumar Singh, Sunit Kumar Nandi, and Sukumar Nandi. A tutorial survey on vehicular communication state of the art, and future research directions. *Vehicular Communications*, 18: 100164, 2019a.

16 Kan Zheng, Qiang Zheng, Haojun Yang, Long Zhao, Lu Hou, and Periklis Chatzimisios. Reliable and efficient autonomous driving: The need for heterogeneous vehicular networks. *IEEE Communications Magazine*, 53(12): 72–79, 2015.

17 Ibrar Yaqoob, Latif U. Khan, S. M. Ahsan Kazmi, Muhammad Imran, Nadra Guizani, and Choong Seon Hong. Autonomous driving cars in smart cities: Recent advances, requirements, and challenges. *IEEE Network*, 34(1): 174–181, 2019.

18 Zhaolong Ning, Peiran Dong, Xiaojie Wang, Xiping Hu, Jiangchuan Liu, Lei Guo, Bin Hu, Ricky Kwok, and Victor CM Leung. Partial computation offloading and adaptive task scheduling for 5G-enabled vehicular networks. *IEEE Transactions on Mobile Computing*. IEEE, 2020.

19 Alan Burns and Robert I. Davis. A survey of research into mixed criticality systems. *ACM Computing Surveys*, 50(6): 82, 2017.

20 Alan Burns, Robert I. Davis, Sanjoy Baruah, and Iain Bate. Robust mixed-criticality systems. *IEEE Transactions on Computers*, 67(10): 1478–1491, 2018.

21 Ashik Ahmed Bhuiyan, Kecheng Yang, Samsil Arefin, Abusayeed Saifullah, Nan Guan, and Zhishan Guo. Mixed-criticality multicore scheduling of real-time gang task systems. In *2019 IEEE Real-Time Systems Symposium*, pages 469–480, 2019.

22 Rolf Ernst and Marco Di Natale. Mixed criticality systems—a history of misconceptions? *IEEE Design & Test*, 33(5): 65–74, 2016.

23 Aurélien Monot, Nicolas Navet, Bernard Bavoux, and Françoise Simonot-Lion. Multisource software on multicore automotive ECUs—combining runnable sequencing with task scheduling. *IEEE Transactions on Industrial Electronics*, 59(10): 3934–3942, 2012.

24 Kyung-Jung Lee, Jae-Woo Kim, Hyuk-Jun Chang, and Hyun-Sik Ahn. Mixed harmonic runnable scheduling for automotive software on multi-core processors. *International Journal of Automotive Technology*, 19(2): 323–330, 2018.

25 Lucia Lo Bello, Riccardo Mariani, Saad Mubeen, and Sergio Saponara. Recent advances and trends in on-board embedded and networked automotive systems. *IEEE Transactions on Industrial Informatics*, 15(2): 1038–1051, 2018.

26 Guoqi Xie, Hao Peng, Zhetao Li, Jinlin Song, Yong Xie, Renfa Li, and Keqin Li. Reliability enhancement toward functional safety goal assurance in energy-aware automotive cyber-physical systems. *IEEE Transactions on Industrial Informatics*, 14(12): 5447–5462, 2018a.

27 Guoqi Xie, Gang Zeng, Yan Liu, Jia Zhou, Renfa Li, and Keqin Li. Fast functional safety verification for distributed automotive applications during early design phase. *IEEE Transactions on Industrial Electronics*, 65(5): 4378–4391, 2018b.

28 Zhe Quan, Zhi-Jie Wang, Ting Ye, and Song Guo. Task scheduling for energy consumption constrained parallel applications on heterogeneous computing systems. *IEEE Transactions on Parallel and Distributed Systems*, 31(5): 1165–1182, 2019.

29 Mingxi Cheng, Ji Li, and Shahin Nazarian. DRL-cloud: Deep reinforcement learning-based resource provisioning and task scheduling for cloud service providers. In *23rd Asia and South Pacific Design Automation Conference (ASP-DAC)*, pages 129–134. IEEE, 2018.

30 Feng Cheng, Yifeng Huang, Bhavana Tanpure, Pawan Sawalani, Long Cheng, and Cong Liu. Cost-aware job scheduling for cloud instances using deep reinforcement learning. *Cluster Computing*, 25(1): 619–631, 2022.

31 Ning Liu, Zhe Li, Jielong Xu, Zhiyuan Xu, Sheng Lin, Qinru Qiu, Jian Tang, and Yanzhi Wang. A hierarchical framework of cloud resource allocation and power management using deep reinforcement learning. In *2017 IEEE 37th International Conference on Distributed Computing Systems (ICDCS)*, pages 372–382. IEEE, 2017.

32 Geetishree Mishra, Maanasa RamPrasad, Ashwin Itagi, and KS Gurumurthy. An efficient hybrid scheduler using dynamic slack for real-time critical task scheduling in multicore automotive ECUs. *International Journal of Embedded systems and Applications (IJESA)*, 5(2): 1–14, 2015.

33 Chung Laung Liu and James W Layland. Scheduling algorithms for multiprogramming in a hard-real-time environment. *Journal of the ACM*, 20(1): 46–61, 1973.

34 Nathan Fisher and Sanjoy Baruah. *Rate-Monotonic Scheduling*, pages 751–754. Springer US, Boston, MA, 2008.

35 Samarjit Chakraborty, Simon Künzli, and Lothar Thiele. A general framework for analysing system properties in platform-based embedded system designs, pages 190–195, 2003.

36 Christos H. Papadimitriou and Kenneth Steiglitz. *Combinatorial Optimization: Algorithms and Complexity*. Courier Corporation, 1998.

37 Iain Bate and Alan Burns. An integrated approach to scheduling in safety-critical embedded control systems. *Real-Time Systems*, 25(1): 5–37, 2003.

38 Iain Bate, Alan Burns, and Robert I. Davis. An enhanced bailout protocol for mixed criticality embedded software. *IEEE Transactions on Software Engineering*, 43: 298–320, 2017.

39 Enrico Bini and Giorgio C. Buttazzo. Measuring the performance of schedulability tests. *Real-Time Systems*, 30(1–2): 129–154, 2005.

40 James Hamilton. Cooperative expendable micro-slice servers (CEMS): Low cost, low power servers for internet-scale services. *Conference on Innovative Data Systems Research (CIDR'09)(January 2009)*. pages 4–7, 2009.

41 T. Renugadevi, K. Geetha, K. Muthukumar, and Zong Woo Geem. Optimized energy cost and carbon emission-aware virtual machine allocation in sustainable data centers. *Sustainability*, 12(16): 6383, 2020.

42 Nirmal Kaur, Savina Bansal, and Rakesh Kumar Bansal. Survey on energy efficient scheduling techniques on cloud computing. *Multiagent and Grid Systems*, 17(4): 351–366, 2021.

43 Biao Hu, Yinbin Shi, and Zhengcai Cao. Adaptive energy-minimized scheduling of real-time applications in vehicular edge computing. *IEEE Transactions on Industrial Informatics*, 19(5): 6895–6906, 2023a.

44 Alessio Botta, Walter De Donato, Valerio Persico, and Antonio Pescapé. Integration of cloud computing and internet of things: A survey. *Future Generation Computer Systems*, 56: 684–700, 2016.

45 Ian Foster, Yong Zhao, Ioan Raicu, and Shiyong Lu. Cloud computing and grid computing 360-degree compared. In *Grid Computing Environments Workshop*, pages 1–10. IEEE, 2008.

46 Mostofa Kamal Nasir, Rafidah Md Noor, M. A. Kalam, and B. M. Masum. Reduction of fuel consumption and exhaust pollutant using intelligent transport systems. *The Scientific World Journal*, 2014: 836375, 2014.

47 Li Shi, Zhemin Zhang, and Thomas Robertazzi. Energy-aware scheduling of embarrassingly parallel jobs and resource allocation in cloud. *IEEE Transactions on Parallel and Distributed Systems*, 28(6): 1607–1620, 2016.

48 Minghui LiWang, Seyyedali Hosseinalipour, Zhibin Gao, Yuliang Tang, Lianfen Huang, and Huaiyu Dai. Allocation of computation-intensive graph jobs over vehicular clouds in IoV. *IEEE Internet of Things Journal*, 7(1): 311–324, 2019.

49 Biao Hu, Zhengcai Cao, and Mengchu Zhou. Scheduling real-time parallel applications in cloud to minimize energy consumption. *IEEE Transactions on Cloud Computing*, 10(1): 662–674, 2022.

50 Biao Hu, Zhilei Yan, and Mingguo Zhao. Workload-aware scheduling of multiple-criticality real-time applications in vehicular edge computing system. *IEEE Transactions on Industrial Informatics*. IEEE, 2023b.

51 Jiawei Zhang, Xiaochen Zhou, Tianyi Ge, Xudong Wang, and Taewon Hwang. Joint task scheduling and containerizing for efficient edge computing. *IEEE Transactions on Parallel and Distributed Systems*, 32(8): 2086–2100, 2021.

52 Biao Hu and Zhengcai Cao. Minimizing resource consumption cost of DAG applications with reliability requirement on heterogeneous processor systems. *IEEE Transactions on Industrial Informatics*, 16(12): 7437–7447, 2020.

53 Yanting Wang, Min Sheng, Xijun Wang, Liang Wang, and Jiandong Li. Mobile-edge computing: Partial computation offloading using dynamic voltage scaling. *IEEE Transactions on Communications*, 64(10): 4268–4282, 2016.

54 Feng Wang, Jie Xu, Xin Wang, and Shuguang Cui. Joint offloading and computing optimization in wireless powered mobile-edge computing systems. *IEEE Transactions on Wireless Communications*, 17(3): 1784–1797, 2017a.

55 Cheng Hu, Yuhui Deng, Geyong Min, Ping Huang, and Xiao Qin. QoS promotion in energy-efficient data centers through peak load scheduling. *IEEE Transactions on Cloud Computing*, 9(2): 777–792, 2018a.

56 Zhaohui Yang, Cunhua Pan, Jiancao Hou, and Mohammad Shikh-Bahaei. Efficient resource allocation for mobile-edge computing networks with NOMA: Completion time and energy minimization. *IEEE Transactions on Communications*, 67(11): 7771–7784, 2019.

57 Ying Chen, Ning Zhang, Yongchao Zhang, Xin Chen, Wen Wu, and Xuemin Shen. Energy efficient dynamic offloading in mobile edge computing for internet of things. *IEEE Transactions on Cloud Computing*, 9(3): 1050–1060, 2019.

58 Weiwei Fang, Shuai Ding, Yangyang Li, Wenchen Zhou, and Naixue Xiong. OKRA: optimal task and resource allocation for energy minimization in mobile edge computing systems. *Wireless Networks*, 25(5): 2851–2867, 2019.

59 Jing Bi, Haitao Yuan, Kaiyi Zhang, and MengChu Zhou. Energy-minimized partial computation offloading for delay-sensitive applications in heterogeneous edge networks. *IEEE Transactions on Emerging Topics in Computing*, 10(4): 1941–1954, 2022.

60 Haitao Yuan, MengChu Zhou, Qing Liu, and Abdullah Abusorrah. Fine-grained resource provisioning and task scheduling for heterogeneous applications in distributed green clouds. *IEEE/CAA Journal of Automatica Sinica*, 7(5): 1380–1393, 2020.

61 Keqin Li. Improving multicore server performance and reducing energy consumption by workload dependent dynamic power management. *IEEE Transactions on Cloud Computing*, 4(2): 122–137, 2015.

62 Biao Hu, Xincheng Yang, and Mingguo Zhao. Online energy-efficient scheduling of DAG tasks on heterogeneous embedded platforms. *Journal of Systems Architecture*, 140: 102894, 2023c.

63 Junlong Zhou, Jin Sun, Mingyue Zhang, and Yue Ma. Dependable scheduling for real-time workflows on cyber–physical cloud systems. *IEEE Transactions on Industrial Informatics*, 17(11): 7820–7829, 2020a.

64 Biao Hu, Zhengcai Cao, and Mengchu Zhou. Energy-minimized scheduling of real-time parallel workflows on heterogeneous distributed computing systems. *IEEE Transactions on Services Computing*, 15(5): 2766–2779, 2021.

65 Nakku Kim, Jungwook Cho, and Euiseong Seo. Energy-credit scheduler: An energy-aware virtual machine scheduler for cloud systems. *Future Generation Computer Systems*, 32: 128–137, 2014.

66 Yao Shen, Zhifeng Bao, Xiaolin Qin, and Jian Shen. Adaptive task scheduling strategy in cloud: When energy consumption meets performance guarantee. *World Wide Web*, 20(2): 155–173, 2017.

67 Bhavani Krishnan, Hrishikesh Amur, Ada Gavrilovska, and Karsten Schwan. VM power metering: Feasibility and challenges. *ACM SIGMETRICS Performance Evaluation Review*, 38(3): 56–60, 2011.

68 Mustafa Daraghmeh, Ismaeel Al Ridhawi, Moayad Aloqaily, Yaser Jararweh, and Anjali Agarwal. A power management approach to reduce energy consumption for edge computing servers. In *Fourth International Conference on Fog and Mobile Edge Computing*, pages 259–264, 2019.

69 Yuyi Mao, Jun Zhang, S. H. Song, and Khaled B. Letaief. Stochastic joint radio and computational resource management for multi-user mobile-edge computing systems. *IEEE Transactions on Wireless Communications*, 16(9): 5994–6009, 2017.

70 Xuan Xiao, Wanbo Zheng, Yunni Xia, Xiaoning Sun, Qinglan Peng, and Yu Guo. A workload-aware VM consolidation method based on coalitional game for energy-saving in cloud. *IEEE Access*, 7: 80421–80430, 2019.

71 Irfan Mohiuddin and Ahmad Almogren. Workload aware VM consolidation method in edge/cloud computing for IoT applications. *Journal of Parallel and Distributed Computing*, 123: 204–214, 2019.

72 Fahd N. Al-Wesabi, Marwa Obayya, Manar Ahmed Hamza, Jaber S. Alzahrani, Deepak Gupta, and Sachin Kumar. Energy aware resource optimization using unified metaheuristic optimization algorithm allocation for cloud computing environment. *Sustainable Computing: Informatics and Systems*, 35: 100686, 2022.

73 Junfeng Guo, Zhaozhe Song, Ying Cui, Zhi Liu, and Yusheng Ji. Energy-efficient resource allocation for multi-user mobile edge computing. In *IEEE Global Communications Conference*, pages 1–7, 2017.

74 Chen Xu, Guangyuan Zheng, and Xiongwen Zhao. Energy-minimization task offloading and resource allocation for mobile edge computing in NOMA heterogeneous networks. *IEEE Transactions on Vehicular Technology*, 69(12): 16001–16016, 2020a.

75 Huned Materwala, Leila Ismail, Raed M. Shubair, and Rajkumar Buyya. Energy-SLA-aware genetic algorithm for edge–cloud integrated computation offloading in vehicular networks. *Future Generation Computer Systems*, 135: 205–222, 2022.

76 Jingchen Yan, Yifeng Huang, Aditya Gupta, Anubhav Gupta, Cong Liu, Jianbin Li, and Long Cheng. Energy-aware systems for real-time job scheduling in cloud data centers: A deep reinforcement learning approach. *Computers and Electrical Engineering*, 99: 107688, 2022.

77 Huned Materwala and Leila Ismail. Performance and energy-aware bi-objective tasks scheduling for cloud data centers. ArXiv:abs/2105.00843,2022.

78 Mehboob Hussain, Lian-Fu Wei, Abdullah Lakhan, Samad Wali, Soragga Ali, and Abid Hussain. Energy and performance-efficient task scheduling in heterogeneous virtualized cloud computing. *Sustainable Computing: Informatics and Systems*, 30: 100517, 2021.

79 Junlong Zhou, Kun Cao, Xiumin Zhou, Mingsong Chen, Tongquan Wei, and Shiyan Hu. Throughput-conscious energy allocation and reliability-aware task assignment for renewable powered in-situ server systems. *IEEE Transactions on Computer-Aided Design of Integrated Circuits and Systems*, 41(3): 516–529, 2021.

80 Sumit Kumar Saurav and Shajulin Benedict. Energy aware scheduling algorithms for cloud environments – A survey. In *2nd International Conference on Advances in Computing, Communication, Embedded and Secure Systems*, pages 50–55, 2021.

81 Leila Ismail and Huned Materwala. Energy-aware VM placement and task scheduling in cloud-IoT computing: Classification and performance evaluation. *IEEE Internet of Things Journal*, 5(6): 5166–5176, 2018.

82 Xu Chen, Lei Jiao, Wenzhong Li, and Xiaoming Fu. Efficient multi-user computation offloading for mobile-edge cloud computing. *IEEE/ACM Transactions on Networking*, 24(5): 2795–2808, 2015.

83 Shihong Hu and Guanghui Li. Dynamic request scheduling optimization in mobile edge computing for IoT applications. *IEEE Internet of Things Journal*, 7(2): 1426–1437, 2019.

84 Jianchao Zheng, Yueming Cai, Yuan Wu, and Xuemin Shen. Dynamic computation offloading for mobile cloud computing: A stochastic game-theoretic approach. *IEEE Transactions on Mobile Computing*, 18(4): 771–786, 2018.

85 Jiao Zhang, Xiping Hu, Zhaolong Ning, Edith C.-H. Ngai, Li Zhou, Jibo Wei, Jun Cheng, and Bin Hu. Energy-latency tradeoff for energy-aware offloading in mobile edge computing networks. *IEEE Internet of Things Journal*, 5(4): 2633–2645, 2017.

86 Kaiyuan Zhang, Xiaolin Gui, Dewang Ren, and Defu Li. Energy–latency tradeoff for computation offloading in UAV-assisted multiaccess edge computing system. *IEEE Internet of Things Journal*, 8(8): 6709–6719, 2020.

87 Xu Chen, Wenzhong Li, Sanglu Lu, Zhi Zhou, and Xiaoming Fu. Efficient resource allocation for on-demand mobile-edge cloud computing. *IEEE Transactions on Vehicular Technology*, 67(9): 8769–8780, 2018.

88 Pengfei Wang, Chao Yao, Zijie Zheng, Guangyu Sun, and Lianyang Song. Joint task assignment, transmission, and computing resource allocation in multilayer mobile edge computing systems. *IEEE Internet of Things Journal*, 6(2): 2872–2884, 2018a.

89 Mingyue Cui, Shipeng Zhong, Boyang Li, Xu Chen, and Kai Huang. Offloading autonomous driving services via edge computing. *IEEE Internet of Things Journal*, 7(10): 10535–10547, 2020.

90 Suzanne Elashri and Akramul Azim. Energy-efficient offloading of real-time tasks using cloud computing. *Cluster Computing*, 23(4): 3273–3288, 2020.

91 Moonju Park. Non-preemptive fixed priority scheduling of hard real-time periodic tasks. In *International Conference on Computational Science*, pages 881–888. Springer, 2007.

92 Neil C. Audsley. Optimal Priority Assignment and Feasibility of Static Priority Tasks with Arbitrary Start Times. 1991.

93 Guangdong Tian, Yaping Ren, and MengChu Zhou. Dual-objective scheduling of rescue vehicles to distinguish forest fires via differential evolution and particle swarm optimization combined algorithm. *IEEE Transactions on Intelligent Transportation Systems*, 17(11): 3009–3021, 2016.

94 Peng Wu, Feng Chu, Nasreddine Saidani, Haoxun Chen, and Mengchu Zhou. Optimizing locations and qualities of multiple facilities with competition via intelligent search. *IEEE Transactions on Intelligent Transportation Systems*, DOI: 10.1109/TITS.2020.3046885, 2021.

95 Edward A. Lee and Sanjit A. Seshia. *Introduction to Embedded Systems - A Cyber-Physical Systems Approach*. MIT Press, 2013.

96 Hermann Kopetz. *Real-Time Systems: Design Principles for Distributed Embedded Applications*. Springer, 2011.

97 Hoang T Dinh, Chonho Lee, Dusit Niyato, and Ping Wang. A survey of mobile cloud computing: Architecture, applications, and approaches. *Wireless Communications and Mobile Computing*, 13(18): 1587–1611, 2013.

98 Mohammad H. Ghahramani, Meng Chu Zhou, and Tin Hon Chi. Toward cloud computing QoS architecture: Analysis of cloud systems and cloud services. *IEEE/CAA Journal of Automatica Sinica*, 20174(1): 6–18.

99 Anton Beloglazov, Jemal Abawajy, and Rajkumar Buyya. Energy-aware resource allocation heuristics for efficient management of data centers for cloud computing. *Future Generation Computer Systems*, 28(5): 755–768, 2012.

100 Keqin Li. Power and performance management for parallel computations in clouds and data centers. *Journal of Computer and System Sciences*, 82(2): 174–190, 2016.

101 Jing Bi, Haitao Yuan, Wei Tan, MengChu Zhou, Yushun Fan, Jia Zhang, and Jiangqiang Li. Application-aware dynamic fine-grained resource provisioning in a virtualized cloud data center. *IEEE Transactions on Automation Science and Engineering*, 14(2): 1172–1184, 2015.

102 Haitao Yuan, Jing Bi, Wei Tan, MengChu Zhou, and Jiangqiang Li. TTSA: An effective scheduling approach for delay bounded tasks in hybrid clouds. *IEEE Transactions on Cybernetics*, 47(11): 3658–3668, 2017.

103 Haitao Yuan, Jing Bi, Wei Tan, MengChu Zhou, and A.C Ammari. Time-aware multi-application task scheduling with guaranteed delay constraints in green data center. *IEEE Transactions on Automation Science and Engineering*, 15(3): 1138–1151, 2018a.

104 Haitao Yuan, Jing Bi, Wei Tan, MengChu Zhou, and K Sedraoui. Warm: Workload-aware multi-application task scheduling for revenue maximization in SDN-based cloud data center. *IEEE Access*, 6: 645–657, 2018b.

105 Haitao Yuan, Jing Bi, Wei Tan, and MengChu Zhou. Profit-sensitive spatial scheduling of multi-application tasks in distributed green clouds. *IEEE Transactions on Automation Science and Engineering*, 17: 1097–1106, 2019a.

106 Yuhua Song, Xiuyu He, Zhijie Liu, Wei He, Changyin Sun, and Fei-Yue Wang. Parallel control of distributed parameter systems. *IEEE Transactions on Cybernetics*, 48(12): 3291–3301, 2018.

107 Kazutaka Katoh, Kazuharu Misawa, Kei-ichi Kuma, and Takashi Miyata. MAFFT: A novel method for rapid multiple sequence alignment based on fast Fourier transform. *Nucleic Acids Research*, 30(14): 3059–3066, 2002.

108 Guoqi Xie, Gang Zeng, Renfa Li, and Keqin Li. Energy-aware processor merging algorithms for deadline constrained parallel applications in heterogeneous cloud computing. *IEEE Transactions on Sustainable Computing*, 2(2): 62–75, 2017c.

109 Kai Huang, Biao Hu, Jan Botsch, Nikhil Madduri, and Alois Knoll. A scalable lane detection algorithm on COTSs with opencl. In *Conference on Design, Automation & Test in Europe*, pages 229–232, 2016.

110 Xiebing Wang, Christopher Kiwus, Canhao Wu, Biao Hu, Kai Huang, and Alois Knoll. Implementing and parallelizing real-time lane detection on heterogeneous platforms. In *IEEE Conference on Application-specific Systems, Architectures and Processors*, pages 1–8, 2018b.

111 Jeffrey D.Ullman. *NP-Complete Scheduling Problems*. 1975Academic Press, Inc.,

112 Qing Zhao, Congcong Xiong, Ce Yu, Chuanlei Zhang, and Xi Zhao. A new energy-aware task scheduling method for data-intensive applications in the cloud. *Journal of Network and Computer Applications*, 59: 14–27, 2016.

113 Seyedmehdi Hosseinimotlagh, Farshad Khunjush, and Rashidaldin Samadzadeh. Seats: Smart energy-aware task scheduling in real-time cloud computing. *The Journal of Supercomputing*, 71(1): 45–66, 2015.

114 Zhen Xiao, Weijia Song, and Qi Chen. Dynamic resource allocation using virtual machines for cloud computing environment. *IEEE Transactions on Parallel and Distributed Systems*, 24(6): 1107–1117, 2013.

115 Yuan Haitao, Jing Bi, and Meng Chu Zhou. Temporal task scheduling of multiple delay-constrained applications in green hybrid cloud. *IEEE Transactions on Services Computing*, 14: 1558–1570, 2018.

116 Haitao Yuan, Bi Jing, and Meng Chu Zhou. Spatial task scheduling for cost minimization in distributed green cloud data centers. *IEEE Transactions on Automation Science & Engineering*, 16(2): 729–740, 2019b.

117 Wenyong Dong and Meng Chu Zhou. A supervised learning and control method to improve particle swarm optimization algorithms. *IEEE Transactions on Systems Man & Cybernetics Systems*, 47(7): 1135–1148, 2017.

118 Yan Hou, Nai Qi Wu, Meng Chu Zhou, and Zhi Wu Li. Pareto-optimization for scheduling of crude oil operations in refinery via genetic algorithm. *IEEE Transactions on Systems Man & Cybernetics Systems*, 47(3): 517–530, 2017.

119 Yulian Cao, Han Zhang, Wenfeng Li, Mengchu Zhou, Yu Zhang, and Wanpracha-Art Chaovalitwongse. Comprehensive learning particle swarm optimization algorithm with local search for multimodal functions. *IEEE Transactions on Evolutionary Computation*, 23(4): 718–731, 2019.

120 Kaizhou Gao, Zhiguang Cao, Le Zhang, Zhenghua Chen, Yuyan Han, and Quanke Pan. A review on swarm intelligence and evolutionary algorithms for solving flexible job shop scheduling problems. *IEEE/CAA Journal of Automatica Sinica*, 6(4): 875–887, 2019.

121 Yang Yu, Shangce Gao, Yirui Wang, and Yuki Todo. Global optimum-based search differential evolution. *IEEE/CAA Journal of Automatica Sinica*, 6(2): 379–394, 2019.

122 ZiYan Zhao, MengChu Zhou, and ShiXin Liu. Iterated greedy algorithms for flow-shop scheduling problems: A tutorial. *IEEE Transactions on Automation Science and Engineering*, 19(3): 1941–1959, 2021.

123 Yangming Zhou, Chenhui Qu, Qinghua Wu, Yawen Kou, Zhibin Jiang, and MengChu Zhou. A bilevel hybrid iterated search approach to soft-clustered capacitated arc routing problems. *Transportation Research Part B: Methodological*, 184: 102944, 2024.

124 Liyun Zuo, Shu Lei, Shoubin Dong, Chunsheng Zhu, and Takahiro Hara. A multi-objective optimization scheduling method based on the ant colony algorithm in cloud computing. *IEEE Access*, 3: 2687–2699, 2017.

125 Guo Ning Gan, Ting Lei Huang, and Gao Shuai. Genetic simulated annealing algorithm for task scheduling based on cloud computing environment. In *International Conference on Intelligent Computing & Integrated Systems*, 2010.

126 R. K. Jena. Energy efficient task scheduling in cloud environment. *Energy Procedia*, 141: 222–227, 2017.

127 Thar Baker, Bandar Aldawsari, Muhammad Asim, Hissam Tawfik, Zakaria Maamar, and Rajkumar Buyya. Cloud-senergy: A bin-packing based multi-cloud service broker for energy efficient composition and execution of data-intensive applications. *Sustainable Computing Informatics & Systems*, 19: 242–252, 2018.

128 Pei Yun Zhang and Meng Chu Zhou. Dynamic cloud task scheduling based on a two-stage strategy. *IEEE Transactions on Automation Science & Engineering*, 15(2): 772–783, 2018.

129 Mohammed Al-khafajiy, Thar Baker, Atif Waraich, Dhiya Al-Jumeily, and Abir Hussain. IoT-Fog optimal workload via fog offloading. *2018 IEEE/ACM International Conference on Utility and Cloud Computing Companion (UCC Companion)*, pages 359–364, 2018.

130 Dawei Li and Jie Wu. Minimizing energy consumption for frame-based tasks on heterogeneous multiprocessor platforms. *IEEE Transactions on Parallel and Distributed Systems*, 26(3): 810–823, 2015.

131 Aman Kansal, Feng Zhao, Jie Liu, Nupur Kothari, and Arka A Bhattacharya. Virtual machine power metering and provisioning. In *Proceedings of the 1st ACM Symposium on Cloud Computing*, pages 39–50, 2010.

132 Chonglin Gu, Hejiao Huang, and Xiaohua Jia. Power metering for virtual machine in cloud computing-challenges and opportunities. *IEEE Access*, 2: 1106–1116, 2014.

133 Xiaomin Zhu, Laurence T. Yang, Huangke Chen, Ji Wang, Shu Yin, and Xiaocheng Liu. Real-time tasks oriented energy-aware scheduling in virtualized clouds. *IEEE Transactions on Cloud Computing*, 2(2): 168–180, 2014.

134 Yassir Samadi, Mostapha Zbakh, and Claude Tadonki. E-HEFT: Enhancement heterogeneous earliest finish time algorithm for task scheduling based on load balancing in cloud computing. In *IEEE International Conference on High Performance Computing & Simulation*, pages 601–609, 2018.

135 Haluk Topcuoglu, Salim Hariri, and Min-you Wu. Performance-effective and low-complexity task scheduling for heterogeneous computing. *IEEE Transactions on Parallel and Distributed Systems*, 13(3): 260–274, 2002.

136 Qingjia Huang, Sen Su, Jian Li, Peng Xu, Kai Shuang, and Xiao Huang. Enhanced energy-efficient scheduling for parallel applications in cloud. In *IEEE/ACM International Symposium on Cluster, Cloud and Grid Computing*, pages 781–786, 2012.

137 Robert P. Dick, David L Rhodes, and Wayne Wolf. TGFF: Task graphs for free. In *IEEE International Workshop on Hardware/Software Codesign*, pages 97–101, 1998.

138 Qichao Mao, Jiujun Cheng, MengChu Zhou, Shangce Gao, and Shoufei Han. An edge computing-based autonomous vehicle group cooperation model in a highway scene. *IEEE Transactions on Vehicular Technology*, 73(7): 9682–9695, 2024.

139 Georgios L. Stavrinides and Helen D. Karatza. An energy-efficient, QoS-aware and cost-effective scheduling approach for real-time workflow applications in cloud computing systems utilizing DVFS and approximate computations. *Future Generation Computer Systems*, 96: 216–226, 2019.

140 Nagma Khattar, Jagpreet Sidhu, and Jaiteg Singh. Toward energy-efficient cloud computing: A survey of dynamic power management and heuristics-based optimization techniques. *The Journal of Supercomputing*, 75(8): 4750–4810, 2019.

141 Cheng Zhuo, Shaoheng Luo, Houle Gan, Jiang Hu, and Zhiguo Shi. Noise-aware DVFS for efficient transitions on battery-powered iot devices. *IEEE Transactions on Computer-Aided Design of Integrated Circuits and Systems*, 39(7): 1498–1510, 2019.

142 Monire Safari and Reihaneh Khorsand. Energy-aware scheduling algorithm for time-constrained workflow tasks in DVFS-enabled cloud environment. *Simulation Modelling Practice and Theory*, 87: 311–326, 2018.

143 Vishakha Singh, Indrajeet Gupta, and Prasanta K. Jana. An energy efficient algorithm for workflow scheduling in IaaS cloud. *Journal of Grid Computing*, pages 1–20, 2019b.

144 Yi Yao, Jiayin Wang, Bo Sheng, Jason Lin, and Ningfang Mi. HaSTE: Hadoop YARN scheduling based on task-dependency and resource-demand. In *2014 IEEE 7th International Conference on Cloud Computing*, pages 184–191, 2014.

145 Yuming Xu, Kenli Li, Jingtong Hu, and Keqin Li. A genetic algorithm for task scheduling on heterogeneous computing systems using multiple priority queues. *Information Sciences*, 270: 255–287, 2014.

146 Tang Xiaoyong, Kenli Li, Zeng Zeng, and Bharadwaj Veeravalli. A novel security-driven scheduling algorithm for precedence-constrained tasks in heterogeneous distributed systems. *IEEE Transactions on Computers*, 60(7): 1017–1029, 2010.

147 Zhiying Wang, Gang Sun, Hanyue Su, Hongfang Yu, Bo Lei, and Mohsen Guizani. Low-latency scheduling approach for dependent tasks in MEC-enabled 5G vehicular networks. *IEEE Internet of Things Journal*, 11(4): 6278–6289, 2023.

148 Qiaoqiao Shen, Bin-Jie Hu, and Enjun Xia. Cuckoo search-enabled task scheduling and cache updating in vehicular edge-fog computing. *IEEE Transactions on Vehicular Technology*. IEEE, 2025

149 Laizhong Cui, Chong Xu, Shu Yang, Joshua Zhexue Huang, Jianqiang Li, Xizhao Wang, Zhong Ming, and Nan Lu. Joint optimization of energy consumption and latency in mobile edge computing for internet of things. *IEEE Internet of Things Journal*, 6(3): 4791–4803, 2018.

150 Zhaolong Ning, Jun Huang, Xiaojie Wang, Joel JPC Rodrigues, and Lei Guo. Mobile edge computing-enabled internet of vehicles: Toward energy-efficient scheduling. *IEEE Network*, 33(5): 198–205, 2019.

151 Guoqi Xie, Gang Zeng, Junqiang Jiang, Chunnian Fan, Renfa Li, and Keqin Li. Energy management for multiple real-time workflows on cyber–physical cloud systems. *Future Generation Computer Systems*, 105: 916–931, 2020b.

152 Guoqi Xie, Xiongren Xiao, Renfa Li, and Keqin Li. Schedule length minimization of parallel applications with energy consumption constraints using heuristics on heterogeneous distributed systems. *Concurrency and Computation: Practice and Experience*, 29(16): e4024, 2017b.

153 Xiaojun Cai, Feng Li, Ping Li, Lei Ju, and Zhiping Jia. SLA-aware energy-efficient scheduling scheme for hadoop yarn. *The Journal of Supercomputing*, 73(8): 3526–3546, 2017.

154 Jiaying Meng, Haisheng Tan, Chao Xu, Wanli Cao, Liuyan Liu, and Bojie Li. Dedas: Online task dispatching and scheduling with bandwidth constraint in edge computing. In *IEEE Conference on Computer Communications*, pages 2287–2295, 2019.

155 Xiaolong Xu, Hao Cao, Qingfan Geng, Xihua Liu, Fei Dai, and Chuanjian Wang. Dynamic resource provisioning for workflow scheduling under uncertainty in edge computing environment. *Concurrency and Computation: Practice and Experience*, page e5674, 2020b.

156 Chubo Liu, Kenli Li, and Keqin Li. A game approach to multi-servers load balancing with load-dependent server availability consideration. *IEEE Transactions on Cloud Computing*, 9(1): 1–13, 2018.

157 Junyan Hu, Kenli Li, Chubo Liu, and Keqin Li. A game-based price bidding algorithm for multi-attribute cloud resource provision. *IEEE Transactions on Services Computing*, 14(4): 1111–1122, 2018b.

158 Xiaojie Wang, Zhaolong Ning, Song Guo, and Lei Wang. Imitation learning enabled task scheduling for online vehicular edge computing. *IEEE Transactions on Mobile Computing*, 21(2): 598–611, 2020.

159 Jian-Jia Chen and Chin-Fu Kuo. Energy-efficient scheduling for real-time systems on dynamic voltage scaling (DVS) platforms. In *Embedded and Real-Time Computing Systems and Applications*, pages 28–38, 2007.

160 Pengcheng Huang, Pranaw Kumar, Georgia Giannopoulou, and Lothar Thiele. Energy efficient DVFS scheduling for mixed-criticality systems. In *Embedded Software*, pages 1–10, 2014.

161 Baoxian Zhao, Hakan Aydin, and Dakai Zhu. On maximizing reliability of real-time embedded applications under hard energy constraint. *IEEE Transactions on Industrial Informatics*, 6(3): 316–328, 2010.

162 Guoqi Xie, Junqiang Jiang, Yan Liu, Renfa Li, and Keqin Li. Minimizing energy consumption of real-time parallel applications using downward and upward approaches on heterogeneous systems. *IEEE Transactions on Industrial Informatics*, 13(3): 1068–1078, 2017a.

163 Yueyue Dai, Du Xu, Sabita Maharjan, and Yan Zhang. Joint load balancing and offloading in vehicular edge computing and networks. *IEEE Internet of Things Journal*, 6(3): 4377–4387, 2018.

164 Keqin Li. Computation offloading strategy optimization with multiple heterogeneous servers in mobile edge computing. *IEEE Transactions on Sustainable Computing*. IEEE, 2019. doi: 10.1109/TSUSC.2019.2904680.

165 Zhenyu Zhou, Caixia Gao, Chen Xu, Yan Zhang, Shahid Mumtaz, and Jonathan Rodriguez. Social big-data-based content dissemination in internet of vehicles. *IEEE Transactions on Industrial Informatics*, 14(2): 768–777, 2017.

166 Jing Bi, Xiangdong Xue, Haitao Yuan, and Jia Zhang. Latency-minimized computation offloading in vehicle fog computing with improved whale optimization algorithm. In *2023 IEEE International Conference on Systems, Man, and Cybernetics (SMC)*, pages 5003–5008. IEEE, 2023.

167 Lei Liu, Chen Chen, Qingqi Pei, Sabita Maharjan, and Yan Zhang. Vehicular edge computing and networking: A survey. *Mobile Networks and Applications*, pages 1–24, 2020a.

168 Jingyun Feng, Zhi Liu, Celimuge Wu, and Yusheng Ji. AVE: Autonomous vehicular edge computing framework with ACO-based scheduling. *IEEE Transactions on Vehicular Technology*, 66(12): 10660–10675, 2017.

169 Arkadiusz Madej, Nan Wang, Nikolaos Athanasopoulos, Rajiv Ranjan, and Blesson Varghese. Priority-based fair scheduling in edge computing. In *2020 IEEE 4th International Conference on Fog and Edge Computing (ICFEC)*, pages 39–48, 2020.

170 Guoqi Xie, Gang Zeng, Liangjiao Liu, Renfa Li, and Keqin Li. High performance real-time scheduling of multiple mixed-criticality functions in heterogeneous distributed embedded systems. *Journal of Systems Architecture*, 70: 3–14, 2016.

171 Guoqi Xie, Gang Zeng, Zhetao Li, Renfa Li, and Keqin Li. Adaptive dynamic scheduling on multifunctional mixed-criticality automotive cyber-physical systems. *IEEE Transactions on Vehicular Technology*, 66: 6676–6692, 2017d.

172 Yang Bai, Yizhi Huang, Guoqi Xie, Renfa Li, and Wanli Chang. ASDYS: Dynamic scheduling using active strategies for multifunctional mixed-criticality cyber–physical systems. *IEEE Transactions on Industrial Informatics*, 17(8): 5175–5184, 2020.

173 Junlong Zhou, Jin Sun, Peijin Cong, Zhe Liu, Xiumin Zhou, Tongquan Wei, and Shiyan Hu. Security-critical energy-aware task scheduling for heterogeneous real-time MPSoCs in IoT. *IEEE Transactions on Services Computing*, 13(4): 745–758, 2019a.

174 Guoqi Xie, Laurence T. Yang, Wei Wu, Keyu Zeng, Xiangzhen Xiao, and Renfa Li. Security enhancement for real-time parallel in-vehicle applications by CAN FD message authentication. *IEEE Transactions on Intelligent Transportation Systems*, 22(8): 5038–5049, 2020a.

175 Guoqi Xie, Laurence T. Yang, Yao Liu, Haibo Luo, Xin Peng, and Renfa Li. Security enhancement for real-time independent in-vehicle CAN-FD messages in vehicular networks. *IEEE Transactions on Vehicular Technology*, 70(6): 5244–5253, 2021.

176 Youcef Gheraibia, Sohag Kabir, Khaoula Djafri, and Habiba Krimou. An overview of the approaches for automotive safety integrity levels allocation. *Journal of Failure Analysis and Prevention*, 18(3): 707–720, 2018.

177 Markus Nager, Marcel Baunach, Peter Priller, and Georg Macher. Real-time multiplexing of mixed-criticality data streams for automotive multi-core test systems. *IEEE Intelligent Transportation Systems Magazine*, 13(1): 120–135, 2018.

178 Marcello Cinque, Luigi De Simone, and Andrea Marchetta. Certify the uncertified: Towards assessment of virtualization for mixed-criticality in the automotive domain. *arXiv preprint arXiv:2205.12596*, 2022.

179 Zhe Jiang, Shuai Zhao, Ran Wei, Dawei Yang, Richard Paterson, Nan Guan, Yan Zhuang, and Neil C. Audsley. Bridging the pragmatic gaps for mixed-criticality systems in the automotive industry. *IEEE Transactions on Computer-Aided Design of Integrated Circuits and Systems*, 41(4): 1116–1129, 2021.

180 Hatem A. Alharbi, Taisir E.H. El-Gorashi, and Jaafar M.H. Elmirghani. Energy efficient virtual machine services placement in cloud-fog architecture. In *2019 21st International Conference on Transparent Optical Networks (ICTON)*, pages 1–6, 2019.

181 Wei Wang, Yongli Zhao, Massimo Tornatore, Abhishek Gupta, Jie Zhang, and Biswanath Mukherjee. Virtual machine placement and workload assignment for mobile edge computing. In *2017 IEEE 6th International Conference on Cloud Networking (CloudNet)*, pages 1–6, 2017b.

182 Wei Lu, Xianyu Meng, and Guanfei Guo. Fast service migration method based on virtual machine technology for MEC. *IEEE Internet of Things Journal*, 6(3): 4344–4354, 2018.

183 Fei Hao, Guangyao Pang, Zheng Pei, Keyun Qin, Yu Zhang, and Xiaoming Wang. Virtual machines scheduling in mobile edge computing: A formal concept analysis approach. *IEEE Transactions on Sustainable Computing*, 5(3): 319–328, 2019.

184 Yuanzhe Li and Shangguang Wang. An energy-aware edge server placement algorithm in mobile edge computing. In *2018 IEEE International Conference on Edge Computing (EDGE)*, pages 66–73, 2018.

185 Tiago Rosado and Jorge Bernardino. An overview of openstack architecture. In *Proceedings of the 18th International Database Engineering & Applications Symposium*, pages 366–367, 2014.

186 David Bernstein. Containers and cloud: From LXC to docker to kubernetes. *IEEE Cloud Computing*, 1(3): 81–84, 2014.

187 Sanjoy K. Baruah, Alan Burns, and Robert I. Davis. Response-time analysis for mixed criticality systems. In *Real-Time Systems Symposium (RTSS)*, pages 34–43, 2011.

188 Junlong Zhou, Mingyue Zhang, Jin Sun, Tian Wang, Xiumin Zhou, and Shiyan Hu. DRHEFT: Deadline-constrained reliability-aware HEFT algorithm for real-time heterogeneous MPSoC systems. *IEEE Transactions on Reliability*, 71: 178–189, 2020b.

189 REVOLTEK. IoT case—AI smart traffic lights make smart cities more efficient and low-carbon. https://www.revoltek.com.cn/, 2025. Accessed: 2025-04-06.

Index

a

Ant Colony Optimization 68
Application Completion Time 11, 65, 98, 112
Auction-Based Bidding Strategy 95, 97
Audsley's Algorithm 46,
AUTOSAR Standard 9
  see also Electronic Control Unit
Autonomous Driving 7, 8

b

Backward Schedule Adjustment 84–86
Bin Packing Problem Analogy 69
Bottleneck Task 79–81
Break-Even Time 106–107

c

Cloud Data Center 38
  see also Virtual Machine
Cloud-Edge-Device Computing Systems 1–6, 141
Context-Aware Task Scheduling 144–148
Criticality Level 119–126
  see also Mixed-Criticality System

d

Deadline-Aware Queue Jump Algorithm 105–106
Demand-Bound Function 10, 16–27
Directed Acyclic Graph Application 95, 120
  Entry Task 69–76
  Exit Task 69–72
Dynamic Programming 129–132
Dynamic Voltage and Frequency Scaling 41, 95

e

Electronic Control Unit 9
Energy Efficiency 3, 5, 37–41, 46, 51, 66, 69, 88, 96, 123
Execution Efficiency 44, 52, 70, 71, 86

f

Fixed-Priority Scheduling 17, 45, 64, 125, 126
  see also Rate-Monotonic Scheduling
Frequency Profile 54–55

Intelligent Scheduling of Tasks for Cloud-Edge-Device Computing Systems, First Edition.

Published 2025 by John Wiley & Sons, Inc.

g

Genetic Algorithm 7, 42, 46, 67, 98
Global Scheduler 7, 14, 17, 23, 24, 27, 35

h

Hard Real-Time Task 7–13, 17, 20–23, 33–35
Heterogeneous Earliest Finish Time Algorithm 87, 104, 111, 128
Hierarchical Architecture 2
Hybrid Scheduling Framework 10, 14, 28, 35

i

Internet of Things 2, 69, 98, 143, 147
  IoT Device 143
  Sensor 1–3, 141–144
Intelligent Transportation System 53

j

Job Group Scheduling 39
  see also Workload Consolidation

l

Local Scheduler 7, 10, 14, 35

m

Machine Learning Model 141, 144
Mixed-Criticality System 11, 120
  Mode-Switch Scheduling 120, 122

n

Nonlinear Integer Programming 29, 37, 64
NP-hard Problem 66

p

Particle Swarm Optimization 40, 63, 67, 134
Power Model 5, 41, 43, 44, 71, 87, 101

q

Quality of Service 8, 38, 119–123

r

Rate-Monotonic Scheduling 15
  see also Fixed-Priority Scheduling
Resource Allocation 7, 8, 11, 39–42, 49–57, 65–71, 75–76, 82, 83, 87, 93, 120–123
  see also Task Offloading
Response Time 37–39, 43, 45, 59, 66, 67, 99, 102–104, 119, 121, 126–131, 139
Roadside Unit 8, 9, 12–14, 27–28, 33, 95, 123
  see also Vehicular Edge Computing

s

Schedulability Test 4, 7, 10, 14, 15, 17, 20–35, 105, 132
Smart Agriculture 143, 144, 147
Supply-Bound Function 16, 17, 21, 27

t

Task Offloading 3, 11, 40
  see also Resource Allocation
Traffic Management 141, 147
Traffic Signal Control 142

u

Upward Rank Value 87, 97, 104, 105, 107, 128, 129

v

Vehicular Edge Computing 5, 95, 119
  see also Edge Computing; Roadside Unit
Virtual Machine 37, 38, 50, 56, 66–72, 87, 120, 129, 130
  VM Creation 39, 48, 49, 57, 120
  VM Placement 42, 123,
Virtual CPU 5, 38, 43, 58, 59–62, 123, 129–130

W

Workload-Aware Scheduling 37, 40, 53, 64, 119, 147
Workload Consolidation 39
see also Job Group Scheduling
Workload-Bound Function 16, 25
Worst-Case Execution Time 12, 13, 15, 24, 27, 29, 33